Hanged Until Dead

Other books by John Kellie:

Ayrshire Echoes
Ayrshire Folk

Hanged Until Dead

Men and Women
Executed in Nineteenth-Century Scotland

John Kellie

CARN PUBLISHING

© John Kellie, 2018.
First Published in Great Britain, 2018.

ISBN – 978 1 911043 06 5

Published by Carn Publishing,
Lochnoran House,
Auchinleck, Ayrshire, KA18 3JW.

www.carnpublishing.com

Printed by Bell & Bain Ltd,
Glasgow, G46 7UQ.

JOHN KELLIE

John Kellie was born in Ayrshire and educated at Pinmore, Kilmarnock and Glasgow. An enthusiastic outdoorsman and freelance writer, over the years his work has found its way into a variety of magazines on both sides of the Atlantic, as well as broadsheet and tabloid newspapers. After teaching English for the best part of three decades both in Scotland and Canada, he seized the opportunity of an early exit and he is now researching and writing full-time.
Hanged Until Dead is his third book.

For my longtime friend, Frances Smith, without whose staunch support and sound advice this book might never have made it.

Contents

Introduction

'Ye're a vera clever chiel, man,
but ye wad be nane the waur o' a hanging.'
(Robert McQueen, Lord Braxfield)

Cast an eye along a shelf of bestselling Scottish paperbacks and it would be hard to avoid drawing the conclusion that, no matter what anyone might tell you, crime most definitely pays. This, it has to be said, isn't anything new or surprising. There has long been an appetite in Scotland for fiction that delves into the darker recesses of the human psyche - look no further than *Dr Jekyll and Mr Hyde* (1886) - and surely it must stand to reason that what's good enough for fiction will be just as effective for material grounded in fact. It was while I was carrying out research for my previous books of local history that I discovered that some of the stories that gripped my imagination most strongly were those which dealt with criminals and crime. It wasn't anything morbid. It was more the fact that, by studying our forebears' vices and misdemeanours, I was provided with a startlingly vivid insight into the times they lived through, the social conditions they endured, the needs and appetites that regulated their lives, and the temptations that all too often they succumbed to. In short, by tracing the ups and downs of our ancestors' lives - the choices they made, and the price that many of them paid - I was enabled to connect with the past in a more direct and personal way than I ever had previously.

By the standards of our own time, there is no question that punishment meted out by nineteenth-century courts was anything other than harsh, and a man found guilty of an apparently trivial crime could find himself in serious trouble with the law - as an Edinburgh blacksmith, John Craik, found out to his cost when he was sentenced to be transported overseas for his first offence of stealing a cheese. When it came to capital crimes the law was applied with equal rigour, and over the course of the nineteenth century rather more than 250 Scotsmen and women died on the gallows for a variety of unlawful acts. Fifty per cent of those executed had been convicted of murder - or, in one solitary case, of attempt to murder. A smaller number - roughly forty per cent - consisted of individuals convicted of theft or robbery, while the remaining ten per cent were those found guilty of fire-raising, forgery, piracy, rape and treason, plus two antiquated crimes which have long since dropped off the statute book, namely *hamesucken* and *stouthrief* - obsolete terms denoting robbery with violence. One in twenty of all those hanged was female.

Out of that number I have selected a couple of dozen, both men and women, whose stories I have told in these pages. Convicted of a variety of capital offences, they went to the gallows in locations right across Scotland - from Dumfries to Inverness, Aberdeen to Edinburgh. It goes without saying that the morality, or otherwise, of the death penalty is a contentious and emotive issue, so the question of whether and to what extent justice was served in each of these cases I leave as a matter for individual judgment. If my own opinion should surface from time to time, the reader is, of course, quite at liberty to take a different view.

During my writing of this book I found *The Encyclopedia of Scottish Executions 1750-1963* by Alex F. Young (Eric Dobby Publishing, 1998) an invaluable work of reference.

John Young : December 1801

Throughout the north-east it was generally reckoned that John Young ran with a dangerous crowd. Born at the latter end of the eighteenth century into a family of travelling folk - invariably at the time branded *tinkers* - he was the son of John Young senior, a former army man who had seen service during the American War of Independence before returning home when hostilities ceased to resume the wandering life once again. Roaming the countryside with donkey and pack, he made his living by fashioning horn spoons for sale and offering to mend such household essentials as pots, pans and kettles. He was known, in addition, for his knack for repairing broken clocks and watches. His wife and constant companion, Sarah Graham - young John's mother - had lost a forefinger during the course of some or other affray but, for all that, was adamant in claiming descent from gypsy aristocracy. Whatever the truth of the matter, what is beyond doubt is that in their customary stamping ground the Young family's reputation was not entirely spotless.

It seems likely that young John grew up in the shadow of an older brother, twelve years his senior, and following whose untimely death something akin to an entire mythology grew up. Just shy of six feet tall, Peter Young was possessed of a formidable physical strength and regularly proved insuperable in such traditional country sports as 'putting the stane' and throwing the hammer. If that wasn't enough, his dexterity with musket, rod and line was sufficient to ensure that his cooking-pot was seldom in danger of lying empty. Such was his fearsome reputation that more often than not Peter's poaching activities went unreported and it was even said that those lairds who opted to turn a blind eye were duly rewarded when he took it upon himself to shield their lands from predation by rival poachers. With his fondness for whisky, he racked up considerable debt with local landlords but was scrupulous in settling his account in full at a later date. As staunch an ally as he was formidable a foe, Peter could be relied upon to repay a kindness as much as to seek redress for an affront.

Still, for all his sterling qualities, from time to time Peter Young found himself at odds with the law when the odd sackful of potatoes was lifted from a farmer's field, perhaps, or a housewife's poultry went missing overnight. It was said, in fact, that there were few jails north of Perth with which he was unacquainted though, even under the trying circumstances of confinement, the better part of his nature had a tendency to rise to the surface. The story is told that, imprisoned in Aberdeen, Peter's remarkably small hands allowed him to free himself from his chains and overpower his jailer whose keys he quickly appropriated and used to liberate his fellow-inmates from their cells - a cute move for sure that would spread the pursuing forces of the law more thinly. The prisoners' joyful exodus was in danger of stalling, however, when they discovered that the outer door of the building was bolted against them from the outside until, true to form, Peter mustered his prodigious strength and shoulder-charged the heavy door, forcing it wide open and making good the men's escape. Despite such occasional brushes with the law, what was never in doubt was the quality of the Youngs' workmanship, as was clearly demonstrated in William Alexander's classic nineteenth-century novel of rural life in the north-east, *Johnny Gibb of Gushetneuk*, where the author uses good broad Scots to praise the family's fine craftsmanship when he refers to 'as protty [*pretty*] horn speens as ever Caird Young turn't oot o's caums' - *caums* being the wooden moulds routinely used by travelling people in the production of horn spoons. When push came to shove, however, neither Peter's skill at his trade nor his legendary strength was enough to save him from the forces of law and order when they finally caught up with him at Montrose. Barely into his twenties, Peter Young died on the gallows in Edinburgh in 1788.

The fact that Peter's younger brother, John, measured five feet ten inches tall did not prevent his mother from affectionately describing him as 'the dwarf o' a' my bairns' - reputedly seven boys in total. In common with Peter, he too was possessed of great strength and, such being the vagaries of folk memory, one account of the Aberdeen jailbreak exists which identifies John, not Peter, as the brawny saviour of the day and recounts how he paused briefly in his flight to pin a mischievous notice on the gaping prison door advertising 'Rooms to Let'. In an age when relatively few Scots were capable of signing their own name, this might seem an unlikely addition to the story but, amongst his various accomplishments, John was apparently a notable exception who 'wrote a good hand.' Generally viewed as honest, he was a familiar figure as he roamed the north-eastern countryside, undertaking a variety of jobs for local people, but at the end of the day what was probably seen as his finest attribute - his great strength - turned out at best to be a mixed blessing.

For his many rivals John Young's impressive physique singled him out as the man to beat, and consistently at the forefront of the challengers was his cousin, Hugh Graham. On any occasion when the two men came face to face a bout of wrestling quickly ensued from which Young would almost invariably emerge victorious. With his pride at stake, Graham persisted over a long period of time in vying for supremacy and what had initially started out as a good-humoured contest soon came to develop rather more of an edge. Conscious of his opponent's growing resentment, Young attempted to ease the situation by advising him to keep his distance but Graham remained obstinate and did precisely the opposite. Matters finally came to head in April 1801 when the two men clashed for the last time near the small Aberdeenshire village of Chapel of Garioch. For each of them, this would prove to be a fateful encounter. Realising that Young was likely to get the better of him yet again, it looks very much as though Hugh Graham finally reached snapping-point when, producing a knife from his clothing, he proceeded to launch a murderous attack on his opponent. Before he was able to inflict any damage, however, Young managed to wrest the weapon from his grasp and in the scuffle that followed the blade penetrated the wall of Graham's stomach, directly below the ribs. In the general melee that ensued even the female members of the two men's respective gypsy bands were said to have become involved but it was too late for Hugh Graham whose lifeblood drained inexorably into the Aberdeenshire turf. Although early nineteenth-century accounts consistently label Graham as the aggressor, nonetheless John Young immediately fled the scene - probably an understandable course of action given the widespread prejudice relating to travelling people that existed at the time.

With a view to apprehending the wanted man, a posse was swiftly assembled that consisted of a combination of strapping Highlanders and fleet-footed gamekeepers, all accustomed to covering rough terrain on foot, plus a more favoured few who were mounted on horseback. It quickly became clear that John Young had no intention of making their task an easy one or of bowing to his fate without putting up a struggle. In a chase that resembled nothing more than a contest between hare and hounds, the hunters' quarry was often tantalisingly within their sight and they are said to have become so fatigued by their exertions that they resorted to 'lying by the springs [and] lapping water with their tongues like dogs.' When he reached the River Dee, immediately to the west of Banchory, the fleeing man was presented with a formidable obstacle which he overcame by leaping courageously over a deep chasm - estimated at some sixteen to eighteen feet across - through which the rushing waters were channelled, an athletic feat that gained him valuable time when none of his pursuers dared emulate his example and which came to be commemorated in later years when the name 'Young's Leap' was attached to the dramatic gorge. In spite of his best efforts, however, at the end of the day the hunted man was forced to submit to the inevitable when his pursuers finally ran him to ground, tied him up securely and conveyed him by cart to Aberdeen. Reports suggested that, by the time that he was captured, Young had led them on a merry dance of something close to thirty miles.

There were to be no dramatic jailbreaks this time before Friday 10 October 1801 when 'John Young, alias Robertson, travelling tinker' appeared before Lords Dunsinnan and Cullen at the Circuit Court of Justiciary in Aberdeen to answer the charge of having murdered 'James Davidson, alias Hugh Graham, tinker.' Despite the fact that it was generally agreed that the man accused had acted in self-defence, nonetheless the members of the jury were unanimous in finding him guilty as charged, and when the law lords spoke it was to advise Young that he would be 'carried from the bar back to the tolbooth of Aberdeen, therein to be detained and fed on bread and water only [...] till Friday the 11th of December next, and on that day to be taken forth of the tolbooth, and hanged by the neck on a gibbet, till he be dead.' 'His body', they added, would 'be delivered to the Lecturer on Anatomy in the Marischal College, to be publicly dissected and anatomized.' The verdict of the jury and judges' subsequent sentencing probably came as no surprise. As a member of the travelling community whose customs, traditions and nomadic existence frequently ran counter to the grain of mainstream society, the chances are that John Young knew better than to expect leniency.

During the two months that he spent in jail, awaiting his fate, Young was reported to have conducted himself with quiet dignity and to have displayed 'every mark of sincere penitence' - a little odd, we might imagine, given that the action that condemned him had been carried out in his own defence. There is, however, an alternative version of events at this time which recounted how he was interrupted one night in the act of burrowing through his cell floor using tools smuggled in by his friends. A strange old anecdote survives from the day of the execution itself. On the morning of his final day, the custom in Aberdeen was for a condemned man to be dressed in his linen shroud by the city hangman, in Young's case one Robert Welsh. In spite of his forthcoming ordeal, the condemned man's spirit was clearly unbroken when he declined to comply, saying that 'I dinna like to hae that cratur, Robbie Welsh's, hands aboot me.' His wishes, it seems, were respected and the office was carried out instead by a helpful local clergyman. Shedding tears and proclaiming his innocence to the end, John Young expressed his appreciation for the minister's kindness and likewise offered thanks to all those who had visited him in jail. On first catching sight of his coffin, placed beneath the gallows, it was noted that he gasped and gave an involuntary shudder but was quick to compose himself and went thereafter to his death calmly and without fuss.

First and foremost, the death of John Young was a deep personal tragedy, though naturally it created a series of ripples that spread rather wider. On any occasion during his father's later life when the old man happened to be questioned concerning the fate of his sons, his poignant reply, we are told, was 'They were a' hanged'. Now, two centuries on, whether the old man's tone was one of quiet resignation or rather of profound sadness is impossible to say. As for the family of the second party involved in events at Chapel of Garioch, it appears that they perhaps were no strangers to loss themselves. Although the exact year is hard to pin down, it has often been written that Hugh Graham's older brother, Charlie, faced the death penalty at Perth, bowing and raising his hand to an acquaintance in the crowd, it is said, before making his final departure.

George Watson : June 1811

When the Circuit Court of Justiciary sat in Ayr in May 1811, no fewer than three of the cases to be heard related to the theft of livestock. The first case involved a spectacularly ham-fisted attempt at horse-stealing to which an Irishman, William Gillespie, had sufficient sense to plead guilty. Having some time earlier purloined a quantity of blankets and various other items, Gillespie found his haul too heavy to carry so he came up with the bright idea of stealing a horse to assist in his getaway. Caught in the act, he ended up with neither blankets nor horse. Sentenced to a year's imprisonment, he may have been cheered - at least a little - by the prospect of release in twelve months' time, on condition that he guarantee his good behaviour for a further three years. With horse-theft still a capital offence in Scotland, there is no doubt that the Irishman got off lightly. 'The appearance of the prisoner indicated extreme wretchedness,' observed a local reporter. 'His meagre and squalid countenance, long beard and projecting teeth, excited in the spectators a degree of horror mixed with compassion.' Poor Gillespie - it was hardly a flattering portrait but, when push came to shove, it was maybe his looks that saved his bacon. The next case to be heard was disposed of fairly quickly when James Campbell and his son - also James - were due to be tried on a charge of sheep-stealing. Young James failed to put in an appearance and was promptly outlawed by the court, and after hearing the case against his father the jury declared itself satisfied that, although Campbell, senior, had been found assisting in the slaughter of a sheep - a little tricky to explain away, you might imagine - there was no proof that he had actually been involved in the animal's theft. He walked out of the court a free man, though his son's ordeal remained to be faced another day.

The third case also centred around a father-and-son partnership who were accused of having two months earlier stolen a pair of horses from adjoining farms near New Cumnock. The circumstances under which the animals were eventually recovered, and the thieves apprehended, are - to say the least - a little unusual. John Kerr of Knockburnie was widely known as a kindly man who would never refuse a passing tinker a dry corner about his farm steading to pass the night in relative comfort. In March of 1811, however, when George Watson, an itinerant seller of stoneware, and his son, also George, stopped off at Knockburnie for the night, Kerr's hospitality was rewarded with an act of stupefying ingratitude. When the farmer got up the next morning, he received a rather unpleasant surprise when he discovered that his guests had slipped away under cover of darkness, taking with them as they went one of his farm horses: a fine, grey Clydesdale mare.

It is likely that his fury was compounded when it became clear that the Watsons had taken a second horse from the neighbouring farm of Marshallmark which was tenanted by John's brother, William Kerr. With no time wasted the two brothers saddled up and set off in pursuit, so confident of catching up with the thieves fairly quickly that they didn't bother to equip themselves with either money or provisions. Gradually it became clear, though, that perhaps they were facing a tougher task than they had initially bargained for. By the time they had covered the twenty-odd miles to Kilmarnock, they had still seen neither hair nor hide of their quarry so they took the decision that William should return home - someone, after all, had to take care of the men's farms - while his brother continued alone. Stopping off at intervals to make inquiries, John followed the Watsons up and over the Fenwick Moor before heading down through the Mearns and on into Glasgow. He managed to track the thieves through the city - a good deal smaller, of course, then than today - and before long found himself heading up Loch Lomondside and into the Highland hills. His task was made easier, it was said, by the fact that his stolen mare had recently cast a half-shoe and her distinctive hoof-prints were clearly recognisable on areas of soft ground.

As one day ran into the next, how, we might ask, did John cope without a penny in his pocket? Possibly he was able to cadge a short-term loan from some acquaintance along the way, or maybe he simply relied on the goodwill of local people who, on hearing his story, might well have been prompted to provide him with the basic necessities. On reaching Tarbet, John veered west to the shores of Loch Long, then set out on the long climb up the Rest and Be Thankful, a dramatic hill pass rising to just short of 1,000 feet. Of course, in the month of March it is quite possible that at this stage he was tracking his Clydesdale's prints through the snow. Now among Gaelic-speakers, John had entered the mountainous heart of the West Highlands, though somehow it is hard to imagine the stolid New Cumnock farmer being remotely daunted by the scale of the landscape. After all, wasn't he well used to the sight of Blackcraig Hill, frowning darkly over the meadows of Glen Afton and forming a backcloth to his home at Knockburnie? Nothing if not tenacious, he continued round the head of Loch Fyne and pressed on to the town of Inveraray where he obtained a warrant from the sheriff there who, when he heard John's story, provided him with two local policemen for the remainder of his journey. Now a posse of three, the men headed north first to Dalmally, then veered west around the head of Loch Awe, riding in the shadow of Ben Cruachan - though whether John displayed any appetite for Highland scenery is not on record. At last, a total of eight days and 150 gruelling miles after leaving his home, John Kerr finally came face to face with the thieving Watsons in an isolated glen north of Oban.

For brevity and understatement, the exchange that followed was one to rival Livingstone and Stanley's legendary encounter in the heart of Africa, and if George Watson got a bit of a shock he made a good job of hiding it. 'I didnae expeck to see you, Knockburnie,' is supposed to have been his bland opening remark, and John Kerr's rejoinder, when it came, was equally terse and to the point – 'An' I didnae expeck ye wad hae stown [stolen] my grey mare.' At this, Watson went on the attack, launching himself at Kerr, but he was soon dragged back and restrained by the accompanying police officers. The captured men were then escorted back to Inveraray, the county town of Argyll, where they spent several weeks in custody before being sent on to face trial in Ayr. As for John Kerr, the chances are that he simply turned on his heel and headed for home, leading his newly recovered horses behind him. No doubt, there are whimsical aspects to Knockburnie's long ride when viewed from our modern standpoint, two centuries on, but in 1811 the affair was viewed very differently. In those pre-mechanised days the horse was essential not only for transport but also as man's invaluable partner in the production of food, and consequently an animal's theft was viewed as a weighty matter.

Well aware of the gravity of his crime, Watson, senior, pled guilty nonetheless and threw himself upon the mercy of the court and, despite the best efforts of the defence, the jury found young George similarly guilty. Both father and son were obliged to wait a further 24 hours before being informed of their fate and, as it turned out, there was to be no mercy. On Friday 3 May, the presiding judge, Lord Meadowbank, took George, senior, to task for his shortcomings as a father. In addressing him, he made no effort to mince his words, accusing him of 'not only committing a capital crime himself but in corrupting the mind of his own son, seducing him to prove an associate in crime - in forgetting every paternal duty and stifling every paternal feeling - of being guilty of a sin against nature by proving the most fatal enemy of one whom he was bound by every tie of nature and obligation of duty to guide in the paths of rectitude.' Watson remained impassive and displayed no emotion, either during Lord Meadowbank's lecture or when the judge informed him that he would be hanged at Ayr in one month's time. When young George's turn came round, he was treated with greater leniency, sentenced to be transported to New South Wales, Australia, for a period of seven years where, the judge suggested, it might be within his power to recover his good name and return ultimately to Scotland. In sharp contrast to his father's stoical front, young George was unable to conceal his distress, as much at his father's fate as at his own.

When George Watson ascended the scaffold at Ayr on 7 June 1811, the executioner presiding was one John High of Edinburgh, a man known familiarly by the name of *Jock Heich* who, in a cruel irony, was rumoured to have taken up his trade in order to escape punishment for having stolen livestock himself, in his case poultry. It was reported that Watson had shown remorse during his spell in prison and when the time came for him to march to the scaffold he did so with composure and apparent indifference to his fate. Poor George Watson - the law relating to horse-theft was to relax some twenty years later and his was the dubious honour of being the last man in Scotland to steal a horse and pay for it with his life. Fortunately for him, young George appears to have fared rather better and, instead of facing the banishment down under that he expected, he is believed to have travelled no farther than the rotting hulks that served as floating prisons on the River Thames in London where, like many another, he remained confined in squalid conditions for a number of years before finally being released. When he regained his freedom, it is by no means impossible that young George Watson set his face to the north and headed for home, and it seems hardly unreasonable to hope that he might just have made it.

Sadly, George Watson, senior, would not be the last Scotsman to face the death penalty for theft of livestock, though in fact John Ritchie was little more than a boy when he died seven years later on the gallows in Aberdeen. Born in the coastal village of Gardenstown, Ritchie was only two years old when he lost his father and his mother likewise passed away while he was still in his early teens. Charged in January 1818 with having stolen thirty sheep - the property of his Grace, the 4th Duke of Gordon - the seventeen-year-old claimed in court that he had been put up by others to carry out the theft, but though he had no previous convictions the cards were inevitably stacked against him. He was found guilty in due course but the entire jury - with one solitary exception - added a recommendation to mercy. Within the local area Ritchie's conviction attracted a great deal of sympathy and a petition was raised on his behalf, appealing for clemency, and though it was endorsed by representatives of a broad spectrum of north-eastern society, the Duke of Gordon's refusal to sign was believed by many to have been instrumental in its failure. When Ritchie appeared on the scaffold on 5 June 1818, prematurely dressed in his graveclothes, there were many who wept and averted their eyes, finding the sight too painful to bear. With quiet dignity he bowed to those around him before the executioner, John Milne, drew back the bolt and sent him plummeting to his death. Mercifully, the young man slipped away, it was said, with very little of a struggle. As a means of thwarting the bodysnatchers who were active at the time, his remains were carried far out to sea before being weighted down and committed to the waves. As things turned out, John Ritchie's death on the gallows, and that of the horse-thief, George Watson, were to be the last two cases in Scottish legal history when a man's life mattered less than the loss of a brute beast.

John Worthington : February 1815

In the late autumn of 1814, venturing on to the rural roads of Ayrshire appears to have been a fairly hazardous enterprise. A farmer on horseback, Mr Dick of Gateside, Craigie, was waylaid near his home by three unknown men, one of whom thrust a pistol in his face. The would-be robber got more than he bargained for, however, when the plucky farmer reached out and wrested the firearm from his assailant's grasp before riding off at speed, startled for sure but otherwise unscathed. He'd had a lucky escape: when he took the weapon to Kilmarnock the following day, it was examined by the town magistrates and found to be loaded and dangerous. A few days later a young man was similarly menaced at Spittal Hill, scarcely a mile from Gateside, by an assailant also brandishing a firearm.

Around the same time, a post rider near Maybole reported being intercepted by two men on foot who threatened his life if he refused to hand over the mailbags. Rejecting their demands, the postman later recounted how he had struck one of his aggressors full in the face - with such force, he claimed, that the man fell instantly to the ground. When his accomplice attempted to discharge a pistol, by sheer good fortune the weapon loudly misfired, causing the postman's horse to bolt and thus preserving both its rider and the mails. When examined more closely, however, the postman's story started to fray until, questioned under oath, he finally confessed that, having picked up news of recent robberies in the local area, he had fabricated the entire episode in what can only be described as a fairly pathetic attempt to gain kudos for having thwarted a similar attempt. When the truth became known, it seems unlikely that the would-be hero would have reaped much by way of glory from his attempted deception.

Despite debunking the postman's colourful fictions, the authorities remained jittery nonetheless concerning an undeniable upsurge in highway robbery, now a far more common event, it was noted, than in previous years. Chaired by Lord Eglinton, a committee of Justices of the Peace issued a proclamation in November 1814 which, in order to reach as broad an audience as possible, clergymen were instructed to read to their congregations. In their announcement, the JPs made reference to 'the very alarming state of the country' due to 'multiplied instances of Highway Robbery, aggravated, in many cases, by wanton and barbarous assaults.' A reward of twenty guineas (£21) was offered to any member of the public who might apprehend a person who was subsequently convicted of 'Murder, Highway Robbery, or Housebreaking.' In addition to the proclamation from the pulpit, the Justices also released a public notice, exhorting farmers and country people in particular to keep a close eye on 'all Vagrants and Suspicious Persons' and to carry out a citizen's arrest if deemed necessary. Innkeepers, the notice suggested, were 'more in the way of observing suspicious characters than any other class of people' and they were therefore urged to pass on any relevant information to Magistrates and Constables. Failure to do so, it was made clear, might result in the loss of a publican's licence to trade. But the JPs did more than simply pontificate. Based on the selection of a sub-committee, 'a very enterprising man', Angus Gunn, was appointed to the post of Head Constable for Ayrshire at the not inconsiderable salary of £80 per annum. Perhaps it was events of several weeks earlier which had served to focus the minds of the authorities. On Thursday, 27 October, the half-yearly feeing fair known as 'Dudsday' had taken place in Kilmarnock, an occasion when the surrounding landward population flooded into the town - as intent on carousing, possibly, as on commerce - with the result that it was normal for a good number of travellers to be late on the road.

During the late afternoon of the Dudsday in question, the publican, James Ballantine's, wife experienced a vague sense of foreboding when four unknown men planted themselves in her husband's establishment in the village of Monkton. Ballantine eyed his customers warily as they drank down two gills of whisky and disposed of fourpence worth of bread - these were meagre times - their voices dropping any time his wife approached to serve them. They did not, she observed to her husband, have the look of men who were engaged in legitimate business. One of the four was a tall man, around six feet in height, dressed in a long, dark coat with yellow buttons and wide, grey trousers. The skin of his nose was disfigured by a conspicuous black blemish and his sallow complexion gave him an unhealthy look. It would later be said that he had something of the appearance of an old soldier.

Of his drinking companions, one was a much smaller man, a little over five feet perhaps, dressed in a brown coat and whose red hair and matching beard were accompanied by a notably florid complexion. The third drinker, by contrast, was dark with copious black whiskers about his face. About five feet six inches tall, he wore grey stockings and a blue coat with small yellow buttons. It did not escape the publican's notice that he had equipped himself with a stout stick. This dark-featured man was the only member of the party able subsequently to be identified. Strangely, nothing is known about the fourth drinker in Ballantine's hostelry. Perhaps his back was kept turned or maybe he was careful to remain in the shadows, outwith the feeble glow of candlelight.

At five o'clock, James Henry, a weaver living nearby, arrived at Ballantine's premises to buy candles from the small grocery store which the innkeeper operated alongside his public house. Indicating the four sinister characters who had come in earlier, the landlord mentioned to his neighbour on the quiet that the men had unnerved his wife and he specifically asked Henry to take a close look at them. When the group of four finally got up and departed, the landlord voiced his strong suspicion that, before the night was out, some of those returning from the Dudsday fair would have been relieved of their wallets.

As it turned out, the first of these was David Dickie, apprentice to a Kilmarnock upholsterer, William Lamont. Dickie had left the fair just after 5 p.m., making for Ayr on horseback, but his journey by moonlight did not go entirely to plan when his pony cast a shoe at Symington, obliging him to continue at a more leisurely pace. A short time later he was nearing the first belt of woodlands at Rosemount when he became aware of four men, travelling from the opposite direction, one of whom blocked his pony's progress by tightly gripping the reins. The young upholsterer was left in no doubt about the man's intentions when he peremptorily demanded Dickie's wallet and, as if to dispel any doubt that he meant business, proceeded to strike him a savage blow to the head with his stick. The pony reared up at this but before it could break free was restrained by the highwayman's three companions, enabling Dickie's initial attacker to take hold of his right leg and thereby dislodge him from the saddle. The men then bundled their victim into a ditch where they proceeded to rifle through his clothing and pockets, searching even the tops of his boots, and taking from him some seven shillings in silver, a pair of gloves and his handkerchief as well as a second black, silk handkerchief that he had been wearing around his neck.

Not yet satisfied, however, Dickie's first attacker demanded that he hand over his pocket-book - or wallet - while at the same time compressing the apprentice's neck in order to ensure his silence. Meanwhile the robber's three accomplices continued to search his clothing in what proved a fruitless search for a pocket-watch. At one point Dickie attempted to break free and make a run for it, but his efforts were thwarted when the smallest of the men produced and threatened him with a pistol. His ordeal only came to an end when, suspecting that someone was approaching, his attackers released him and slipped away quietly into the darkness. Shocked and badly shaken, Dickie was forced to resume his journey on foot, making his way down the brae to Rosemount smithy where he was fortunate to find his pony waiting. The only detailed description that he was subsequently able to provide was of his initial attacker who was, he reported, a swarthy, dark-complexioned man with a long beard who had been wearing a medium-length blue coat with small yellow buttons. Interestingly, he felt it worth mentioning that, because the highwaymen had been careful to keep their voices lowered, he was unable to say whether any of them had spoken with an Irish accent.

David Dickie was not the only unsuspecting soul who fell among thieves that late October evening. The upholsterer was still recovering from his ordeal when two more men arrived at Rosemount smithy with similar reports of having fallen prey to the violent gang. Monkton farmers, James Ferguson of Newlands and Alexander Paterson of Aikenbrae, had left Kilmarnock Fair together, travelling on horseback, but by the time that Ferguson arrived at the sixth milestone from Ayr - somewhere in the vicinity of present-day Hansel Village - his companion had fallen some way behind. As he passed the Rosemount plantation, Ferguson was riding alone and the attack he suffered there was as merciless as it was unexpected. In a similar manner to David Dickie before him, the farmer's horse was seized by its bridle, allowing him to be pulled to the ground. Despite being threatened with a pistol and beaten about the head with sticks, Ferguson refused to surrender his valuables without a struggle. Even as his pockets were being rifled, he managed to rise to his feet and drag his attackers across the road. Ultimately, however, force of numbers prevailed and he was overpowered and robbed of his possessions: a one pound note, some shillings and other small coins and (something he only became aware of the following morning) the keys to his desk. For all his cuts and bruises, perhaps the Newlands farmer got off relatively lightly: he was said to have been carrying a larger sum of money, secreted about his person, which the robbers failed to locate.

Following on behind, Alexander Paterson rode into an identical ambush. Hauled from his horse and brutally assaulted, his red leather pocket-book, containing the considerable sum of £19 in pound- and guinea-notes, was snatched from his pocket. In addition to cash, he also lost a silver pocket-watch, numbered 47,599. When finally released, Paterson struggled on and overtook James Ferguson and the two men made their way down to Rosemount smithy where they found the gang's earlier victim, David Dickie, still recovering from his own ordeal.

It is hard to imagine that the publican, James Ballantine, and his neighbour, James Henry, were unduly surprised when word reached Monkton of the violent robberies that had taken place some two miles up the road. A posse of twenty or so men (including Henry) was quickly assembled who armed themselves with sticks and made their way directly to Rosemount, encountering Ferguson and Paterson along the way. In spite of their injuries, the two doughty farmers had retraced their steps in search of their attackers, having first taken the precaution of equipping themselves with the Rosemount blacksmith's poker. (David Dickie, by contrast, had clearly had enough by this time and was content to resume his journey to Ayr.) Arriving at Rosemount, the Monkton men combed the surrounding countryside but of the four highwaymen there was not a trace.

Perhaps what put the men of the Monkton posse off the scent was Alexander Paterson's impression that, in the aftermath of the ambush, his attackers had made off in the direction of Kilmarnock. For entirely understandable reasons, however, it turned out that the bruised and battered farmer was mistaken. In reality, the four highwaymen had veered east, following back-roads in the direction of the village of Craigie, where they carried out their fourth robbery of the evening - a crime too far, as it turned out. Around 7 p.m., they waylaid a third local farmer, Robert Guthrie of Townhead of Drumley, and, in a violent attack, dragged him from his horse and robbed him of his valuables. Unfortunately for one of his assailants, Guthrie recognised the man as a hawker who routinely travelled the local countryside, selling items out of a green pack. He named the man as Witheredge.

It turned out that the name provided by Robert Guthrie wasn't too far off the mark. The man, in fact, was John Worthington, an itinerant pedlar who at one time had based his operations at Kilmarnock before later relocating to Glasgow. Around 8 p.m. on the evening of the Dudsday fair, Worthington and a single companion - by his speech an Irishman - turned up on the doorstep of Robert Hamilton, a Kilmarnock weaver with whom Worthington had lodged some three years earlier. Hamilton would later claim to have been uneasy at the hawker's unannounced arrival, knowing full well that he had previously been banished from Ayrshire as a consequence of his criminal activity, but he took him in nonetheless. The presence in Hamilton's home that evening of Worthington's young son and daughter, the latter having arrived from Glasgow earlier in the day, may put a different complexion on matters, giving the contrary impression that, despite the weaver's assertion, the arrival of his guests was not perhaps entirely unexpected. Once settled, Worthington produced a £1 note and sent his son out to buy a mutchkin of whisky - something short of a modern-day pint - but when the twelve-year-old returned empty-handed, saying that no change was to be had, his father handed him instead the sum required - two shillings - in silver. During the course of his visit, Worthington revealed nothing to his host of his movements earlier that day, and when he and his companion finally got up to go he indicated his intention to carry on to Irvine. As he left, Worthington passed two shillings and sixpence to Robert Hamilton's wife to pay for a new shirt for his son. Margaret Hamilton would later state her suspicion that the pedlar might also have given his daughter a sum of money to provide for her return journey to Glasgow. At no point in the Hamiltons' account of events is there any reference to the children's mother.

Worthington did not go to Irvine. Reunited with all three of his companions, he appears instead to have made his way to Rose Fenwick, a small settlement on the site of present-day Laigh Fenwick, arriving there shortly after 10 p.m. Though the landlord of the Black Bull Inn, David Taylor, had already shut up shop and was on the point of retiring for the night, in response to the men's knocking, his wife, Jean, unbolted the door and allowed them in. Although Jean Taylor did not know any of her visitors by name, their faces were familiar and Worthington in particular she had known for several years as a travelling salesman. Settling themselves in the kitchen of the public house, the four men talked for an hour or so, consuming as they did so two half-mutchkins of spirits, after which they approached the landlord's wife to request overnight accommodation. Supplying them with a candle and a third half-mutchkin of spirits, the landlord's wife showed her late-night guests to an upstairs room containing a bed. She would later recall overhearing John Worthington at this time saying that they still had business to be settled.

Jean Taylor's suspicions had been aroused. From the kitchen below, she could hear the chink of money being counted, so she tiptoed upstairs in her stocking soles and, peering one-eyed through a gap in the lathing, spied on her guests - something she would later insist that she was not in the habit of doing. Seen through the narrow cranny, banknotes had been laid out on a table, and, as the intrigued landlady continued to observe, she saw Worthington place a number of shillings on top of each. From the snatch of conversation that she overheard, Jean Taylor formed the impression that there was some disagreement over the division of the money. Having seen enough, she slipped quietly back downstairs and, not long after, the men descended, made their excuses and promptly vanished into the night. It would not be the last that Jean Taylor of the Black Bull would hear of her four shady guests.

In spite of his traumatic experience, Alexander Paterson, the farmer of Aikenbrae, was not one to let the grass grow under his feet. On Friday 28 October, the day after the Dudsday fair, he and James Henry travelled to Kilmarnock, hoping to spot the robbers in the streets, but without success. Continuing to Glasgow at the Sheriff-Depute's request, the two men drew a similar blank in the city. Some weeks later, however, Henry's luck turned. He travelled again to Glasgow and on this second occasion was able to identify John Worthington as one of the four drinkers that he had seen in Ballantine's public house on the afternoon of Kilmarnock Fair day. Whether he came face to face with Worthington by chance or, probably more likely, after the hawker had already been picked up by the authorities is not on record. Whatever the circumstances, the accused man was duly transferred to Ayr where witnesses, including James Ballantine and David Dickie, confirmed him as one of the four highway robbers.

During his spell in Ayr tolbooth we are provided with a rare glimpse of Worthington the man. It seems that throughout his time behind bars his spirits remained buoyant and, for whatever reason, he never doubted his impending acquittal. A joker of sorts, he is said to have indulged in various antics at his fellow inmates' expense, frequently donning an old bonnet in dark parody of the infamous black cap worn by a judge when passing the death sentence. In early December, he was removed from Ayr and conveyed for trial to the High Court of Justiciary in Edinburgh, travelling, as it happened, in the company of John Anderson, a sailor on board the brig Amity, who was accused of murdering his wife by throwing her from the parapet of the Auld Brig in Ayr. Anderson was subsequently acquitted but, as things turned out, John Worthington's earlier optimism proved ill-founded. Despite his plea that on the day of Kilmarnock Fair he had been more than a hundred miles away, visiting Lochgilphead as part of a selling trip to the West Highlands, the Edinburgh jury remained unconvinced. The dismissal on a technicality of one of the charges - that relating to the attack on Robert Guthrie near Craigie - did nothing to save him. By a unanimous verdict, John Worthington was found guilty of three charges of highway robbery and was accordingly sentenced to death, the execution to be carried out two months later, on Friday 17 February 1815.

An unusual aspect of the arrangements for John Worthington's execution was the court's stipulation that the sentence should be carried out as close as possible to the scene of the highwayman's crimes. Consequently, on the appointed day - Candlemas Friday - a deputation of Ayrshire's great and good processed across the Fenwick Moor to Floak where, at the county boundary, the man at the centre of it all, John Worthington, was passed by the Renfrewshire authorities into their hands. Sheriff Eaton and Procurator Fiscal Murdoch formed part of the reception committee, as well as the recently-appointed Head Constable, Angus Gunn, in whose charge the condemned man was placed. Travelling rather grandly in a horse-drawn coach, Worthington then proceeded to Kilmarnock, escorted all the while by a troop of the Second Regiment of the Queen's Cavalry, later augmented by twelve special constables on horseback from Wallacetown, Ayr, all men who had expressly volunteered for the task. As the cavalcade wound its way down past Fenwick, we might wonder whether the landlady, Jean Taylor, watched it pass and thought back to the evening four months earlier when she had spied on Worthington and his partners in crime in an upstairs chamber of the Black Bull.

A little farther down the road, at Kilmarnock, the condemned man was obliged to trade his horse-drawn comfort for the ignominy of an open cart. He requested, and was granted, permission to see his young son, an apprentice shoemaker in the town, and it was reported that the boy's acute distress was evident to all present. Unsurprisingly Worthington too grew emotional but succeeded in composing himself before saying his final goodbye. The fateful caravan resumed once more, accompanied through Kilmarnock by the town magistrates plus a further 120 special constables who escorted Worthington as far as the burgh boundary at Riccarton Bridge. From there, the condemned man had only a short distance to travel - five or so miles - before arriving at Symington Toll, the setting for his ordeal to come.

What must Worthington have thought when he came within sight of the vast multitude of men, women and children who had converged on this place to view his final torment? As he readied himself for death, the band of the Ayrshire Militia played to a holiday crowd while a detachment of the 91st Regiment, stationed at Ayr, remained on hand to maintain good order. The precise location of the whole morbid extravaganza is no longer certain, though it was said at the time that the Sheriff had made a point of positioning the gallows in a spot which ensured a clear and unobstructed view for all in attendance. One suggestion is that it was erected on the brow of Helenton Hill - a conspicuous, green knowe to the east of Jeanfield farm - and this may well have been the spot where the Glasgow hangman, Thomas Young, prepared for his first call to duty, anxiously testing and re-testing his rope-work and knots. When an inquisitive jackdaw landed on the crossbeam and promenaded back and forth, a flutter of speculation as to its significance rippled through the crowd. A carriage that pulled up from Ayr was found to contain Worthington's son-in-law, temporarily released from jail, it was said, in order to take his final farewell.

Amid the morbid razzmatazz, it may be that the condemned man was afforded at least some degree of solace by the two Roman Catholic clergymen - Mr Paterson of Glasgow and Mr Scott of Paisley - who had accompanied him on his final journey and who prayed with him now at the foot of the gallows. In the moments immediately prior to his ascending the platform, Worthington happened to overhear a sympathetic onlooker who had referred to him as a 'poor man'. His response was instantaneous when he replied - 'I am not a poor man today.' His message seems clear and unambiguous. Even faced with imminent death, Worthington's spirit had not been entirely crushed. Though reviled and condemned and poised now on the brink of eternity, his defiant utterance was a final assertion of his pride and human dignity and it may well be that those were his last ever words. Once atop the platform, Worthington showed no inclination to address the crowd and wasted no time in signalling his readiness to die. At twenty minutes past three o'clock in the afternoon, Tam Young drew back the bolt and the highwayman, Worthington, was sent plummeting to his death. He expired quickly, it was said, and with no apparent struggle.

But, even as his body dangled at the end of a rope, the sorry tale of John Worthington was not yet quite at an end. After being left to hang for the best part of an hour, the body was then cut down, placed in a coffin and transported to Kilmarnock to be interred in the yard of the Laigh Kirk. Those of his friends who attended the burial were surprised at the shallowness of the grave and surmised that a deliberate attempt had been made to facilitate the work of resurrectionists who were known to be active at the time. In order to thwart the body-snatchers' macabre pursuits, two of Worthington's associates used a spade to prise open the coffin lid, after which they poured a large bottle of vitriol and a bucket of quicklime over the corpse with a view to accelerating the process of decomposition and thus rendering the body unsuitable for dissection. An eye-witness observed wryly that Worthington's grave was 'reekin' like a lime kiln.'

A strange sequel to events at Symington Toll involved William Evans, the Duke of Portland's overseer at Troon. Riding by on the day of Worthington's execution, Evans was asked by the elderly toll-keeper whether he intended to wait in order to view the forthcoming spectacle. 'I attend no such gatherings, sir,' came Evans's haughty reply before he galloped off at speed. Little more than a year later, however, the Duke's overseer made a notable exception when he was present in May 1816 at an execution in Ayr. The crime on that occasion was one of forgery and the man who was hanged was William Evans himself.

Margaret Crossan : October 1817

In the early morning of Monday 5 May 1817 smoke was seen rising from the farm of Carsegowan, by Newton Stewart, but by the time the alarm was raised and potential helpers assembled the blaze was already out of control. Fanned by the breeze, the flames curled around the walls of the outbuildings, generating such heat as they did so that none of the shocked onlookers dared approach and every so often the sound of an almighty crash signalled that one or other of the rafters inside had splintered and collapsed. More distressing by far, however, was the bawling of cattle, trapped within the byre and maddened with fear. By the time that the fire had finally exhausted itself, the entire steading - stable, barn and byre - had gone up in smoke, with the stackyard's valuable stock of hay and straw reduced to nothing more than a heap of blackened cinders. Worst of all, of all the beasts in the byre not one was found to have survived the blaze. The tenant of Carsegowan, a farmer by the name of McKean, insisted that no naked lights or any other flammable material had been kept anywhere near the steading, and examination of the charred remains revealed that fire had broken out in three separate locations, raising a very strong suspicion that the blaze had been started deliberately. Apart from the damage to the buildings themselves, McKean estimated his losses at some £200, and a reward of one hundred guineas (the equivalent of nearly £10,000 today) was quickly put up for anyone informing on the person, or persons, responsible.

It took little more than a month for a suspect to be identified, apprehended and lodged in Wigtown jail. Born in County Tyrone, Ireland, in the late 1780s, Margaret Crossan had left her native land in search of a better life. A slim, attractive woman in her twenties, she had settled in the part of Scotland that was closest to home - Wigtownshire - but after a few years in her adopted country things went badly awry. Why relations had soured is not clear, but her landlord - McKean of Carsegowan - was determined to evict both her and her child from their home and, when Margaret showed an unwillingness to move, he reacted by threatening to burn the house down over their heads. Without a leg to stand on, she had no option but to comply but, even after finding new accommodation, the way McKean had treated her continued to rankle and she resolved to repay him like for like. But, as so often when acting in haste, it turned out to be a mistake.

Following her arrest, Margaret was charged with 'maliciously setting fire to ... the farm of Carsegowan, in the County of Wigton [*sic*], by which the greater part of the premises were consumed, and particularly, twelve cows, a bull and three calves, in the byre.' Her first reaction was to deny everything but in a second declaration to the authorities, she backtracked somewhat and admitted to being responsible for the blaze, giving as her reason the resentment she had felt following her eviction. Unexpectedly, she went on to implicate an accomplice. On the morning in question, she stated, she had got up early and, with her plan of revenge in mind, had removed a live coal from the grate which she then placed in a can and carried to her former landlord's farm. She was accompanied on her mission by a friend, Isobel Logan, and on arriving at Carsegowan the two women paused outside the barn while Margaret broke the coal into two halves, keeping one half for herself and giving the other to Isobel who carried it to the opposite end of the building. At the same time as Margaret dropped her own half-coal into the barn through 'one of the wickers' (a narrow window-space), her friend did likewise at the opposite end. The bone-dry contents of the barn - hay, grain and straw - instantly caught light, the flames spread to the neighbouring outbuildings and, as we know, the entire farm was destroyed as a result. Margaret's revenge was thus complete, but what a price she would have to pay for it.

Following her arrest, Margaret Crossan was confined behind bars for a period of four months before her case came to court on Thursday 11

September at Ayr, with the notoriously hard-drinking septuagenarian, Lord Hermand, occupying the judge's seat. First to take the witness stand, McKean was backed up in his evidence by his farm-servant, McAlister, and by the neighbouring farmer, McQueen - namely, that the steading of Carsegowan had been burned to the ground by a fire which had been set in three different places. Following on after was Isobel Logan who denied any involvement in the crime, but recounted for the court how a few days after the fire Margaret Crossan had been in her house and had admitted to having set the barn alight, claiming that she did so in response to her quarrel with the farmer. According to Isobel Logan, Margaret had gone on to express regret about the cattle's gruesome death, suggesting that she would have been better pleased if McKean himself had taken the place of the unfortunate beasts. She had finished, Isobel stated, by saying that if the steading were to be rebuilt at any stage in the future she would willingly walk twenty miles 'to give them another whiz' - that is, to do the same again. Logan's testimony was backed up by various others: Sarah Boden, to whom Margaret had apparently given a similar account; Henry McGhie, a local labourer, who had overheard the incriminating conversation between Margaret and Isobel Logan; and John McGraa, a constable, who testified that Margaret had made a similar confession during her time in jail.

Once all of the witnesses had had their say, the Crown prosecutor gave way to Margaret's lawyer, Thomas Maitland, who - unfortunately for her - was able to produce no evidence in her defence. The outcome looked like a foregone conclusion, and it came as no surprise when the spokesman for the jury announced that its members had found Margaret Crossan guilty of wilful fire-raising. At that, the day's proceedings wound to a close, with the judge intimating that, for whatever reason, sentencing would be deferred for 24 hours. After what must have been an excruciating wait, Margaret was brought back to the bar the following day where Lord Hermand duly sentenced her to death by hanging, the execution to take place at Ayr in a month's time, on Friday 17 October, between the hours of two and four o'clock in the afternoon. Despite the 'horrid crime' of which she had been convicted, it was reported at the time that Margaret nonetheless attracted a degree of sympathy by virtue of 'her age, sex, appearance and dreadful situation', a sentiment seemingly shared by the normally-crusty Lord Hermand when he indicated that he was 'unwilling to add affliction to the afflicted' but felt obliged in the circumstances to advise Margaret that he held out no hope of any reprieve. With her fate spelled out in the starkest of terms, Margaret collapsed, unable to walk unassisted, and had to be carried back to her prison cell by the jailor and his orderlies.

Execution day, when it came, turned out to be a noteworthy occasion in the history of Ayr: the one and only time during the nineteenth century when three executions were scheduled to be carried out on a single day, and unsurprisingly the prospect of such a morbid spectacle generated an inordinate amount of interest among the population at large. By an odd coincidence the other prisoners to be hanged that day were two cousins, Joseph Cairns and William Robertson, who had also committed their crimes of robbery in Wigtownshire, not far from Carsegowan. During the course of the forenoon the scaffold was assembled in front of the town jail, while a large body of law-enforcement officers - Special Constables; members of the Ayrshire Militia; plus a party from the 1st Regiment of Royal Dragoons - were assembled to assist the Provost and Magistrates of the Burgh in the disposal of their duties. At shortly after half past two a large crowd watched agog as the three prisoners were brought from their cells to the place of execution, one after the other at regular intervals and each accompanied by a clergyman of the appropriate denomination. Robertson led the way, followed by Cairns, while Margaret Crossan came last, dressed for the occasion in a white robe and cap knotted with black ribbons, and attended by a representative of the Roman Catholic church in Glasgow. (It was into this clergyman's care that Margaret's young child was passed but what became of the infant thereafter is impossible to know.) Scrutinising the prisoners closely, members of the crowd noted that Robertson appeared tearful, Cairns detached and unconcerned, while Margaret wore on her face 'a smile, but not that of levity.' The chances are that, such was the depth of trauma she had endured, she was barely conscious of what was taking place around her.

First to ascend the scaffold, Robertson appeared faint as the noose was being placed around his neck and he was forced to lean back for support against the prison wall. Taken in hand by his accompanying minister, he succeeded in recovering himself before turning to address the vast assemblage of onlookers. Sabbath-breaking and night-walking, he told them, had led him to this place but he had reconnected with religion during his time spent in prison. 'Thank God,' he concluded, 'since I came to this jail, I have spent the happiest days of my life.' The two remaining prisoners now took turns in climbing on to the platform, Cairns with a slow and steady pace and Margaret with 'a rather hasty, but firm step' - a sure sign of nerves. As the executioner, James Aird, carried out his final preparations, the voice of William Robertson was heard clearly by all around as he prayed loudly and without pause. By previous arrangement Joseph Cairns had been nominated to give the signal and, after verifying that his fellow-prisoners were ready and in agreement, he did so, whereupon the drop fell and then ... silence. Not a sound, not a cry, not even a murmur arose from the vast assembled throng. Robertson, they observed, died without a struggle, but the other two, less fortunate, were for some excruciating moments 'considerably convulsed'. When the last signs of life had finally departed, all three corpses were left to hang for the following hour, before being cut down, lowered into coffins and carted back to the prison, to be interred at a later point in the burial ground of the Auld Kirk of Ayr. It was noted in the aftermath of the execution that the crowd was greater than any previously known for a hanging in Ayr, many of those in attendance having reportedly travelled in from the surrounding countryside. There were, however, no disorderly scenes and the spectators were said to have dispersed quietly and without incident.

During her time spent in jail while awaiting execution, Margaret is on record as having expressed regret for her wrongdoing and acknowledged the justice of her sentence, and yet, for all that, she persisted in her story that she had not acted out of 'any vindictive spirit of her own' but had been instigated in her actions by 'another woman with whom she kept company.' Tried, sentenced, condemned and the date of her execution fixed, what could she have hoped to gain at this stage by lying, and what might her possible motive have been? What seems strange in the immediate aftermath of the fire is that Margaret should have spoken so freely to her neighbours regarding her own involvement - unless they too were similarly involved - and fishier still is how the labourer, Henry McGhie, just happened to be within earshot at the very moment when one such conversation was taking place *inside* Isobel Logan's house. It is hard, frankly, not to smell a rat. That Margaret had a hand in the Carsegowan blaze seems beyond question, but whether she was acting alone is another matter entirely. Let us not forget that the person whom she implicated in her second declaration - Isobel Logan - was one of the witnesses who subsequently testified against her in court. Is it possible, we might ask, that Logan colluded with her fellow-witnesses in order to keep her own part in the affair hidden and to leave the outsider, Margaret Crossan, to carry the can alone? After all, it was one such fellow-witness - the eavesdropper, Henry McGhie - who benefited from the blaze to the tune of one hundred guineas, though we might wonder how many others expected a cut.

François Gautiez & Peter Heaman :
January 1822

On a July morning in 1936 when the landlady of a Helensburgh boarding-house went to check on two of her elderly guests, she made rather a grim discovery. Approaching their bedroom door at around seven o'clock, she became aware of the smell of gas and, investigating more closely, was shocked to discover that, although the window had been left slightly open overnight, the ladies' room had apparently filled up with fumes and that Janetta Miller, aged 92, and her sister, Johanna, 90, had perished from asphyxiation, side by side in their bed. Further investigation concluded that one of the ladies had got up during the night to brew a pot of tea on a small gas-ring and, when finished, had failed to screw the tap off fully. Though resident in Morningside, Edinburgh, the two unmarried sisters had strong Hebridean connections where their descent could be traced back to the celebrated Jacobite heroine, Flora MacDonald, and one of the ladies was reportedly wearing her illustrious forebear's ring, containing a lock of Bonnie Prince Charlie's hair, at the time of the Helensburgh tragedy. Another family keepsake which the sisters had gifted to a friend in Stornoway shortly before their death consisted of two unusual Spanish coins, dating back more than a century and with a curious tale attached.

When the schooner, *Jane*, set sail from Malta in mid-May 1821 her captain, Thomas Johnston, and his eighteen-year-old Maltese cabin-boy, Andrew Camelier, faced the prospect of a lengthy voyage to come.

Stopping off briefly at the vessel's home port of Gibraltar, they took on a further six crew members plus a cargo of oil, olives, beeswax, raisins and silk and, last of all, a total of eight barrels, carried on board at sunset and intended for delivery to a certain Joao Miguel Dias de Faria at the port of Salvador in Brazil. It was said that Captain Johnston alone was privy to the barrels' contents but, in an unguarded moment, he let slip to the ship's mate that secreted within them were, in fact, some 38,000 Spanish silver dollars, commonly known as 'pieces of eight' - an unimaginably vast sum at the time. On 19 May, as *Jane* sailed westward into the open Atlantic and the rock of Gibraltar receded steadily behind her, Captain Johnston could scarcely have predicted the price that he would end up paying for his moment of indiscretion.

Crewing the ship as she set out that spring morning was a total of three Scots seamen: nineteen-year-old Arbroath man, Peter Smith; a second native of Angus, Robert Strachan, also nineteen; plus a third Scot, James Paterson, who had been appointed as the schooner's helmsman. The remaining crew consisted of the mate, Peter Heaman, a Swedish-born seaman in his mid-thirties, now resident with his family in the Sunderland area of north-east England; and François Gautiez, a 23-year-old Frenchman who was engaged as ship's cook but who understood no English. The sixth and final crew-member was Johanna Dhura (otherwise known as John Hard), a man in his mid-twenties of Italian origin who was proficient in English and also knew a little French. The captain, Thomas Johnston, was generally reckoned a just and even-tempered master, not given to vices such as strong drink, but there could be little doubt that, as he directed his vessel out to cross the Atlantic, the lure of Spanish treasure, deep in the hold, had placed his authority in grave doubt.

Just over a fortnight out from Gibraltar, some distance west of the Canary Islands, it all kicked off. Andrew Camelier, the cabin-boy, was awakened one night from his slumbers when the deafening sound of a gunshot, accompanied by a blinding flash, rang out through the darkness of his cabin. Startled, he rushed on to the deck where he was shocked to see the mate, Peter Heaman, viciously attacking the helmsman with the butt end of a musket. Unarmed and unable to defend himself, James Paterson cried out as he crumpled to the ground where Heaman continued to beat him mercilessly - the price, it later transpired, of the helmsman's loyalty to his captain - until eventually all movement ceased. Fearing a similar fate, the cabin-boy wept as he pleaded for his own life to be spared. Meanwhile Captain Johnston had appeared on deck, distressed, apparently disorientated, and uttering the words - 'What is this? What is this?' He held one hand pressed firmly to his forehead where Camelier noticed blood oozing from what looked like a fresh gunshot wound. At this point François Gautiez stepped out from the shadows and struck the captain a savage blow with the butt end of a musket, knocking him to the deck where he continued to attack him ferociously. Above the sound of Captain Johnston's agonised groans, the cabin-boy heard the voice of Peter Heaman, crying 'Don't come up!' as other members of the crew, on hearing the commotion, began to emerge from their sleeping quarters in the fo'c'sle.

John Hard made it on to the deck but Robert Strachan and Peter Smith were prevented from following by Heaman who by this time had added to his authority by wielding an axe. Ordered to assist in disposing of the bodies, Hard and the cabin-boy had no option but to cooperate as James Paterson's body was heaved overboard with an iron weight attached to one of his feet. Similar treatment was then meted out to Captain Johnston whose clothing was weighted down with rocks taken from the ballast before his body too was cast into the sea. While Hard appeared reluctant, François Gautiez was by contrast an enthusiastic participant in these proceedings, though perhaps surprisingly the mate, as Camelier observed, took no part. Chillingly, the cabin-boy would later recall that, as Captain Johnston's body was consigned to the deep, signs of life were still evident. His blood-stained bedclothes followed some time later along with official paperwork relating to the ship, but the cook was careful to take possession of the captain's pocket-watch while his watch-chain, with its various small trinkets attached, was appropriated by the mate.

The horrors did not end there and events aboard the *Jane* proceeded to take what can only be described as a bizarre turn. Presumably uncertain of their loyalty, Heaman set about confining Peter Smith and Robert Strachan in their quarters within the fo'c'sle, battening down the hatches which he went on to ensure were securely nailed down. He then set about stacking up firewood, impregnated with tar, which he subsequently set alight using gunpowder, the resulting smoke to penetrate Smith and Strachan's cabin through holes that had been drilled in the bulkhead. Heaman was meticulous, even going so far as to caulk any cracks through which smoke might escape or fresh air enter, using for the purpose a paste made up from a solution of flour and water. The fire, once lit, burned intermittently for a day and two nights and, when the hatches were finally opened up, it was by no means clear whether the crewmen within would be found dead or alive. As it happened, it transpired that both Smith and Strachan had survived their smoky ordeal, though - understandably - both were found to be in a debilitated condition. Following a plea by their shipmate, John Hard, a little bread was handed down to them before they were released some time later from their smoke-blackened cell. Why the pitiless duo of Heaman and Gautiez elected to spare the two Scots' lives at this stage rather than simply finishing them off is not entirely clear. Perhaps the intention all along was not so much to suffocate the two men but rather to terrify them into compliance.

Smith and Strachan had not yet, however, earned the murderers' trust. On being released, both men were obliged to kiss the Bible, then swear that they would remain forever silent concerning recent events that they had witnessed aboard the *Jane*. The murderers' motive was never in doubt. While Gautiez took control at the helm, the barrels of Spanish dollars were brought up on deck and the money placed in bags before being stowed beneath the bulwarks of the ship. In an effort to destroy incriminating evidence, the barrels themselves were then burned. With no longer any reason to complete the Atlantic crossing, the ship's course was duly altered and, following discussion, she turned her face to the north and set sail for Scotland. Flying an American flag, Heaman took it upon himself to take on the role of captain, while his accomplice, François Gautiez, promoted himself to the position of mate.

It seems likely that the pirates sought to avoid busy, populated areas, making first landfall at the southernmost end of the long Hebridean chain where Heaman, Smith and Strachan went ashore on the island of Barra and, using false identities, exchanged 60 Spanish dollars for a small fishing-boat. Leaving Barra, the *Jane* sailed north once again, this time making for Orkney, until rumours of a customs vessel operating in the vicinity brought about a rethink and the somewhat drastic decision was taken to hole the vessel using a crowbar and scuttle her in the seas off the Isle of Lewis. This done, the pirates then used the boat bought at Barra to ferry their treasure ashore where they divided it up, initially counting the coins by hand and then, when that was found to be too time-consuming, using a tin pot as a scoop. Once the money was all accounted for, it emerged that each man was to benefit to the tune of more than 6,000 dollars, a tidy enough haul for sure, though it escaped no-one's notice that Heaman allocated to himself the lion's share. The sailors' first priority now was to conceal the money, burying most of it in bags and money-belts beneath the shoreside shingle while a smaller sum was deposited in their sea-chests. As they worked feverishly to conceal their treasure, what the men were unaware of at this time was the fact that their attempt to scuttle the *Jane* had proved singularly unsuccessful and, propelled by a fresh easterly wind, the vessel had been driven on to craggy rocks near Tolsta Head where she had quickly been spotted by local people and attempts made to salvage what remained of her cargo.

It was inevitable that the men's own arrival had also been noted. As they set up home in a makeshift tent, erected on top of their boat, a band of curious locals appeared on the scene, followed soon after by Roderick MacIver, customs officer at Stornoway, to whom Peter Heaman suavely introduced himself as one George Shadwell. From the outset MacIver was inclined to be sceptical of Shadwell's tale of how his ship, the Betsy, had been wrecked off Barra Head, her entire cargo of North American tobacco and cotton lost to the waves, and he took an even keener interest in the stranded seafarers when, suspecting smuggled goods, he opened up the men's sea-chests and came across, not French wine or brandy as might have been expected, but rather a substantial quantity of Spanish silver dollars. Posting a guard at the shoreside camp, MacIver set out to return to Stornoway for reinforcements and, by so doing, provided Andrew Camelier with just such an opportunity as he had been waiting for. In the blink of an eye, the plucky cabin-boy eluded his guards, sprinting out of the makeshift camp and catching up with the customs officer, where he breathlessly blurted out the truth about what had taken place aboard the *Jane*. Convinced of the cabin-boy's sincerity, MacIver immediately co-opted men from the nearby settlement at Swordale to reinforce the existing guard, then hastened back to the town where he set about assembling a posse to bring the suspects in. It must surely have been a red-letter day as the crew of the *Jane*, bound with ropes, were led through the Stornoway streets, but even greater drama followed soon after when a cartload of silver dollars, unearthed from the sands of Swordale, trundled its way toward Customs House. The crewmen themselves were detained at Stornoway until the customs vessel *Prince of Wales* arrived to transport them to Edinburgh.

Unsurprisingly, once investigations had run their course, the two men facing charges of piracy and murder in the High Court of Admiralty on 26 November 1821 at Edinburgh were Peter Heaman and François Gautiez. Able counsel was provided for the men's defence and the French consul, Monsieur Hugot, attended throughout as an observer. On hearing the charges read out against them, both of the accused pled not guilty and in the hours that followed testimony was provided, not only by the other members of the Jane's crew, but also by more than thirty other witnesses who had contributions to make. Central to proceedings was the evidence of the Stornoway customs officer, Roderick MacIver, who recounted in detail the part he had played in apprehending the men accused, while a fellow resident of the Isle of Lewis, sixty-year-old John Murray of Melbost, required the services of a Gaelic translator in describing Heaman's obvious agitation at Swordale when it was discovered that his cabin-boy had given him the slip. A London associate of the *Jane*'s owner, Moses Levy of Gibraltar, related how he had organised insurance for the schooner's cargo to the value of £2,000. When his own turn came to be questioned, Peter Heaman was at pains to paint the picture of an unhappy ship, depicting Captain Johnston as a violent and tyrannical figure who routinely stirred up resentment through his mistreatment of the seamen under his command. As tensions steadily mounted aboard the *Jane*, Heaman recounted, matters finally came to a head when Captain Johnston got wind of rumblings of discontent among his crew and, in what might seem like a major over-reaction, mistook James Paterson at the helm for one of the principal agitators - François Gautiez - and promptly 'blowed his brains out.' Following this outrage, the mate related how Johnston had gone on to pistol-whip the Frenchman, breaking his left arm in the process, before being collectively restrained by the remainder of the crew. During the altercation that followed, Heaman claimed that he was uncertain as to which man had struck the blow that ended the captain's life but he was adamant that the entire crew had participated in pitching the body overboard - himself excepted. He did, however, emphasise the part played in Johnston's death by the cabin-boy, Andrew Camelier, who was, he insisted, 'the most bloodthirsty of the whole.'

With the predictable exception of his co-accused, François Gautiez, Heaman's version of events was one that no other witness was prepared to corroborate and whether the tale the two men spun would be credible enough to convince the fifteen-man Edinburgh jury remained to be seen. As proceedings drew to a close, the Lord Advocate, Sir William Rae, summed up for the Crown, acknowledging that the jury had already absorbed nearly sixteen hours of testimony before he moved on to point out one of the most singular aspects of the case: 'It is to the punishment of offences committed in Scotland,' he observed, 'that the attention of juries in Scotland is demanded. But here you see we are called upon to judge in a case which occurred many thousand miles distant from the nearest corner of the kingdom.' That unusual circumstance, he insisted, did not detract from the fact that the men on trial were guilty both of piracy and murder, charges which he believed had been substantiated beyond reasonable doubt. Speaking for the defence, the best that Thomas Maitland could do was to attempt to discredit the prosecution witnesses by highlighting certain minor inconsistencies in their evidence but, clearly aware of the uphill struggle he faced, he chose to conclude his remarks by recommending that the jury find the charges against both men 'not proven.' Speaking last, the Admiralty judge, Sir John Connell, provided the jury with a clear indication of his own opinion - as well as an unmistakable nudge - when he described Andrew Camelier, the Maltese cabin-boy, as 'as candid a witness as ever appeared in a court of justice.' And it appears that that the jurymen took the hint, returning some hours later to convey their unanimous view that both of the accused men were guilty as charged of piracy and murder.

The resulting sentence was, of course, a foregone conclusion and Sir John Connell didn't mince his words. 'If the law of this country permitted a punishment greater than death,' he told the two convicted men, then 'that punishment would be inflicted on you.' Quashing any hope of a reprieve, he made it clear that their fate was 'finally and irretrievably fixed' and exhorted them to use what time they had left in this world to repent of their sins in preparation for facing divine justice to come. All that was left now was for Heaman and Gautiez to be 'carried from the bar back to the tolbooth of Edinburgh' where they would be 'fed on bread and water only' until several weeks hence when they would 'be taken forth of the said tolbooth to the sands of Leith, within floodmark, and then and there ... hanged by the neck, upon a gibbet, by the hands of the common executioner, until they be dead.' The men's bodies were then to be cut down and delivered to Dr Alexander Monro, Professor of Anatomy at Edinburgh University, for the purpose of public dissection. On learning their fate, the two convicted men remained composed throughout, bowing respectfully to the court, but the anguished cries of Heaman's wife, present throughout the trial, were distressing to all who heard.

In the days that followed, a platform was duly erected on the Leith sands, close to the Naval Yard and immediately below the tideline. On the day appointed - 9 January 1822 - crowds waiting outside Edinburgh's New Jail were rewarded at around half past nine in the morning when the gates swung open and a procession of three carriages emerged, the foremost carrying four Edinburgh bailies in their robes of office, wearing white gloves and carrying white staves. A Roman Catholic clergyman, Rev. Wallace, was among those in the second carriage, whose responsibility it was to attend to François Gautiez' final spiritual needs; and travelling in the final vehicle were representatives of the Church of Scotland - a local minister, Rev. Dr John Campbell and Rev. James Porteous, the Edinburgh prison chaplain. A simple cart followed on behind containing a bench on which the two condemned men were seated facing the horse's tail and, last of all, the hangman, Thomas Williams, brought up the rear on foot. Public order was maintained by a cavalry detachment of the 3rd Dragoon Guards, backed up by city officials bearing halberds as well as a large contingent of duty police officers. During the course of his final journey Peter Heaman rose to his feet, removed his hat and, clutching a copy of the New Testament in one hand, bowed repeatedly to the immense crowds of spectators that thronged the streets and peered from the windows of their homes and businesses - an expression of gratitude, it was suggested, for the Edinburgh folk's generosity toward his wife and four children, lately departed for their home in England. François Gautiez by contrast remained seated, seemingly preoccupied with his thoughts and paying little heed to the bustle of activity around him.

As the procession arrived on the sands and the two condemned men ascended the scaffold, it was clear to all that strain was taking its toll. Peter Heaman, for his part, was observed to shed tears - the only time during the entire proceedings that he did so - while François Gautiez appeared bewildered and required at times to be supported. By the time that a portion of the 51st psalm was sung - specifically chosen as a plea for divine forgiveness - Heaman, it was noted, had succeeded in composing himself and he participated heartily in the singing but, knowing little English, Gautiez remained kneeling throughout, attended to in his private devotions by the accompanying priest. When the psalm ended and the crowd fell silent, Rev. Campbell addressed those present on Heaman's behalf, acknowledging his guilt and commending in addition the fairness of his trial and the justice of the sentence imposed. Bowing to the crowd, Heaman added a few words of his own, cautioning his audience concerning the hazards presented by bad company and the danger of neglecting religious duties, both of which, he recognised, had contributed to his melancholy fate. He kneeled as Rev. Campbell offered up a final prayer.

When the minister's voice fell silent, Heaman and Gautiez took up their final positions where, in an affecting scene, the two men shook hands in a last farewell. The bell of the South Leith Church tolled sonorously in the background as cords were placed around their necks. After standing quietly for some time with his hands uplifted, Heaman uttered his final words - 'Lord Jesus, receive my soul!' - and immediately gave the signal, at which point the hangman drew back the bolt and the two men were plunged into space. For Heaman death came mercifully swiftly, but reports suggested that his companion, Gautiez, was less fortunate and faced a tougher struggle in departing this life. To both men's credit, however, it was generally agreed that each had appeared contrite and resigned to his fate, and Shakespeare's well-known line - 'Nothing in his life became him like the leaving it' - might with a degree of justice have been applied to either. As the crowd of some 40-50,000 dispersed, it was noted that there were no untoward events. What no-one who had witnessed the hangings could have realised that day was that these would be the last ever executions to take place in Scotland for the crime of piracy.

Moving on then to the 1930s, how might it have come about that a number of the Jane's silver dollars fell into the hands of two elderly Morningside spinsters? The answer perhaps is to be found in the memoirs of Evander MacIver, for many years the Duke of Sutherland's (unpopular) factor on his Scourie estates, who, in recalling his boyhood on Lewis, recounts how a significant portion of the Jane's treasure mysteriously vanished from the barn at Swordale where it was being stored overnight, but the identity of those responsible never came to light. Whether more of the pirates' hoard might have found its way out of the cart and into various pockets along the road to Stornoway, who can say? However, it came about, such was the leakage of silver dollars, MacIver suggests, that for several years afterwards they became an accepted part of the local currency and it was well-nigh impossible to make a purchase on the Isle of Lewis without incurring the risk of receiving Spanish coins among your change.

Malcolm Gillespie : November 1827

Assisted by moonlight, he spotted a rowing-boat as it peeled away from the sailing ship on the bay and turned towards the north. Familiar as he was with every cove and inlet of the coast, he could guess the small boat's likely destination and was confident too that he knew what cargo she was carrying. Taking care not to be seen, he followed the shoreline, always keeping the boat within sight, until he reached Sandend where a narrow arm of the sea cut into the land. Scouting around in darkness, the only spot he could find that overlooked the tiny creek, but where crucially he would still be screened from view, was beneath a rocky overhang whose roof unfortunately was too low to allow him to stand upright, so his only option was to muster his resolve, take a deep breath, then lower himself down into a pool of icy seawater.

And surely the wait must have seemed interminable as frigid seawater permeated his clothing until at last he heard the voices of men and caught sight of their rowing-boat pulling towards him and edging its way into Sandend's narrow creek with precious little room to spare. When he heard the gravelly crunch as it nosed on to the shingle of the beach, he knew that it was now or never. One man against several, he leapt out and presented his firearm, frightening the boatmen into flight and taking possession of their craft. As he had suspected, its cargo was indeed contraband spirits, but his task was not yet complete and it was far too early yet to claim victory. As he manoeuvred the boat back out of the creek, a welter of rocks and stones rained down on him, launched by the would-be smugglers from the cliff above and putting his life at serious risk until he managed to pull the boat beyond their range and out into Collieston Bay. A heavy sea was running in a stiff easterly breeze as he rowed, drenched and chittering, a full two miles to the fishing village of Ward of Cruden where not a soul could be found at such an hour of the night who might have rendered him assistance. Working single-handedly, he lugged the majority of the heavy wooden casks ashore and deposited them at a safe distance from the boat before rousing the occupants of the local inn who, when they accompanied him back to the foreshore, found that the rowing-boat and what remained of its cargo had been reclaimed by the smugglers and was already out of reach. At that point Malcolm Gillespie had no option but to let matters rest, and be content with what he had.

It was only one of many such tales, and in his role as a north-east customs officer - or 'gauger' - Gillespie's exploits were legendary and his commitment to duty unquestionable. Originally a native of Dunblane, Perthshire, at the age of seventeen he had enlisted in the army where he served for three years before leaving to become a customs officer at Prestonpans with responsibility for supervising the activities of salt manufacturers who operated in that area. By now a husband and father, he was successful in uncovering and clamping down on various fraudulent practices within the industry. After two years in East Lothian he was transferred by his own request to the north-east, a part of the country where smuggling had long been rife. By making use of inside information he quickly became the scourge of the local smuggling fraternity and was responsible for detecting many foreign ships and their illicit cargoes. Not all contraband goods, of course, came by sea and, in order to deal with those arriving from the inland districts, he took a fairly radical step when he chose to enlist the services of a somewhat unorthodox partner.

At considerable expense, so we are told, he acquired a bull terrier - a sturdy, tenacious breed - which he went on to train in preparation for its intended occupation. Once its education was complete, the dog received its first test when Gillespie intercepted smugglers and horses, laden with casks of whisky, near Midmar Lodge. During the melee that ensued, the dog soon proved his mettle by lunging into battle and creating havoc among the horses to such an extent that many of them panicked and bolted, scattering whisky casks far and wide - which, of course, were quickly secured by Gillespie and his men. Sometime later, the terrier earned his keep yet again when his master got wind of another plot, this time to smuggle whisky down from the hilly country of Upper Donside. In the hope of taking the smugglers by surprise, Gillespie set up an ambush, concealing his men in a gravel-pit where they settled down quietly to wait. For the time being the dog was restrained on a leash. Some hours later, a gang of eight or nine smugglers came into view, emerging with their packhorses from the hills. The gaugers sat tight until the optimum moment when Gillespie stepped from the shadows and demanded surrender. The hillmen, however, were in no mood to throw in the towel quite so easily, and while some of their number held the excisemen at bay, their companions attempted to head off the horses, back towards the hills. Drawing his pistol, Gillespie fired a shot which punctured one of the whisky barrels, then, calling for his dog to be released, he set it upon the smugglers' horses till, one after another, they bucked and shied and shed their loads. It was said at the time that in the aftermath of the scuffle the scene resembled a battlefield, with *ankers* (eight-gallon barrels), blue bonnets, tartan plaids and items of the horses' harnesses strewn all over the ground. At the end of the day, it was in large part thanks to Gillespie's plucky terrier that the full consignment of illegal whisky was seized by the gaugers, the total haul on this occasion some thirty or forty gallons, with a further thirty or so spilled from broken barrels.

As he gained more experience, the bull terrier showed remarkable initiative and learned very quickly to ignore unloaded horses and tackle only those which were carrying barrels, frequently seizing these unfortunate animals by the nose and holding on tightly with his teeth until the goods on their backs were dislodged. Hardly surprisingly, the dog was a source of aggravation to the smugglers, many of whom would gladly have done it a mischief; and yet, for all that, when the creature finally met its end it came about purely by accident. It so happened that Malcolm Gillespie heard tell of a party of smugglers who were travelling down from the high country on their way to Aberdeen and, making a calculation of their likely route, he resolved to intercept them when they crossed the River Don at the Brig o' Dyce. Accordingly, he assembled his men close to the bridge shortly before midnight, and half an hour or so later the creaking of horse-drawn wagons heralded the smugglers' imminent arrival. Within a few minutes four carts trundled into view, accompanied by eight men, a number of whom were notorious criminals who had previously been outlawed by the courts. When challenged, the smugglers refused to give up their whisky but instead turned tail and drove off their carts at high speed. In an effort to thwart their escape, Gillespie fired off a shot which killed one of their horses but, nonetheless, the smugglers continued on their flight from the law. Turning off the main road, they hurtled down a narrow avenue where the darkness was so intense that Gillespie, riding ahead of his men, was said to have followed them solely by sound. What the smugglers hadn't bargained for, however, was the existence up ahead of a locked iron gate that forced them to turn and stand at bay. Arriving a few moments later, Gillespie heard one of the cornered men call out his name, followed by a threat that his brains would be blown out if he dared take another step. This was the point when, by sheer bad luck, a stray shot through the darkness struck and killed the bull terrier which was standing, muzzled and leashed, beside his master. Despite being upset, Gillespie entered into negotiations with the smugglers who finally agreed to surrender their goods on condition that their horses and carts would not be confiscated. It was an arrangement that netted for the gaugers a total of 200 gallons of illicit whisky, but there is no doubt that for Gillespie the confrontation at the Brig o' Dyce amounted to a pyrrhic victory. Saddened by the loss of his dog, he was heard to remark that he 'would not have parted with him for a hundred guineas.' Unfortunately, the valiant terrier's name is no longer known.

During his time in office, Gillespie covered a considerable stretch of the north-east, and when a rumour reached him that the crew of a lugger - a small sailing ship - had slipped ashore a quantity of contraband goods near Stonehaven, he hurried to the scene as quickly as possible. When he arrived, he found much of the Kincardineshire coast under blockade with various officials - excisemen, tidewaiters and other assistants - busily in attendance. He set to work immediately and, in a surprisingly short time, his keen eye and long experience of skulduggery brought him success where his fellow officers had singularly failed. To general astonishment, he located, buried between the high and low watermarks on the sand, a cache of no fewer than ten casks of brandy and 29 ankers of gin - all under the nose of local officials who in previous days had repeatedly passed to and fro. Ensuring that his haul was in safe hands, Gillespie went on to explore a neighbouring stretch of coastline where, concealed among the dunes, he discovered several longstanding hiding-places for illegal spirits, some in recent use, which he immediately set about destroying - much to the chagrin of suspected local smugglers who were monitoring proceedings from afar. Their dens among the dunes were believed to have been in use for more than fifty years and were capable, it was claimed, of concealing an entire ship's cargo. Gillespie's final act was to uncover the identities of those involved in the local smuggling trade and pass on their names to the authorities. In addition to damaging the interests of legitimate merchants, it was reckoned that during the course of any given year smugglers had defrauded the Exchequer out of thousands of pounds.

All things considered, Gillespie's performance as an exciseman was impressive. During the course of his 28-year career he was successful in seizing many thousands of gallons of illicit alcohol - both foreign and home-produced - and of destroying a good many more. He confiscated a large number of horses and carts, and located and dismantled several hundred illegal whisky stills. Never at any point was he bested by his adversaries, and he always managed either to make a seizure or at the very least foil the wrongdoers' plans. Surviving all manner of scrapes, on one infamous occasion he escaped being throttled only by clamping his assailant's thumb between his teeth and biting as hard as he could. But Gillespie's successes as a gauger came with a price attached, for at the end of the day he ended up out of pocket and in debt. The reason for this strange irony lay in the system for remunerating customs officers at that time. In lieu of regular income, Gillespie was entitled instead to a share in the proceeds of each seizure he made. All well and good, you might think, for such a successful officer but when government taxes were taken into account, as well as transportation costs in relation to goods seized and solicitors' fees to be paid, his terms of employment seemed a good deal less enticing. In addition to funding out of his own pocket the wages and accommodation costs for several assistants, he was also expected to slip a backhander to those informants whose tip-offs were so vital to his success. When all of these expenses were taken into account, a successful operation and consequent seizure would often result in a nett loss for

Gillespie, and what must surely have grated was the irony of a situation whereby other excisemen of his acquaintance, though markedly less effective than himself, appeared to fare rather better. As well as taking its financial toll, his years as a customs officers had also had an adverse effect on his health, and he was said to have received no fewer than 42 wounds to his person, all of them sustained in the line of duty. Now a fifty-year-old widower with sole responsibility for his children, when faced with the prospect of bankruptcy and disgrace he came up with a rather desperate plan which he hoped might shore up his flagging finances.

Realising that his friend was in dire financial straits, a wealthy farmer, Alexander Smith of Blackhills - a man approaching ninety - attempted to assist Gillespie by writing to the manager of the Aberdeen Town and County Bank requesting that he accept documents known as 'bills of accommodation' against which Gillespie was entitled to withdraw funds, to be repaid by a given date. In addition to Smith's own signature, a guarantor was required for each bill, but what neither Smith nor the bank manager realised at the time was that, on each of the bills thus presented, the guarantor's signature had been forged by Gillespie's assistant and confidant, Skene Edwards. As a means of foiling detection, Gillespie made a point of arranging with the bank that all communication relating to the bills should be directed in the first instance to himself, on the understanding that he would then personally forward any such letters to their individual addressees. A constant worry though it must surely have been, the possibility of being unmasked as a forger was not Gillespie's only source of anxiety. Sometime before undertaking the financial scam, he had embarked upon another project with a view to boosting his finances, equally underhand and just as dishonest. Having first insured his home - Crombie Cottage, near Skene - with the Palladian Life and Fire Assurance Society of London for £530, and with the Phoenix Assurance Society for a further £300, he proceeded to store various highly flammable substances in the cellar and adjoining barn. Then, immediately before his planned departure to attend a trial in Edinburgh, he had two of his servants - John Edwards (a maritime man, and brother of Skene) and George Brownie - spread turpentine and gunpowder throughout the house, treat the furniture with melted rosin, and pack kindling made from broken beds between the joists and under the roof-thatch. Shortly before leaving, he assembled a number of his servants -

his housekeeper, Jessy Greig; Skene and John Edwards; and another employee, William Jenkins - and, speaking obliquely, suggested to them that if his cottage happened by any chance to burn down during his absence, then it would do him no harm; indeed, it might very well have the opposite effect and ease his current financial predicament.

His indirect message escaped no-one, and accordingly Gillespie's staff formed their plans during the evening of Wednesday 21 February 1827. Shortly before midnight they gathered in Crombie Cottage where each was given a dram by the housekeeper, Jessy Greig. George Brownie then lit two candles, one of which he passed to another trusted servant, Lexy Campbell, who carried it down to start a fire in the cellar, while Brownie himself set light to the room next door. Once the fire had got a grip, Brownie left Crombie Cottage for his own home a short distance away, instructing the others to allow him time to get into bed before raising the alarm. According to plan, Crombie Cottage was burned to the ground but, when he returned home from Edinburgh, Gillespie carefully avoided asking any awkward questions, commenting only that the job had been 'genteelly done'. But, just when he might have imagined that there was light at the end of the financial tunnel, disaster struck.

For a time Gillespie's financial wheeling and dealing had all gone to plan. He had managed to meet his obligations regarding repayment of the 'bills of accommodation' by their due date, but his scheme began to unravel when a letter requesting payment happened to bypass him and went directly to its alleged counter signatory, Joseph Low of Bogfairlie - a man not entirely innocent of a spot of illicit distilling of his own. Hearing of the letter's arrival, Gillespie approached Low and attempted to convince him that he had simply forgotten having signed the bill while under the influence of drink, and even when he learned that the farmer was totally illiterate he continued to press him to sign, pleading rather desperately that 'it wad save his neck fae the rope.' Low, however, refused to budge. When news of the affair got out, an investigation was immediately launched which revealed in due course that not a single one of the countersignatures on the bills was genuine. Some of the guarantors, it transpired, were entirely fictitious, and one - a farmer named Robert Lawson - had apparently appended his signature from somewhere beyond the grave. By the time that the scam came to light in the spring of 1827, Gillespie had presented to the bank a total of 22 fraudulent bills and netted for himself in the process the tidy sum of £554 and ten shillings. In desperation, he turned for assistance to his old benefactor, Alexander Smith of Blackhills, but Smith's wife (remarkably, some sixty years his junior!) would have none of it, threatening to report him to the Procurator Fiscal and request that the Aberdeen bank write directly to all of the supposed guarantors. Hearing this, Gillespie cried out in alarm, 'For God's sake, my good madam, don't do that; for if the Fiscal was to get notice o't, I might as weel cut mysell to pieces.' The woman's irritation is entirely understandable in light of the fact that her husband had been the one - the only one - who lost out financially when it was left to him to settle the bills.

But by now the cat was well and truly out of the bag. Sleeping in a small bothy not far from the burnt-out shell of his former home, Gillespie was still in bed on Monday 20 April when he found himself on the receiving end of a rather rude awakening. When presented with a warrant for his arrest by Aberdeen's Messenger at Arms, John Fyfe, he is said to have blurted out, 'Good God! I'm a gone man', before begging Fyfe to 'let me disappear until this matter be settled.' His request, of course, was denied, and along with Skene Edwards - incapably drunk at the time - he was escorted to Aberdeen where the two men were imprisoned in the city tolbooth. Their case was heard five months later - on Friday 28 September - at Aberdeen Circuit Court of Justiciary before Lords Alloway and Pitmilly. In front of a packed-out public gallery, both Gillespie and Edwards pled not guilty to the charges against them of forgery and 'uttering' - that is, passing off counterfeit money or, in this case, false financial documents. The case for the prosecution was led by the Advocate Depute who opted to tackle only seven of the 22 bogus bills of accommodation which Gillespie had encashed. Supported by the testimony of George Brownie, Lexy Campbell and Jessy Greig - each given a pass from jail to appear as a witness - the main thrust of Gillespie's defence was to place the blame solely and squarely at the door of Skene Edwards, a line of attack which singularly failed to take account of the fact that it was, not Edwards, but Gillespie himself who turned up at the Town and County Bank to exchange the bogus bonds for cash.

It was only after a marathon fifteen-hour session that the members of the jury were dismissed to consider their verdict, and half-past one in the morning - Saturday 29 September - before they returned, drooping and weary, to announce their decision. But not yet. Owing to the lateness of the hour, they were instructed by the judges to return with their verdict at 10.30 a.m., allowing the jurors to snatch a few hours of much-needed sleep. On their return, however, there was yet another delay when it was discovered that one of their number, James Davidson of Kinmundy, had inexplicably vanished. Four hours later Davidson was retrieved from his home, seven miles away, and explained to the court that he had assumed that once a verdict was reached he had been free to leave. He received a reprimand from the bench. Once that small matter had been attended to, mercifully there were to be no more hitches. When the foreman of the jury stepped forward and passed an envelope to the judges, the more sharp-eyed among the public would have noticed its ominous black seal and, just as it had seemed to portend, the outcome for Gillespie was gloomy. On all seven charges of forgery and uttering the members of the jury found him guilty. His co-accused, Skene Edwards, was likewise guilty of forgery but cleared of uttering, and following representations from his lawyer, his case was referred for clarification to the High Court in Edinburgh.

Following Gillespie's conviction, Lord Pitmilly gave voice to the sadness he felt when recalling the prisoner's previous appearances before him when he had occupied a quite different role. His 'zeal and activity as an Officer of Revenue,' Pitmilly continued, '[have] not been absent from my mind a single moment since this trial commenced, and I could scarcely make myself believe that so sad a reversal has taken place.' Despite his feelings of regret, the judge was candid about his agreement with the verdict reached by the jury, and he advised Gillespie that the sentence he must face was one laid down by statute and over which neither he nor Lord Alloway had any discretion. When his turn came to speak, Lord Alloway stated that the duty he was about to perform was a painful one and, placing the black cap upon his head, he turned to address Gillespie. 'You are a man of good education,' he told him, 'a man certainly of great talent [but] you have been found guilty of one of the highest crimes that can be committed in a commercial country.' He urged him not to waste what time he had left in nursing vain hopes of a pardon, but instead to devote his attention to more spiritual matters. In conclusion, the judge told Gillespie that he would be taken back to the tolbooth, 'therein to be detained till Friday the 16th day of November next to come, and upon that day, between the hours of two and four o'clock afternoon, to be taken from the said tolbooth to the common place of execution in Aberdeen, and there, by the hands of the common executioner, to be hanged by the neck upon a gibbet until he be dead ... which is pronounced for doom.' Though clearly aware of the gravity of his position, it was noted that throughout the duration of his trial Gillespie had conducted himself with dignity and restraint. After hearing his sentence read out, he bowed respectfully to the bench and the jury before stepping down from the dock.

The question of arson, of course, remained to be dealt with and, following Gillespie's conviction, Alexandrina Campbell and George Brownie were brought before the court, charged with wilful fire-raising and intent to defraud. Initially they pled not guilty, but part-way through the trial both of them changed their plea to guilty of fire-raising but not of attempted fraud. They claimed that, in burning down Crombie Cottage, they had acted in accordance with their master's instructions, though they had no inkling of his reasons for wanting them to do so. Improbable perhaps, but the Crown nonetheless accepted their revised pleas and, after highlighting the seriousness of their crime, Lord Alloway sentenced each to be transported overseas for a period of seven years. He added that, by changing their plea, Brownie and Campbell had undoubtedly saved themselves from the rope. As for Skene Edwards, when his case was heard in Edinburgh in late November, he too was fortunate to escape the death penalty but was sentenced instead to a seven-year term of transportation.

Disregarding Lord Alloway's advice, Gillespie set great store by the belief that influence in high places would be brought to bear and secure for him a reprieve, and he seemed to have grounds for optimism. Based largely upon his reputation as an efficient customs officer, testimonials in his favour were sent to the Secretary of State in London by such distinguished figures as William Gordon, MP for Aberdeenshire; the Right Honourable Lord Viscount Arbuthnott; Sir Alexander Keith, Knight Marischal of Scotland; and the Honourable General Duff MP. While awaiting news of how their appeal for clemency was received, never at any stage was Gillespie prepared to admit to wrongdoing, and he devoted much of his time and energy to producing a 'Dying Declaration' in which he strove to clear his name. Skene Edwards, he would have his readers believe, was the villain of the piece, himself a mere innocent victim. Written in near-flawless prose, it falls nonetheless some way short of being convincing. When, three days before his execution, Gillespie was informed of the petition's failure his shock was palpable. Distressed and tearful, his first reaction was to exclaim, 'Oh! my poor family! Poor orphans!', before managing to pull himself together. Only now did he appear genuinely responsive to the ministrations of the prison chaplain, Rev. McCombie, and various other clergymen who had spent time preparing him for what was to come.

On the eve of his execution Gillespie received a last visit from his daughters whom, in an emotional scene, he joined in singing the final verse of the eighth Paraphrase:

> So days, and years, and ages past,
>   Descending down to night,
> Can henceforth never more return
>   Back to the gates of light;
> And man, when laid in lonesome grave,
>   Shall sleep in Death's dark gloom,
> Until th' eternal morning wake
>   The slumbers of the tomb.
> O may the grave become to me
>   The bed of peaceful rest,
> Whence I shall gladly rise at length,
>   and mingle with the blest!
> Cheer'd by this hope, with patient mind,
>   I'll wait Heav'n's high decree,
> Till the appointed period come,
>   When death shall set me free.

The relevance of these lines to Gillespie's situation is not hard to see. As they left the prison, his daughters were unable to contain their grief when they witnessed preparations for the erection of the scaffold.

The night before his execution Gillespie slept tolerably well. In the early afternoon he was led, dressed in mourning, into the Old Court Room where he stood before Bailie Milne who asked him whether there was anything that he wanted to say. Gillespie said that he wished to thank those magistrates and clergymen who had visited him in prison, and singled out his jailor, George Cockburn, for the kindness he had shown. The focus then turned to spiritual matters as, by Gillespie's request, the group came together in singing a number of verses of the eighth Paraphrase, after which prayers were conducted by Rev. Dr Kidd. Shortly after this Gillespie came over faint, but after drinking a glass of water he had recovered sufficiently to ask leave to address the magistrates - on the grounds, he said, that he 'did not want to die with a lie in [his] mouth.' Granted permission, he spoke at some length, claiming that at no stage had he had any intention to defraud, and once again declaring himself innocent of the crimes for which he had been convicted. And then, having said his piece, he made his way to the foot of the gallows where he said his final farewells before submitting himself to an unknown hangman and mounting the scaffold steadily, without hesitation. In front of a vast array of spectators, the lever was drawn at approximately 2.40 p.m. and, as he plunged from the scaffold, Gillespie claimed his place in history as the last man in Scotland to be hanged for the crime of forgery. Death, it was reported, came mercifully swiftly and with little apparent struggle. His body was cut down some time later and placed in a coffin to be conveyed to Skene, some miles west of the city, for burial. It was noted that the large numbers of spectators at Gillespie's execution had conducted themselves appropriately throughout, and dispersed quietly once proceedings were complete.

A man with a fatal flaw, there is something of the tragic hero about Malcolm Gillespie. As was highlighted by Lord Pitmilly during his trial, critical errors of judgment led him from his former high position on an inexorable downward path which ended in death and disgrace. Or so it might have seemed. There is a curious postscript that requires to be added to Gillespie's story. The tale has been told of how, at some point in the early twentieth century, his coffin was exhumed from its lair in Skene kirkyard and, when opened up, was found to contain not bones, but rather in their place a quantity of rocks and earth, thus giving rise to the rumour that Gillespie had been cut down from the gallows while still alive. Is there a possibility, then, that the Aberdeen forger cheated the hangman, assumed a new identity perhaps and restarted his life elsewhere? An intriguing notion for sure, but when considered in the rational light of day - perhaps regrettably - it seems highly unlikely.

David Little : January 1831

Standing on top of the scaffold with his arms strapped firmly behind him, beset by the jeers and catcalls of a hostile, Glasgow mob, he must surely have never imagined that it would come to this. A crime committed five years earlier; a flight from justice across the sea; successfully dodging the law for weeks, months, years; and yet, for all of his bobbing and weaving through life's highs and lows, there was no way now that David Little could escape his past. His chickens had well and truly come home to roost.

Built only recently, Gartloch House must surely have presented the local criminal fraternity with a tempting target in 1825. Situated seven miles east of Glasgow in what was then open countryside, the house occupied an elevated site overlooking the waters of the Bishop Loch, a stone's throw to the south. The name says a lot. Gartloch - 'the garden by the loch' - was considerably more than a standard, everyday dwelling and was, in fact, something more akin to a mansion, sitting in its own grounds of more than 500 acres. Fronted by well-groomed lawns, the house was entered through a splendidly pillared portico which led into the grand hallway, flanked on one side by the library and on the other by a billiards room. To the rear, the drawing and dining rooms faced south over the loch and gave access, weather permitting, to a sunny outdoor terrace. In order to blend in with the house's grandeur, it seems certain that the furniture, artwork and interior decor must surely have been of the highest quality. Upstairs, on the first floor, were a total of six bedrooms, three with adjoining dressing rooms, and on the top floor a further six attic rooms. Two more bedrooms were tucked away in the basement along with the kitchen and larder, wine-cellar, laundry and the servants' hall. Outside, the house was surrounded by wooded policies containing offices and stables, a large walled garden and a small ornamental lake. Pleasant pathways led down to the shore of the Bishop Loch and, a short distance across the fields, the estate had its own Home Farm. Granted, the cost of building had not been cheap but, given the house's exceptional location and manifold amenities, the £12,000 tab seemed not unreasonable. On the face of it, then, life at Gartloch looked idyllic, cushioned and comfortable, but for the family who lived there something irreplaceable was missing. Sadly, the proprietor of the house, a lawyer named James Hill, had died in his mid-fifties, a few short years after his country retreat was completed. And the chances are that potential housebreakers in the area would have known that Gartloch was a house of women.

James Hill was survived by his widow, Margaret, and the couple's four daughters: Margaret, Elizabeth, Charlotte and Mary. In the early hours of Tuesday 20 September 1825, the peace of their home was disturbed by something more like a military raid than a run-of-the-mill, opportunistic burglary. The first to be aware of the presence of intruders were the two housemaids, Christian McLean and Catherine Campbell, who slept in one of the basement bedrooms. Somewhere between two and three o'clock in the morning Christian was awakened by the sound of footsteps in the lobby, and a few seconds later a masked man materialised at the foot of her bed with a candle in one hand and what looked like a soldier's bayonet in the other. Two other men followed on behind, the first similarly masked and the second with an old black hat drawn down over his face in an effort to conceal his identity. Fearful for her life, Christian sat up in bed and asked what the men wanted, to be told peremptorily, 'Hold your peace - not a word'. The speaker went on to threaten the maid with violence should she be so foolish as to try to call out. Realising that she was entirely at the men's mercy, Christian attempted to hide beneath the blankets but rough hands soon pulled her out again, and there was nothing she could do to prevent her wrists from being bound tightly with twine. The second maid, Catherine, received similar treatment in due course before the strangers left the women's room, closing the door behind them.

In her first-floor bedroom, Margaret Hill's eldest daughter, also Margaret, was disturbed a little later by sounds coming from downstairs: someone moving furtively, she fancied, in the dining room directly below. She got up out of bed, quietly opened her bedroom door and stood listening for a few moments, but when she heard nothing more she dismissed her fears as simply the product of an over-active imagination. No sooner had she lain down again, however, than a scream rang out through the darkness, chilling her to the quick, and which she recognised immediately as having come from her sister's room next door. Rising once again, this time Margaret saw a strip of light beneath her bedroom door so she slipped quietly into her dressing room from where she could see three shadowy figures on the landing, one carrying a lighted candle and all three armed with pistols and daggers. Making as little noise as possible, Margaret tiptoed back to her bedroom and quietly turned the key in the lock. A few seconds later she heard the bell in her sister's room, normally used for calling a housemaid, ringing out wildly and the voice of a man barking in response, 'You need not ring - your servants are bound.'

Margaret's sister too had sufficient presence of mind to lock her door, but it did not take long for the intruders to work out that they could access the shared dressing room between the girls' bedrooms but could go no farther. Speaking from the landing, a gruff voice assured the quaking sisters that they need not be afraid since what he and his companions were interested in was money, plain and simple. A curious conversation then took place between Margaret, on one side of the door, and the housebreakers' spokesman, on the other. When asked to come out and point out where the money was kept, Margaret refused, giving as her reason the fact that she was dressed only in her nightclothes. An uncompromising reply came back to the effect that this was no time for modesty, and that if she failed to cooperate then the simple fact was that her bedroom door would be forced. Alarmed at the prospect, Margaret offered to tell him where to find the key to a chest of drawers containing cash. In the circumstances, who could have blamed her? Her shock at waking up to find three unknown men in her home in the dead of night, armed and in disguise, is virtually unimaginable. Anyone's first instinct would be to cooperate, no matter the cost.

The key, Margaret told them, could be found in the pocket of clothing in her dressing room and the cabinet that it opened was only a few paces away. When at first the key refused to turn in the lock Margaret realised that the burglars had picked the wrong cabinet and she quickly corrected their mistake. This second time they were more successful, finding some £10 or £11, but it was not enough to satisfy them. Clearly it was specifically cash they were looking for since she heard one man say to the others, 'Don't touch any bills or letters' - documents equivalent to a present-day cheque. While the men were preoccupied in rifling the drawers of the cabinet, Margaret took advantage of the moment to open her bedroom window and call out for help - a courageous action which, she later admitted, she had carried out more in hopes of alarming her unwanted visitors than in any real expectation of being heard by the grieve (farm manager) or the gardener, whose cottages lay at some considerable distance from the main house. Perhaps, for all that, Margaret's ploy paid off since, after warning her that it would go badly for her if she dared follow them downstairs or were foolish enough to repeat her call for help, the intruders prepared to depart, one reminding the others to gather up their weapons and leave nothing behind. As soon as she was certain they were gone, Margaret unlocked her door and she and her sister joined forces to hurry along to their mother's room where they found her in a state of alarm but unhurt. Finally, when she was confident that the coast was clear, Margaret ventured downstairs to the dining room where she found a large broken pane in one of the windows on which traces of tar could be seen. (It was standard practice at the time for housebreakers to coat a rag with tar, glue or grease and press it hard against a windowpane in order to muffle the sound of the breaking glass.) The only mementos of their visit that Gartloch's nocturnal callers had inadvertently left behind them were a quantity of *spunks* - matches - and a single, solitary glove.

Asleep in his basement bedroom, the first that a male house-servant, James Wilson, knew of the burglary was when he heard a voice in the darkness, hissing, 'Bind him, bind him; tie him, tie him.' With remarkable self-control, the footman decided to pretend to be asleep with the result that, in preference to waking him and tying him up, the housebreakers opted instead to lock him in his room and steal away quietly - a serious error of judgment, as it later turned out. Wilson risked opening his eyes just in time to catch a glimpse of three vague forms, lit from beneath by a candle, sidling out of his bedroom door, after which he heard the key turn in the lock. Sensibly he stayed put for a time before hurriedly dressing and exiting via the back window. As he ran in the direction of the estate offices he had an inkling that he was being followed, so he put on an extra spurt and called out, 'Robbers! Robbers!' Two other members of the Gartloch staff, James Robertson and his son - also James - were roused by Wilson's cries and, after he had gasped out his tale, they wasted no time in accompanying him back to the big house. Before setting out, the younger man took the precaution of arming himself with the shaft of a garden rake. Between slipping out of his bedroom window and arriving back at the big house with the Robertsons, Wilson estimated that around twenty minutes had elapsed and that he had run a full mile.

Reaching Gartloch, the men quickly got down to business, patrolling the immediate vicinity of the house. While combing an area of shrubbery at the rear of the building, they stumbled across two housebreakers who immediately sprang up and made off at speed. With no thought for his own personal safety, the younger Robertson immediately gave chase and once he had gained sufficiently on the slower of the two he swung his wooden rake and fetched the stranger a mighty blow to the side of the head, toppling him instantly to the ground. Robertson, senior, took a few seconds to catch up with the action and, when the felled man began to recover his wits, he recounted for his captors a very strange story. The previous evening, he told them groggily, he had been assaulted on the Stirling road by two men bearing pistols who had then compelled him to accompany them against his will on a criminal mission to Gartloch House. It was a tall tale, to say the least, but clearly the best he could come up with on the spur of the moment. There can be no doubt that the elder Robertson for one remained unconvinced for, when the man attempted to get to his feet, he lashed out with a poker he was carrying and knocked him out cold. Leaving him where he lay, the Robertsons continued their search of the grounds but of the other two burglars there was nary a trace. When they returned to the shrubbery they discovered that their third man, having presumably regained consciousness, had likewise shown a clean pair of heels - though there seemed to be little doubt that he would have suffered from a pounding headache for some time to come. In one near-contemporary account of the Gartloch robbery there is a fourth housebreaker who remained outside in the garden throughout the operation, acting on behalf of his accomplices as a lookout. His job complete, this elusive fourth man - if he ever existed - slipped quietly out of the story.

If the burglars thought that fleeing the crime scene would get them off the hook, then they were to be sadly mistaken. Before the main business of conducting trials got underway at the Autumn Circuit Court of Justiciary in Glasgow on Monday 25 September 1826 - a whole year after the Gartloch burglary - a number of men whose whereabouts were unknown were declared outlaws. These included Michael Griffin, wanted for murder; Peter Kelly, for rape; Hugh Twaddel and Robert Ingram, for forging and presenting bogus banknotes; and William Bennie, Torrance Braidy, Robert Hutchison, Donald O'Hara and Michael O'Neill, all alleged to have carried out serious assaults. Also on the list of those outlawed by the court that day were three (not four) individuals who were wanted in connection with the crime of *stouthrief* - a term in use at the time to denote robbery with violence - and their names were David, Mathias and William Little. Having been identified as suspects, we may assume from the fact that the men were declared outlaws that they had already taken the initiative and decamped.

Tracing David Little's movements in the aftermath of the burglary is tricky, but he is believed to have kept on the move, hiding out with friends in various locations and picking up jobs wherever he could find them. It has been suggested that he caught a ferry for Ireland, before moving on again, this time to England, where he seems to have accepted the king's shilling but deserted from his regiment sometime later at Chatham in Kent. What we do know for sure is that by 1830 he had drifted north again to Manchester where he found work in a factory in Miller's Lane, some say as a cotton spinner. Around this same time he became involved with a local woman whom he was foolish enough to entrust with his dark secret - a serious mistake, as he found out to his cost when the relationship went pear-shaped. In the aftermath of the break-up, his lady-friend, whoever she might have been, felt sufficiently aggrieved to have gone to the authorities and passed on details of her former lover's past, whereupon he was taken into custody on Saturday 31 July by a local policeman, Thomas Williamson. Puzzled as to the reason for his arrest, the penny must definitely have dropped when he was told that 'it was for something done in Glasgow, or the neighbourhood'. At some point during his journey to Manchester's New Bailey Prison, Little admitted his part in the burglary to Williamson, saying that it was pointless to deny it.

But when his case came to court in Glasgow on Friday 7 January 1831 - a full five years after the crime had been committed - he changed his tune. To the charge of having broken into Gartloch House - 'armed with pistols, a cutlass, or dagger, and pick-axe' - and having stolen '£8 [sic] in notes, silver tea spoons, a gold mounted and a silver mounted eye-glass, also a silver watch, and several other articles', David Little pled not guilty. It soon became clear that he had an uphill struggle on his hands. Mary Laing, who in autumn 1825 had lived in the home of the prisoner's father, John Little, in the Drygate, Glasgow, testified that she remembered the morning after the burglary seeing David Little 'with his head tied up in a napkin.' He had, she added, several visible cuts to his face. That same day a lodger in the house, Charles Kerr, saw him dressing his cuts with 'sticking-plaister'. Little had proceeded to give an account of his previous night's work to Kerr, and shown him some of the proceeds. Possibly the most theatrical moment of the whole thirteen-hour trial occurred when James Robertson, senior, took the stand and was asked to indicate where exactly on the prisoner's person he had struck him with the poker. Stepping across the courtroom, Robertson pointed without hesitation to where a scar was still visible - five years on - immediately above Little's eyebrow. Once the evidence of all the witnesses had been heard, Lord Moncrieff dismissed the jury whose members, despite the fact that the robbery had not involved violence, found David Little guilty of stouthrief. They were, however, unanimous in appending a recommendation to mercy in consideration of the fact that he had no other criminal convictions to his name, and at the time when the Gartloch robbery took place he had been no more than seventeen or eighteen years old. In spite of the jurymen's view, Lord Moncrieff made it clear to the prisoner that he held out little hope of a reprieve and concluded proceedings by sentencing him to be executed a fortnight hence, on Thursday 27 January. As throughout his trial, Little remained impassive on hearing his fate spelled out, and showed no visible reaction. Though it could not have been known at the time, he turned out to be the last man in Scotland ever to face the death penalty for committing the crime of stouthrief.

In spite of the fact that his solicitor, James Crawford, submitted no fewer than five character references in support of David Little, Lord Moncrieff's pessimism in court was shown to have been well-founded when, a week after the trial, word came through to the effect that 'the law must be allowed to take its course.' In jail, Little was ministered to by Rev. Duncan Macfarlane, Principal of Glasgow University, to whom, it is said, he responded both positively and with courtesy, even going so far as to acknowledge the justice of his sentence. On execution day itself he appeared stoical and he maintained his composure throughout all stages of the gruesome procedure. Out of the three men who took part in the Gartloch robbery, David Little alone faced the vengeance of the law which came down heavily on a man who, when push came to shove, was little more than a thief. By this time, his brother, Mathias, was dead while William Little, for his part, appears to have dropped off the radar completely. Now, the best part of two centuries on, times have changed and attitudes with them. For David Little's crime today, a first-time offender might reasonably hope to escape a custodial sentence altogether, while, for the stunts they pulled with rake and poker, our two have-a-go heroes, the feisty Robertsons, would almost certainly do time behind bars.

Hugh MacLeod : October 1831

In April 1830 a Drumbeg boy, John Mackenzie, happened to be passing along the shoreline of one of the myriad freshwater lochs that stud the landscape of north-west Sutherland. Following a recent dry spell, the water-level on Loch Torr na h-Eigin was unusually low and as he walked along the banks John was startled to see, floating on the surface, what was unmistakeably the body of a man. Overcoming his shock, the schoolboy wasted no time in reporting his discovery to his neighbours and, as word quickly spread, some fifty curious locals gathered by the lochside to watch as the body was recovered. Once ashore, it was immediately apparent that the corpse was remarkably well preserved, the result, it was suggested, of antiseptic properties possessed by the mosses that grew in profusion around the rim of the loch, and it was quickly identified as the body of a well-known packman, Murdo Grant, although there was no trace to be found of either his money or his goods. As they watched events unfold, a flurry of speculation arose among the local people as to the possibility of foul play.

By the very nature of his trade, a nineteenth-century Highland packman had a demanding and insecure existence. Tramping through far-flung districts of the land where locals had little or no access to shops and markets while shouldering his heavy pack, the solitary pedlar presented a tempting target for any ruthless individual who was prepared to risk taking the law into his own hands. His merchandise of lowly household items - buttons, perhaps, or needles and bobbins of thread - and the meagre income they fetched might seem like slim pickings today, and even such small luxuries as ribbons, handkerchiefs and bows would add up to a modest enough sum, but for a great many Scots of the time money was a scarce commodity and wealth a relative concept. Even for a burly man in his mid-twenties, Murdo Grant's patch was not by any standards an easy one. A kenspeckle figure in his tartan coat and waistcoat, he operated from his base at Strath Beg, near the head of Little Loch Broom, and his customary stamping-ground took in some of the most remote and scattered communities of Scotland's far north-west at a time of social change and hardship caused by the Highland Clearances. In early March 1830 Grant set out on a routine visit to the isolated Sutherland district of Assynt, carrying in his pack an estimated £40 worth of linens, cottons, stockings and suchlike. In his red-coloured wallet he carried cash to the tune of £15 or £16. During the course of his trip, he planned to conduct new business as well as collect sums of money already owing to him. We know that on 11 March he was present at the wedding of Betty Fraser and Angus Matheson and that he decided to remain in the Assynt area for a further week, confident of finding overnight accommodation with his friends and regular customers. On Thursday 18 March, he visited the village of Drumbeg where money was due to him, and spent the night there in the home of Alexander Graham. The following morning, he packed up once again and set off in the direction of Nedd, a small coastal settlement a few miles away. And that was the point where things went awry. The young packman was never seen alive again. It was as though he had simply vanished into thin air. For a number of reasons, it took some time for his disappearance to be noticed. In Assynt, it was taken for granted that he had completed his business there and headed home, while at Strath Beg, on the other hand, there was no reason to doubt that he was still in the process of completing his rounds. On top of that, Grant was a bachelor whose only close relative was a brother living in Ross-shire. Accountable to no-one for his movements, consequently there was nobody to raise the alarm if he failed to return home by a given date.

Immediately after the macabre discovery at Loch Torr na h-Eigin, a curious old ritual was enacted. In line with an ancient belief that a murder victim's corpse will bleed when touched by the hand of his killer, the local people stepped forward one by one to lay hands upon the dead man's body and thus demonstrate their innocence. If, on the other hand, death had been the result of suicide, then it was believed that such physical contact would have the effect of allowing his spirit to be released. Standing apart from the community, a young schoolteacher, Hugh Macleod, chose not to participate but few eyebrows were raised. That an educated man should give no credence to an age-old superstition was hardly surprising. When the suggestion was made that this same Macleod might be the one most qualified to inform the local minister, the teacher appeared reticent, citing as the reason his aversion to undertaking a solitary twelve-mile journey on foot just as darkness was falling. His objection was countered, however, when a local boy, Donald Graham, was deputed to act as his companion. During their long walk the boy chattered excitedly about the possibility of robbery and murder, and at one point the teacher turned to him and asked, 'Do you think that I would do it?' Taken aback at the directness of the question, Donald Graham quickly replied that he would as soon suspect his own little brother, John. His reply went down well. 'You are right, my lad,' said Macleod approvingly and once again the two resumed their march.

Sometime later they arrived at the manse where the schoolmaster quickly informed the minister of the reason for their visit. Hearing of the gruesome discovery, Rev. Gordon pressed him for details concerning the corpse's condition and how its presence in the loch had become known. During the course of his reply, Macleod voiced his opinion that the various scratches and abrasions on the body were most likely to have been caused by contact with underwater rocks, and he was insistent that the packman had most probably been responsible for his own death. Like everyone else in the area, the teacher was presumably well aware of recent suicides in the area where Grant had been found. Meanwhile back at Loch Torr na h-Eigin the assembled locals looked on as the dead man's corpse was consigned once again to the water, a method used since time immemorial for preserving the freshness of newly-caught salmon. Early the following morning, in the presence of Rev. Gordon, Grant's body was brought to the surface a second time, then placed in a coffin and given temporary burial by the lochside. It was obvious to all that there were a number of highly suspicious circumstances relating to the packman's death which could not be ignored: the injuries on his head were wounds, not scratches; his pockets appeared to have been turned inside out, as though rifled for cash; and his pack and merchandise, of course, had still to be located. Hugh Macleod, it was said, had slept too late to be present at the burial but his lonely form was spotted from time to time, observing proceedings from a vantage point on a distant hillside.

The schoolmaster's early origins were undeniably humble. Born in Assynt in 1809, he was the only son of tenant crofters who from the outset entertained grand ambitions for his future. With their hopes pinned on education, he underwent a programme of instruction directed by his father, Roderick Macleod, but within a very few years, it seems, he had outstripped his parent's abilities in reading and writing. With no school within reach, the only available option was to engage a private tutor, a costly arrangement which lasted for two years until a school was established locally where Hugh immediately enrolled and from that point on he fell into the habit of attending classes in winter while working on his parents' croft during the summer months. There is no doubt that he was overindulged but, even so, the family income was not without limit and, as a means of offsetting the cost of his education, Hugh was obliged to undertake employment, first as a shepherd, then for a time on board a fishing boat. Some would have it that mixing with other working men was what triggered his fall from grace and that under their negative influence he cultivated for the first time such vices as drinking, gambling, resorting to bad language and what was seen at the time as the monstrous sin of exercising his sheepdogs on a Sunday. Whatever the reason, Hugh became a regular at the Lochinver Inn where, in an effort to impress the opposite sex, he took to dandifying his appearance. Tall and athletic, he cut quite a dash with the ladies and reputedly enjoyed a measure of romantic success, thus adding to an already healthy self-esteem.

At the age of eighteen, Macleod's chequered reputation did nothing to prevent his being appointed assistant schoolmaster at Coigach, a craggy coastal area of Wester Ross lying immediately to the south of Assynt. His new-found professional role, however, did nothing to rein in the excesses of his social life and, if anything, he found that his good looks, lively conversation and polished manners (quite a contrast to his habitual behaviour back on the farm) were more in demand than ever. He felt an obligation to dress the part which naturally came at a cost and before long his expenditure had overtaken his modest income and he had no choice but to devote the entirety of each month's salary simply to servicing existing debts. The future was looking precarious in the extreme until, faced with the prospect of ruin and disgrace, he came up with a desperate solution.

Macleod's answer to his problems was burglary, plain and simple. In June 1829, he forced his way into a local shop, emptied the till of its contents and carried off a length of tweed which he then concealed beneath a cairn of stones at a suitable distance from his home. Once the initial hue and cry had died down, he slipped back to retrieve the stolen cloth which he subsequently had made into a smart new suit of clothes for himself, making out that he had purchased the material from an unnamed travelling salesman. Under the flimsy pretext of having no shoes to wear, he dodged attendance at church one Sunday but took advantage of his elderly neighbour's absence to enter her cottage and abstract a sum of £2 from where it had been concealed within the kist-neuk - or hidden compartment - of her locked trunk, her entire earthly savings, so it was said. It seems suspicious that the key he used to open his neighbour's chest was one of a small collection already in his possession. Just how many similar acts of dishonesty Macleod was responsible for is impossible to know, but it would seem puzzling in the small community of Coigach if no whiff of suspicion attached itself to the showy, young schoolteacher, recently arrived from the north. The explanation may simply be that, with nothing concrete to pin on Macleod, speculation in the area never rose above the level of *sotto voce* gossip.

But, as the old adage makes it clear, there is a tendency for one thing to lead on to the next and, sure enough, flushed with the success of his earlier criminal ventures, the young schoolmaster began to tinker with the notion of pushing his boundaries yet further. For whatever reason - and we might well wonder - by 1830 he had left his post at Coigach and was back in Assynt, living with his parents once again and teaching in the nearby school at Nedd. A telling account of a conversation, alleged to have taken place between Macleod and one of his pupils, has survived from this time. 'We are poor, Donald,' said the teacher, 'and there are plenty of travelling merchants here about. Though we should kill one of them and take his money there would be no harm.' Presumably much aghast, Donald Wilson gasped out his reply - 'But we could not do that without being found out.' 'Would you tell?' probed the teacher, 'For if you would not tell we could do it easily enough.' 'Oh, Hugh! Hugh!' came the boy's reply - 'Though I should conceal it, God would not conceal it.' And that, it would seem, put paid to that. But surely there is something wrong here. The stilted conversation, the repetitive wording and the notion that even Macleod would have risked making a serious criminal suggestion to a school-age child must surely be taken with a generous pinch of salt. And if that wasn't all, common sense suggests in addition that for a pupil in nineteenth-century Scotland to be on first-name terms with his local dominie would be more than a little irregular. All things considered, we might reasonably conclude that the reported exchange between Hugh Macleod and Donald Wilson was a mythical addition to the schoolmaster's story, attributed retrospectively in the light of revelations about to be made.

When news of the grim discovery at Loch Torr na h-Eigin reached James Brander, the Procurator-Fiscal of Sutherland, he instantly smelled a rat. After undertaking the seventy-mile journey from Dornoch, Brander visited the remote, moorland loch on Thursday 29 April in the company of the Sheriff of the county, Hugh Lumsden, and two local doctors. In marked contrast to the day of the burial, on this occasion Hugh Macleod made sure of his position at the forefront of the assembled crowd and even assisted, it is said, during the exhumation of the packman's body. The dead man was promptly identified by Alexander Grant as that of his brother, Murdo, before an extempore post-mortem examination identified fearful head-wounds as the cause of death - inflicted, so the doctors believed, by a heavy, blunt instrument such as a hammer. During the course of the Sheriff's subsequent inquiries Macleod proved highly useful in his ready ability to translate local people's statements from Gaelic, but at the end of the day the formal investigation revealed nothing new. No-one came forward with any additional information, and the whereabouts of the deceased man's belongings remained as mysterious as ever.

Within the local community, however, suspicion was rife about the part played by Macleod in relation to the packman's disappearance. While Sheriff Lumsden was transacting business in the local post office, the postmaster happened to let slip that he had recently been tendered a

Bank of England £10 note by 'a person who, he did not think, *should* have had so much in his possession.' A fairly obvious tip-off, the postmaster's remark directed the attention of the authorities to the obvious contrast that existed between Macleod's finances before, and then after, Grant's disappearance. On the basis of this and other statements received from local people, the teacher found himself arrested and removed to Dornoch where his garbled, longwinded protestations of innocence were insufficient to prevent him from being charged with the packman's murder and placed accordingly behind bars. When questioned, he attributed certain bloodstains on his clothing to a gamebird which he had recently shot for the pot, and when it was pointed out to him that the stockings he was wearing at the time were identical to those sold by Grant he denied any connection outright. Confinement in jail, however, did not completely put an end to his opulent lifestyle and it seems that he contrived to obtain whisky, passed through the window of his cell and which he paid for, according to some, using the money of his victim. On one notable occasion, he tossed his empty snuffbox out on to the street along with a £1 note and a brief message requesting a refill. A passing cobbler, Alexander Sutherland, was willing to oblige but only, it seems, under his own terms when, in payment for his trouble, the wily shoemaker shortchanged the hapless prisoner by a hefty margin. For all his creature comforts in prison, Macleod did on one occasion make an unsuccessful attempt to escape.

One of his most regular visitors in jail was a local clergyman, Rev. Kennedy, who was sufficiently convinced of the schoolmaster's innocence to be prompted to pray repeatedly for the identity of the genuine guilty party to become known. During one of these visits, the prisoner recounted details of a disturbing dream which he had experienced the previous night. Macleod told the minister that during the course of his nightmarish vision he had found himself standing in an unfamiliar burial ground, watching an old man who was engaged in the task of digging a grave. His job complete, the old man turned and for the first time looked directly at Macleod who was shocked to recognise the gravedigger's face as that of his father. 'Hugh,' the old man said, 'here is your grave; lie down in it now, for your time is come.' Shocked and fearful, Macleod pleaded for a reprieve until the elderly gravedigger finally relented. 'Well, Hugh,' he said, 'go this time, but remember that in a year your coffin will meet you. Mark that! Do not forget.'

Hugh Macleod was not the only one around this time who claimed to have been in receipt of otherworldly communication. While the schoolmaster remained locked up in jail, drinking whisky and tolerably comfortable, elsewhere dramatic developments were taking place. At Clachtoll, not far from Drumbeg, a drinking crony of Macleod's called Kenneth Fraser - otherwise known as 'Kenneth the Dreamer' - recounted to the authorities how he had heard in his sleep a man's voice speaking to him in Gaelic. 'The pack of the merchant,' the voice told him, 'is lying in a cairn of stones in a hollow.' Fraser's mysterious correspondent proceeded to provide him with a detailed description of the cairn's location which he was subsequently able to identify as lying in an area to the south-west of Loch Torr na h-Eigin. Initially a search of the hollow in question revealed nothing but, as the scope of the hunt widened, five silk handkerchiefs belonging to Murdo Grant were found not far away, hidden among stones on the banks of a burn.

While all this was taking place Hugh Macleod was transferred from Dornoch to Inverness where he appeared before the High Court of Justiciary on Wednesday 22 September 1830 and listened from the dock as his indictment was read out to him. It soon became clear, however, that the case would be unable to proceed when, after counsel for the accused had objected to two potential jurors and the prosecution had similarly ruled out a third, insufficient jurymen remained and there was no alternative but to postpone proceedings for the time being. The court reconvened six months later, in April the following year, but progress stalled once again when the Advocate-Depute requested a further postponement on the grounds that a material witness, George Mackenzie of Lochinver, had failed to turn up. Macleod's third appearance did not take place until five months later, on Tuesday 27 September, when he faced charges of having assaulted and murdered Murdo Grant in March of the previous year and stolen from his victim banknotes, a sum of money in silver and goods to the value of £40. With Lords Moncrieff and Medwyn presiding, the case for the Crown was made by the Advocate-Depute, while the accused was defended by Charles Neaves, himself later a high court judge (and who will be encountered once again at a later point in this volume). Without hesitation Macleod pled not guilty. More than fifty witnesses were called upon to disclose what they knew, making use where necessary of the services of a Gaelic translator, Rev. Dr

Mackintosh Mackay of Badenoch, a distinguished Highland historian and scholar. Some of the most harrowing testimony came from Doctors Grant and Ross whose examination of Murdo Grant's body at Loch Torr na h-Eigin had revealed a number of fatal head wounds, some that had 'penetrated to the bone', as well as a fractured jawbone and other injuries. Death, they believed, had not been instantaneous, though they thought it likely that the murder victim had perished before being immersed in the loch. In the opinion of the two doctors, the packman's injuries could not possibly have been caused by contact with rocks underwater.

From the outset things went badly for the accused. Prior to Murdo Grant's disappearance Macleod was shown to have been penniless and in debt, a situation that appeared to change overnight when, days later, he was seen flashing high-value banknotes, treating his associates to rounds of drinks, and adding to the contents of his own wardrobe. It was observed that his spending money was kept in a red-coloured wallet. His sister, Anne, testified that on the morning of Friday 19 March, the date of Grant's disappearance, her brother had left for school as per usual, but the fact that he never turned up there only added to the weight of circumstantial evidence that was steadily piling up against him. His cousin, Isabel Kerr, stated that she had met Macleod in the vicinity of Loch Torr na h-Eigin some weeks before Grant's body was discovered. 'You need not be telling that you saw me,' he told her without further explanation. On top of all that, the court was informed of the fact that the stockings he was wearing at the time of his arrest were of an identical type to those sold by Murdo Grant from his pack. For a supposedly intelligent man, Macleod showed surprisingly little awareness of the need to cover his tracks. Perhaps his ego was such that he felt no need to.

It was well past midnight when the final witness was called for the prosecution in a courtroom now illuminated by candlelight. Kenneth Fraser - 'the Dreamer' - didn't allow the lateness of the hour to prevent him from playing the part of the Highland seer, stating theatrically that his only knowledge of the whereabouts of Murdo Grant's possessions had come by occult means. Fraser's declaration, it has been claimed, was the one and only verifiable occasion when an incidence of second sight was admitted as evidence in a Scottish court. When 'the Dreamer' left the stand, it was made known that no witnesses were to be called for the defence. In his summing up, the Advocate-Depute managed to occupy a further two hours which Charles Neaves for the defence came painfully close to matching. Anxious - for understandable reasons - to bring matters to a speedy conclusion, the jury by contrast took a mere fifteen minutes to return a unanimous verdict of guilty. Hearing this, Macleod leapt to his feet, crying 'The Lord Almighty knows that I am innocent. I did not think one in this country would be condemned on mere opinion'; but, with no right of appeal yet on the statute-book, his fate was sealed. Lord Moncrieff duly assumed the black cap and sentenced the 22-year-old schoolmaster to death, informing him that on Monday 24 October, between the hours two and four o'clock in the afternoon, he would be executed at Inverness. His corpse would then be packed in salt and delivered to the Professor of Anatomy in Edinburgh for the purposes of dissection, one of the last bodies of a criminal, as it turned out, to be disposed of thus in Scotland. And at that the court finally rose at nine o'clock in the morning following a marathon session of 24 hours without a break. As the building emptied, there must surely have been many who were breathing colossal sighs of relief.

Macleod, of course, saw things differently and, left alone with his thoughts, it wasn't long before he changed his tune. In the presence of two witnesses - Sheriff Lumsden and Rev. Clark - he made a full confession in which he admitted to having formed and executed a plan to murder and rob Murdo Grant. Under the impression that he wished to buy up the packman's entire stock, Grant had agreed to a meeting at twelve noon on Friday 19 March in order to finalise the details. By whatever method, Macleod persuaded his intended victim of the need for secrecy. On the morning in question the schoolmaster rose early and, in an act of stupefying irony, prayed for God's blessing on his enterprise that day. He then picked out as his weapon of choice a heavy mason's hammer whose handle he shortened for ease of carrying and also, presumably, concealment. As a final precaution, he opted to wear a bulky overcoat belonging to his father, beneath which he hoped that the weapon would go unnoticed. Setting out on the road to Nedd, he arrived at the agreed meeting-point well in advance of midday and was obliged, he told his two listeners, to spend several miserable hours, sheltering from the wind and rain in a nearby cave. When the packman eventually appeared, the two men set off across country, ostensibly aiming for Macleod's home at Lynnmeanach. More than once, he said, he had been tempted to launch his attack but on each occasion held back for fear of being seen from the hills.

The two men were walking single-file around Loch Torr na h-Eigin, with Macleod in the lead, when he finally took the bull by the horns. 'I suddenly turned around,' he recalled, 'and with a violent blow under the ear felled him to the ground. He lay sprawling in great agony, but never spoke. I took the money out of his warm pocket and put it into mine. There was about £9 in all.' Macleod's gruesome revelations did not end there. 'I gave him two or three violent blows,' he continued, 'and dragged the body into the loch, as far as I could with safety to myself. Even then life was scarcely gone, for the air kept bubbling up from the mouth.' Macleod then disposed of the murder weapon, hurling it into the loch, before systematically going through the pedlar's goods, removing what could be carried and sinking the rest in a *moss-loch*, or peaty quagmire, far out on the moor. Foolishly, he waited some time before he parted with his victim's red wallet, eventually burying it too, but not before it had been seen in his possession by several people. Throughout the following days and weeks, Macleod had to pass the murder scene twice each day, walking to and from school, and as the water-level in the loch dropped steadily during a dry spell of weather he noticed with trepidation that Grant's body, the evidence of his crime, was in danger of resurfacing. For fear, he explained, of being seen, he failed to react to the situation and this was what led inexorably to the discovery of his crime. So - confession duly made, we might be tempted to regard the matter as done and dusted. Well, no. There remains a niggling sense that there is something about Macleod's account, as passed down to us, that does not ring true. It is easy to see why a man on the cusp of eternity might wish to make a clean breast of his crimes - and unburden his conscience in the process - but why Macleod should have chosen to cast his actions in such a lurid light is a good deal harder to understand. All things considered, it seems reasonable to doubt whether his words were recorded entirely verbatim. What we do know for sure is that, facing imminent death, Macleod fell back on religion, whether moved to repentance by the earnest ministrations of Rev. Clark or - as the more cynical might suspect - as a last, desperate means of keeping his soul free of the fires of hell.

On the morning of his final day, Macleod was roused by Davidson, the jailer, at seven o'clock and he indicated that he had slept soundly. He took breakfast at nine o'clock and a blacksmith was summoned an hour later whose job it was to remove the leg-irons with which he had been shackled during his imprisonment. By the afternoon, a crowd, estimated at 7,000 or 8,000, had gathered in Inverness to witness a grim spectacle that harked back to medieval times. Declining the offer of a cart to ride on, the condemned man, dressed in a full-length black robe and wearing a white nightcap on his head, was led through the streets by the hangman, Donald Ross, by a rope around his neck. He held in his hands an open Bible from which he was observed to read during much of his journey to where the scaffold had been erected by the seashore. Ascending the gallows, he addressed the crowd in Gaelic, holding himself up as an example of the dangers of succumbing to the temptations presented by alcohol, gambling and women. 'Though I would live one hundred years,' he told them, 'I would never again put a glass of whisky to my lips.' As his speech neared its conclusion, he finished up by pointedly absolving his friend, 'Kenneth the Dreamer' - to whom some degree of suspicion had attached itself - of any involvement in Murdo Grant's death. In what can only be described as a poignant gesture, he handed over his Bible, requesting that it be sent to his parents along with a letter which he had penned the previous day. During the singing of the 51st psalm, likewise in Gaelic, he participated wholeheartedly, then, with no time wasted, he dropped his handkerchief as a signal to the hangman who immediately drew back the bolt. Uttering the words 'The Lord receive my spirit', Hugh Macleod plunged from the scaffold and it was noted by many of those present that he departed this life without any appearance of a struggle.

It seems inevitable that during his final, dark days in prison Hugh Macleod's thoughts must have returned repeatedly to his dream in Dornoch jail in which the shadowy gravedigger had foretold the timing of his death. Call it coincidence, chance or perhaps something more, but the old man's prophecy - that death would come within a year - had missed being accurate by a mere matter of weeks.

Samuel Waugh : January 1832

The two opposing armies met face to face near the old corn mill that operated on the Water of Girvan. Those several hundred marchers who had arrived from the north, brandishing banners, swords and staves, were fronted by a handful of men bearing firearms. Directly ahead, their opposite numbers made up for their lack of fire-power by a hail of rocks which they rained down upon the visitors' heads while the two groups' leaders engaged in negotiations. Struck on the face by a flying stone, one of the northern gunmen finally snapped and, raising his weapon to his shoulder, took careful aim before firing. In the pitched mêlée that followed a goodly number of combatants on both sides were to suffer grievous injuries and not everyone would emerge from the fracas with his life intact. So - a scene dating from late medieval times, perhaps, as competing factions fought out a turf-war in a bid to establish local precedence? Not so. For the Bridge Mill confrontation took place less than two centuries ago, a few short years before a youthful Queen Victoria acceded to the British throne.

The lead-up to the disturbance at Bridge Mill was a time of great unrest. Parliamentary reform was in the wind and up and down the land its supporters were engaged in conducting meetings and congregating in marches and processions. With the permission of the authorities, Ayrshire pro-reformers picked out a local holiday, Monday 25 April 1831, to march through the town of Girvan, holding aloft the radical political symbol of a tricolour on which the words 'Reform' and 'Loyalty' were emblazoned. Not everyone, however, was in agreement with the marchers' aims. At that time, the population of Girvan totalled some five thousand, an estimated two thirds of whom were believed to be Irish in origin. For some of the Protestant Irish the passage through parliament two years earlier of the Roman Catholic Relief Act - under whose terms Catholics were entitled for the first time to hold many public offices, including that of Member of Parliament - had already been a step too far, and they viewed with displeasure the prospect of further parliamentary concessions, the principal beneficiaries of which, they believed, would once again be their Catholic neighbours.

For these reasons Girvan's community of Orangemen resolved to take action. During the course of the April demonstration, they intercepted the pro-reform marchers at the street known as the Sandy Raw (now Duncan Street), tore down their tricolour and carried out a number of violent assaults. In a show of defiance, the pro-reformers regrouped the following day and once again hoisted the tricolour with a view to resuming their march but they found their way barred a second time by Orangemen wielding sticks, pokers and hammers. At this point the local authority stepped in, calling a meeting on Wednesday 27 April during which all future processions were banned in an effort to stem further disorder. The injustice of the decision outraged many local people and, following a fairly widespread indignant reaction, the ban was quickly revoked with the result that on Thursday 28 April a large pro-reform procession, with a body of magistrates at its head, marched through the streets to a mass rally at Girvan Green. Flags were displayed - tricolours among them - as well as banners proclaiming pro-reform slogans. Speeches were made and three cheers raised for eminent local reformers, such as Thomas Francis Kennedy of Dalquharran and Dunure, the popular MP for Ayr Burghs, and Richard Oswald of Auchincruive, a future Whig member for Ayrshire. The event passed off without incident and, when proceedings were complete, the crowds dispersed in an orderly fashion. This time the local Orangemen kept their distance, the occasion perhaps a little too grand for their brand of bully-boy tactics.

Trouble wasn't inevitable. Around the same time as Girvan's problematic march, Kilmarnock staged a similar event on what can only have been a highly impressive scale. A mile-long procession of several thousand marchers, attended by a hundred men on horseback, made its way through the town streets with representatives of Kilmarnock's principal trades to the fore, each displaying its own distinctive flag and emblem. Numbers were swelled by pro-reform delegations from much of the surrounding area - from Ayr, Cumnock, Fenwick, Galston, Irvine, Kilmaurs, Newmilns, Stewarton and Tarbolton - and the vast throng that assembled on the site of the present-day Howard Park was estimated at considerably more than 10,000. The crowd was addressed by various pro-reform speakers, and rousing musical entertainment was provided by local bands. Arguably the day's most poignant moment came about immediately after the voice of the final speaker fell silent. In a dramatic and moving gesture, a vast array of 130 pro-reform banners were simultaneously unfurled and held aloft while the sonorous sound of a drum-beat rolled out across the park. A sense of fate seemed to hang in the air - of change for the better within reach - and, when the rally dispersed, it was noted that there were no instances of drunkenness or disorder and that the pro-reformers returned to their homes in a sombre and law-abiding fashion.

What happened at Kilmarnock was by no means unique in Ayrshire. The town of Largs hosted a pro-reform rally during which some five hundred marchers and sixty mounted men expressed their political opinions in an orderly manner, while 1,100 turned up at a similar event in Beith. At Cumnock more than a thousand people, many of them elderly and at least one man walking assisted by crutches, took to the streets in order to demonstrate their hunger for change. In an echo of an earlier display of people-power, some of the pro-reformers carried swords and banners that dated back a century and a half to the days of the Covenanters, and one of the flags in use was said to have been flown at the Battle of Drumclog in 1679. Another flag, borne aloft by the people of Ochiltree, was reputed to have been carried by Richard Cameron, immediately prior to his martyrdom at Airds Moss in 1680. Meanwhile the townspeople of Stewarton expressed their gratitude to Colonel Charles MacAlister, who had cast his vote in the recent general election for a pro-reform candidate, by unyoking his carriage and drawing it manually through the town streets. As they hauled him all the way from Stewarton to his home at Kennox House, a distance of more than three miles, a piper accompanied the procession and struck up the cheerful tune of *Charlie Is My Darling*.

But at the southern end of the county resentment continued to smoulder. Still smarting from the Orangemen's spoiling tactics in April, Girvan's pro-reformers drew up plans to thwart traditional Orange celebrations on 12 July to commemorate King William III's victory in 1690 over his Catholic rival, James II. Learning of their intentions, the Orangemen, for their part, made contact with sister-lodges at Maybole, Crosshill and Dailly, inviting their members to show solidarity by swelling the Girvan Orangemen's ranks. When councillors were presented with representations from concerned members of the public, they immediately issued a statement prohibiting the march but, apparently fearful that their ban would be disregarded, they also sent word to the Sheriff Substitute for Ayrshire, William Eaton, alerting him to the potential for conflict.

Responding to their nervy communication, Eaton arrived for an overnight visit to Girvan on Monday 11 July, a mere 24 hours before the scheduled time of the march. He spent time in discussions with local magistrates before meeting leading figures in the Orange community whom he cautioned, both face to face and in writing, about the risk of serious disorder if the procession were to go ahead as planned. A deal was struck when the Girvan Orangemen agreed to call off their march. As it was too late now to cancel arrangements already made with the Maybole and district lodges, they undertook to intercept the visiting Orangemen at Bridge Mill and convey them to the Doune Park by a route through the town which would avoid the principal thoroughfares. After refreshments, the Maybole Orangemen would follow the same route out of Girvan. The chances are that the Sheriff Substitute breathed a mighty sigh of relief when his eleventh-hour efforts appeared to bear fruit. The truth was that he had no other card up his sleeve, having been advised by the Solicitor General in Edinburgh that he had no legal means at his disposal to ban the procession outright. In addition, the council's request that a military force be dispatched to Girvan in order to keep the peace had been declined, for all that the two opposing parties were known to be making preparations for armed conflict. In the absence of military assistance, responsibility for maintaining order fell entirely to the town's special constables and, following negotiations with William Eaton, an additional one hundred Girvan residents were co-opted specifically for duty on 12 July. Accompanied by one of the town bailies, James Henderson (a local slater and plasterer), and equipped with staves and batons - but without firearms or swords - these were the men who were posted to await the Maybole Orangemen's arrival at Bridge Mill. Behind them trailed a small army of townsfolk, consisting, it was said, mostly of women and children.

When the Maybole Orangemen first appeared, they were seen to be marching in orderly fashion, four or five abreast, bearing colours and accompanied by fifes and drums. Despite the presence of a heavily-loaded cart, dispensing generous shots of whisky, the mood was hardly festive: of an estimated two or three hundred marching men, roughly half were described as being armed with weapons that ranged from swords and bayonets to pikes and guns. When the marchers reached Bridge Mill they stopped a hundred yards short of the waiting constables, two of whose number stepped forward to inform the Orangemen's leader of the change of plan as agreed by the Girvan lodges. It looked as though there might be a peaceful outcome when the chief Orangeman agreed to the constables' demands and made to redirect his men accordingly. But things started to crumble when it became obvious that a number of the men under his command were unwilling to cooperate.

During the wrangling that ensued, a number of stones were lobbed from behind a hedge towards the stalled procession. Predictably the Orangemen responded in kind with the result that, despite the special constables' best efforts, a barrage of missiles was soon raining down on both sides. The stone which struck one of the Orangemen and possibly broke his jaw was the one fated to ignite the touchpaper. Witnesses recounted how a lean man, no longer young, stepped out from the fifth or sixth file of Orange marchers, raised his rifle in a methodical manner and took careful aim before firing. At this stage in proceedings the Girvan constables were a mere ten or fifteen yards away and the unfortunate soul on the receiving end of the Orangeman's bullet was Alexander Ross, a fisherman to trade, who was heard to utter the words 'Oh! I've been shot' before crumpling to the ground with his hands pressed to his stomach. Ross died within minutes with a bullet lodged in his spine.

As several more shots rang out, panic seized the crowd whose members scattered and fled, some into the fields, others back towards the town, while a smaller number made good their escape by swimming the

River Girvan. One of those who did so, a blood-spattered constable, was stoned by the Orangemen as he struggled across, fortunate possibly to reach the far bank without drowning. It was only a single instance of what quickly developed into an inexplicable wave of brutality. Finding the remaining constables powerless to halt their advance, the Orangemen surged into Girvan, rampaging through the streets and wreaking havoc wherever they went, egged on, it was later alleged, by Irish Protestants living locally. Anyone unfortunate enough to come within reach - whether man, woman or child - was viciously attacked. While attempting to disarm Alexander Ross's killer, Alexander Stevens was struck on the head from behind and knocked unconscious. An elderly man, Gilbert Davidson, was accosted as he attempted to make his way out of the town in order to work in the fields. Assaulted and left for dead, the old man was fortunate to survive. A weaver, David McQueen, lost the sight of one eye as a result of a stab-wound but perhaps the most shocking case of all related to a constable by the name of Orr who was assaulted close to the council buildings. Knocked to the ground by his attacker, he was battered and slashed before a second assailant entered the fray and set about unleashing repeated kicks to his body. Orr's worst moment, however, was yet to come when a third attacker discharged a pistol in his face but by sheer good fortune the bullet merely grazed the side of his head, thus enabling the beleaguered constable to survive by the skin of his teeth.

When the marauding Orangemen arrived at their destination at the Doune Park they were received as guests by representatives of Girvan's Orange lodges. Meanwhile the rest of the town's inhabitants set about arming themselves as best they could in anticipation of the mob's return. To this end a four-pounder cannon was hauled from Bailie Anderson's garden, loaded chock-full of grapeshot and set up in a prominent position overlooking the municipal buildings. But the townsfolk's anxieties, as it turned out, proved unfounded. Whether word had reached the Orangemen concerning Bailie Anderson's formidable ordnance or rather they were already sated with gratuitous violence, in the event they elected to leave Girvan via the back door, ironically by following the route that had been allocated for their arrival.

As the dust gradually settled, feelings throughout the town continued to run high. Throughout the entire episode, the Sheriff Substitute had been *persona non-grata* for his perceived inaction. Handfuls of gravel had been thrown at the window of his accommodation in the King's Arms Inn and he had been harangued in the streets to the extent that he was forced to retreat to his lodgings. Leaving Girvan in the aftermath of the riot, his carriage was pelted with stones and his coachman mistreated by the angry townspeople. As darkness fell, armed citizens patrolled the town's bullet-scarred streets but peace had once again been restored and no further trouble was encountered. Of Girvan's resident Orangemen there was nary a trace. Fearful of recriminations, it was believed that they had abandoned their homes and fled to the country.

It would be entirely understandable if the Sheriff Substitute was a little put out by the rough handling he had been subjected to at Girvan but, whether or not, he still had a job to do and a killer remained at large. Eaton's first stop was at Maybole where he orchestrated the arrests of ten men who were suspected of involvement in the recent atrocity. The following day 21 men, some displaying obvious injuries, were transported by cart from Maybole to Ayr where they were secured under lock and key. A suspect had emerged for the shooting of Alexander Ross and the Sheriff Substitute dispatched a party of men in his pursuit. It appeared that Samuel Waugh, an Irishman living in Maybole and a former soldier with the Downshire Militia, had taken to the wild hills beyond Barr, making for Newton Stewart, possibly in the hope of ultimately finding a passage across the Irish Sea. Some accounts suggest that Waugh's pursuers caught up with him at the Suie, an isolated shepherd's house and toll on the very fringes of Ayrshire. Arrested and escorted back to Ayr, it was noted that his jaw had been broken in two places - whether from his involvement in the riot or the result of his resisting arrest is impossible to know. Following investigations by Sheriff Archibald Bell (who had by now travelled to Ayrshire from his base in Edinburgh), Sheriff Substitute William Eaton, and the local Procurator Fiscal, Samuel Waugh was charged with the murder of special constable Alexander Ross. The acknowledged leader of the Orange procession, John Ramsay, faced an identical charge, while a number of other men from the Maybole district were charged with offences relating to mobbing, rioting and assault.

It was three or so months before Waugh and Ramsay appeared before the Court of Justiciary at Ayr in late September. Proceedings soon ground to a halt, however, when counsel for the accused made representations on his clients' behalf, requesting that their trial be removed out of Ayrshire to a neutral venue where opinions were liable to be a little less entrenched. It transpired that the presiding judge, Lord Gillies, was willing to assent - probably aware that sectarian tension in Ayrshire showed no signs of easing. A number of Girvan Orangemen and their families had been obliged to seek refuge in Maybole, having allegedly been forced from their homes. There were those, however, who characterised events rather differently, suggesting rather that the Orangemen had left Girvan by choice and had decided to instigate a little trouble prior to their departure.

Around the same time, Alexander Goldie, an Orangeman facing charges in relation to the riot who was currently released on bail, and his wife, Margaret Davidson, fell victim to what appeared to be a savage tit-for-tat attack on a country road near Girvan Mains, as did another Irishman, William Young, who was assaulted at the place known as 'Blue Sky', near Houdston Farm. So severe were Goldie's injuries, it was said, that he had to be transported to Ayr by cart. Two weavers, Alexander McBroom and Andrew McGarva, were subsequently convicted of the assaults and each was sentenced to a nine-month jail term. Robert Sloan, a juvenile who had also been party to the crimes, received a lesser sentence of three months' imprisonment and all three were bound to keep the peace for a further five years. A relatively new phenomenon to Scotland, Orange sectarianism was regarded sufficiently seriously as to merit parliamentary attention at Westminster. A House of Commons select committee report into Orange institutions expressly referred to events at Girvan - the murdered constable, Alexander Ross, was named specifically - as well as noting the curious detail that, unlike other Scottish counties, a significant proportion of lodge members in Ayrshire were not Irishmen by birth but native Scots. No reason for this was suggested. The report's authors were clear in their observation that for the most part Orange lodges were concentrated in the west of Scotland and this circumstance is likely to have influenced the decision to relocate Samuel Waugh and John Ramsay's trial to Edinburgh.

Their case came to court during the dark days at the tail-end of the year. As well as mobbing, rioting and assault, both men were charged with having been responsible for Alexander Ross's murder, Waugh with having pulled the trigger and Ramsay having given him the order to do so. Both pled not guilty. Given the chaotic conditions at Bridge Mill on 12 July and the entrenched positions of most of those present, sifting fact from fancy was never likely to be easy and much of the evidence provided by witnesses proved conflicting. During his testimony, special constable James McClure stated his firm belief that none of the townsfolk had been armed with a gun but a witness from the Orange party was equally adamant that the first shot had come from the Girvan side. Asked to substantiate his opinion, he insisted in all seriousness that he had seen with his own eyes a puff of smoke produced by the gunshot. A number of eyewitnesses denied categorically that John Ramsay had ever issued any order to shoot, one man going so far as to recount how he had seen the Orange leader step in to obstruct an Orangeman who was in the act of firing. Constable McClure, on the other hand, confidently asserted that Ramsay had given the command to fire. A further bone of contention cropped up over the question of whether Samuel Waugh had been struck by a stone before or after Ross's death - or indeed whether he had been struck at all. Whatever the truth of the matter, Gilbert Gray of Fauldribban, near Girvan, had no hesitation in confirming Waugh as the man who had fired the fatal shot. From the Orange side, James Farrell described how he had watched Waugh load his weapon carefully prior to the shooting but the Crosshill weaver stopped short of confirming that Waugh's bullet had been the one responsible for ending Ross's life.

For all the confusion, there was enough sound evidence to convince the jury. By a majority verdict, Samuel Waugh was found guilty of murder and sentenced to be executed at Ayr on 19 January 1832, his body to be subsequently given over for medical dissection. On learning his unhappy fate, the prisoner reportedly remained impassive. His co-accused, John Ramsay, fared a good deal better when the charge of murder against him was unanimously found 'not proven' - perhaps more a reflection of the conflicting evidence than of the jury's faith in his innocence. In relation to the lesser charges that he faced, the court accepted the Orange leader's plea of not guilty to the charge of assault and sentenced him to nine months' imprisonment for his part in the mobbing and rioting at Girvan. Four weavers similarly accused were given jail terms that varied between nine and twelve months.

For Samuel Waugh it looked as though the game was well and truly up but one final straw remained to be clutched at. In a last-ditch bid for clemency, an account of the circumstances relating to his case was commissioned by the Lord Justice Clerk and sent for consideration by government officials in London. The fact that as many as six out of the fifteen Edinburgh jurors had judged the accused man guilty of no more than culpable homicide had provided his supporters with a glimmer of hope but it was quickly dashed when word came back from the south that there was to be no reprieve. Although he was said to have received the news with stoicism, it seems that Samuel Waugh was never able to reconcile himself to his own culpability and insisted to the very last that 'his own blood and the blood of Alexander Ross lay upon the people of Girvan'. Not everyone, of course, would agree that the pitching of stones merited gunfire in response.

Alexander Ross's grieving friends and family were not the only ones whose lives were damaged by Waugh's crime and the convicted murderer's own nearest and dearest also suffered collateral damage. While awaiting execution, the Orangeman received a final visit from his distraught wife, her distress compounded, it was reported, by the recent loss of her only child. Waugh's sisters also travelled to the prison to say their last farewells. Attended by various clergymen, the prisoner freely admitted to having fired the shot that struck down Alexander Ross but persisted in his claim that his intention had never been to kill either him or anyone else. During his time in jail, Waugh was described as remaining remarkably calm, declaring himself ready to meet his maker and confident of a fair hearing in the world to come.

The prisoner's last earthly journey took place on Tuesday 10 January, just over a week before the date assigned for his execution, when he travelled from Edinburgh back to Ayrshire. He was met at the county boundary by a company of the Ayrshire Yeomanry plus a deputation of local officials including the Chief Constable of the county and the Sheriff Substitute, William Eaton, into whose custody he now passed. Given the publicity surrounding Waugh's case, it is hardly surprising that his execution generated a good deal of interest in the local area. In line with standard practice, the scaffold was erected outside Ayr prison the night beforehand and from first light onwards on the day of the hanging itself the first members of the public started to congregate. Given the current sectarian tensions, a heavy security presence had been put in place in the form of a squad of armed constables, some specially sworn in for the occasion, plus a detachment of soldiers on horseback. During the day local officials, including the Sheriff and Provost, took their places among the spectators whose estimated number had risen to more than 5,000. It was early afternoon before the condemned man finally appeared and, as he was seen ascending the scaffold's fateful steps, a hush descended on the crowd. For a man whose previous actions might indicate an uncertain temper, it was reported that Waugh proceeded to his death coolly and with no theatricals. He was granted a few quiet minutes to prepare himself for what was to come before the hangman, John Murdoch of Glasgow, drew back the bolt and, as he plunged from the scaffold, Samuel Waugh paid for his inexplicable moment of rashness with his life.

Allan Mair : October 1843

Born a few short weeks after the death of his father, Allan Mair did not have a promising start in life. Following his mother's remarriage, he is said to have left home and struck out on his own at the tender age of nine and, though aware of advertisements that she placed in the press seeking his whereabouts, for his own reasons he chose not to respond. He travelled south from his home in Stirlingshire and found work as a drover in England, a trade he pursued for a number of years before crossing the Atlantic to undertake the task of driving eight score of Merino sheep, the property of the Earl of Selkirk, to the new Red River settlements in Alberta. On completion of the job, Mair received payment of 160 guineas - one guinea per sheep - but, after spending a few weeks on the western prairie, he headed back east where he embarked on a new venture. In the city of New York, he was engaged by a major shipping company as a buyer of grain and such was his proficiency in the business that not only did he earn a substantial wage, but he was also promoted to a responsible position aboard one of the company's ships, trading regularly between New York and Kingston, Jamaica. After a number of years at sea, he made the decision to return home to Scotland where, armed with the tidy sum of 2,000 guineas, he embarked on a legal battle in an effort to overturn the will of his late father, in which he had apparently been overlooked. Very quickly, however, he found that the greater part of his nest egg had been swallowed up in legal expenses, and it was this experience, according to some, that embittered him and pitted him against the world for the rest of his days.

Back home in Stirlingshire, Mair took on the tenancy of the small farm of Heatherslacks where he lived with his common-law wife, Mary Fletcher, but female company did little to sweeten his outlook. Within the local area he soon came to be recognised as a dyed-in-the-wool curmudgeon, notorious for challenging anyone who dared set foot on his land and involving himself in numerous disputes with his neighbours. He and Mary remained on the farm, so it is said, for the best part of three decades until the spring of 1842 when, both by then in their eighties, they flitted to a house a few miles away at Candie End where it did not take their new neighbours long to recognise that marital relations were, to say the least, strained. One kindly near neighbour, Helen Nimmo, fell into the habit of paying Mary a visit once or twice each day, and she found the old lady to be a gentle soul who plainly had a great deal of difficulty when walking and who suffered cruelly from back-pain. According to Helen, she looked every one of her 85 years. For her part, Mary sensed that Helen was someone in whom she could trust and revealed to her that her husband regularly deprived her of food and, although he ate well himself, he made a point of ensuring that all food in the house was kept under lock and key. Overhearing the women's conversation, Mair viciously berated his wife, telling her that he wished her in hell with her soul burning. 'Oh, Allan,' the old lady replied, 'we could live like the king on the throne, although we are poor, if you were good to me.' (It appeared to have escaped Mary's notice that the king had been dead for nigh-on six years and the nation had a new young queen. In the circumstances, she can surely be forgiven.) Any time thereafter that Helen spotted Mair leaving home, she grasped the opportunity to take food to Mary and, learning of the old lady's plight, other neighbours did likewise. But Mair's abusive tendencies did not end there, and it was not long before his habit of beating his wife became widely known.

A year or so after the Mairs' arrival at Candie End, Helen Nimmo overheard a commotion at their house and, when she approached to investigate, she saw Mary lying on the ground, weeping profusely, while Mair stood over her with a spade in his hands. All of a sudden he struck Mary a frightful blow, prompting Helen to intervene on the old lady's behalf which - for the moment, at least - stopped him in his tracks. What a pity that she did not report the matter to the authorities in the light of what followed three weeks later. On the evening of Sunday 14 May, Helen paid a routine visit to her elderly neighbour, bringing a meal which Mary tucked into heartily and, returning to her home, she went to bed at her usual time. Shortly after hearing the clock strike eleven, she was disturbed by an urgent knocking at her door. On the doorstep she found Jean Letham, the Mairs' immediate neighbour, who breathlessly told her to get herself dressed as something was badly wrong next door. It was then that Helen heard a cry of 'Murder!' and straight away recognised Mary's voice. A few moments later, as the two women stood at the Mairs' front door, they heard the sound of heavy blows being struck - in Helen's words 'like the blows of a hammer' - and Mary's voice pleading in response, 'Let me lie, and die in peace, and don't strike me anymore.' Mair replied that he would leave her alone once she had 'put in the sneck of the bed' - that is, use a latch to fasten the doors of the box-bed she was lying in - a simple enough matter, you might think, but Mary could not see to do this in the dark. Listening from outside, Helen called through the door, telling him to leave his wife alone, but he was in no mood to comply and shouted back, threatening to shoot anyone who dared to interfere. Knowing that he possessed firearms, Jean Letham had had enough and retreated to her own home, and, even though the disturbance was still ongoing, sometime later Helen did the same. It seems puzzling, to say the least, why neither of the two women made any attempt to seek outside help. Surely by now they must have had grave doubts relating to Mair's state of mind, and how they could have left the frail old lady to be beaten and misused is hard to understand. Possibly in early-Victorian Scotland the notion of coming between a husband and his wife was viewed as a very last resort.

Anxious about her elderly friend's welfare, Helen called on Mary first thing the following morning and it was Mair who answered the door. Treading gingerly for fear of reigniting his wrath, she inquired after his wife's health, to which Mair replied that she had been wrestling through most of the night with the doors of her box-bed. Helen risked asking what it was that had made him so angry during the night and he explained that the doors of the box-bed banging had prevented him from sleeping. He was going now to the manse, he told her gruffly, where he intended to instruct the minister 'to make a snuff box of Mary' - a possible reference to the macabre practice at the time of making novelty snuff boxes in the shape of a coffin, sometimes even with the carved figure of a corpse inside. If that was indeed Mair's meaning, then he had spoken prematurely because Helen found Mary still alive but only precariously so, crouched at the foot of her bed. The front of the old lady's nightclothes were stained with blood and the blankets, Helen could see, were also badly discoloured. When offered tea, Mary was unable to raise her right arm and had to use her left hand to hold the cup. Indicating her husband, she stated - quite superfluously - that it was he who had been responsible for her bruises and cuts. At this point Helen finally took the bull by the horns and sent belatedly for the police. That evening an officer turned up at Candie End and when he learned of the previous night's events he had no hesitation in taking Allan Mair into custody. By the time that the old man appeared before the sheriff, however, Mary had already died of her injuries so he was consequently charged with his wife's murder and committed to jail in Stirling.

When his case came to court five months later, Mair pled not guilty to having 'with a stick, or other weapon, beat[en] and abused Mary Mair, of which injuries she came by her death.' In his defence, his lawyer claimed that at the time when Mair assaulted his wife he had been suffering from a form of insanity, though he undermined his own argument by conceding that his 'loss of reason' had not extended to his dealings with others - something which was surely open to question. But the weight of evidence against Mair was overpowering and, following an absence of twenty minutes, the jury returned to the courtroom where their spokesman delivered a unanimous verdict of guilty. At this, the judge, Lord Moncrieff, donned the black cap and sentenced Mair to be executed on Wednesday 4 October between eight and ten o'clock in the morning, his body to be buried within the precincts of the prison. Taken back to his cell, Mair refused food for four consecutive days but on the fifth he was overcome by pangs of hunger to the extent that his resolution crumbled and he accepted a meal. (That he made any connection between his own self-imposed starvation and the ordeal he had previously put his wife through seems unlikely.) Given any opportunity, he was vociferous in protesting his innocence and, although no-one was remotely convinced, the Provost and Magistrates of Stirling got up a petition in the hope of winning for him a reprieve. Given the brutality of Mair's crime, however, it was always likely to be a long shot and in the end proved unsuccessful. When the news was broken to him in prison he reportedly broke down in tears. 'Weel,' he said resignedly, 'I maun submit.' As it turned out, however, he did not live up to this stated intention.

On the eve of his execution - Tuesday 3 October - he retired to bed before midnight, but was awakened in the early hours by the sound of hammering as workmen assembled the scaffold in front of the prison. 'What a horrible thing,' he was reported as saying, 'to be hanged like a dog.' For the rest of the night he was unable to settle and woke up every hour. Frail and unrested, in the morning he had to be half-carried into the courtroom where he wept and wrung his hands repeatedly during a short religious service. Offered a glass of wine, he declined. When the executioner, John Murdoch of Glasgow, set about the job of pinioning his arms, he turned to him and said, 'Oh, dinna hurt me, dinna hurt me! I'm auld - I'll mak nae resistance.' Carried on to the scaffold, he expressed a wish to address the crowd of onlookers and, unable to stand without assistance, he was provided with a chair. Feeble or not, he soon made it clear that he had no intention of going quietly, and spoke out loudly in what the *Stirling Observer* described - rather sniffily - as 'an antiquated Scottish dialect, now fast dying out.' The newspaper rendered Mair's speech into a more genteel, standard English before publication, but a local author, William Drysdale, was less mealy-mouthed and reported his words verbatim: 'People, wan an a', listen to me! I caw upon the hale company o' ye, great as it is, and mair especially those wha cam' frae my ain parish, to listen to what I hae to say, as I've no' been gien a single opportunity ever since I was grippit and ludged in jile to prove that my innocence was as clear as the noonday sun! The minister o' the parish invented lees - lees against me!' Growing increasingly animated, he hurled accusations not only against the minister, but also the police, the Fiscal, the Sheriff, and those neighbours who had testified against him, and called down a plague on all their houses. 'People, yin an' a',' he thundered in a final broadside, 'mind I'm nae murderer! I ne'er committed murder, and I say it as a deein' man wha is juist aboot to pass into the presence o' my Goad! I say again I was condemned by the lees o' the minister, by the injustice o' a sheriff an' fiscal, and by the perjury o' the witnesses. I trust for their conduct that a' thase parties shall be owertaen by the vengeance o' Goad, and sent into everlasting damnation!' It was a bravura performance, a classic fire-and-brimstone rant that lasted a full ten minutes, and perhaps he believed every word of it. Given his age and mental state, it is possible that he was convinced in his own mind that he was a victim of injustice and, even as the white cap and noose were being placed over his head, he continued his tirade. At just before a quarter to nine the hangman drew back the bolt, but the drama was not yet over. One of the prisoner's hands had been incorrectly pinioned, and at the very last moment he reached above his head and seized hold of the rope in what looked like an effort to save himself. But all to no avail and, after a short, convulsive struggle, his grip slackened and his life ebbed away.

At 84 years old, Allan Mair was - and remains - the oldest man on record to have been executed in Scotland and, at the end of the day, it is hard to know what to make of him. Sifting fact from fiction is not entirely straightforward but almost certainly he suffered from some form of dementia - the point, we might suppose, that his lawyer attempted to argue in court. After his death, he began to be mythologised as sketches of his early life appeared in print, frequently at odds with one another, and not always in keeping with the carnaptious old man he had become. It was suggested that during his roving days in the Caribbean he had been a bit of a dandy, wearing his hair fashionably long and developing a reputation as a ladies' man which was the envy of many. One story related how, on returning to Scotland, he had become known as a dedicated bird-fancier who kept for his pleasure an aviary of ornamental birds, and was widely credited with having been the first person to introduce the canary to his home country. There was, however, a distinctly darker side to some of the stories, and the tale was routinely told that during his execution he was left choking and gasping at the end of the rope until the hangman finally took pity on him, gripped him by the legs and pulled with all his might until he heard his neck snap. It was a lurid tale, to be sure, but one with no more basis in fact than a rumour that did the rounds concerning a ghostly presence that haunted the prison cell where he had spent his final hours.

Aside from such tittle-tattle, Allan Mair's execution created ripples that spread rather wider, perhaps, than might have been expected. For one thing, his death opened up discussion of capital punishment more generally, and raised the question of whether hanging an 84-year-old man - viewed by some as 'an act of barbarism' - in any way served the public interest. And, secondly, it piqued the interest of devotees of phrenology - a pseudoscience, popular in Victorian times, based on the notion that the size and shape of a person's skull were instrumental in determining his or her character and mental capabilities. An amateur local enthusiast was John Christie, a Stirling shopkeeper, who was called upon to assist when a plaster cast was made of Allan Mair's head. Based on study of the model, a report was produced whose findings made for interesting reading. 'It was the practice of sheep-farmers, before the discovery of Phrenology, to choose persons for shepherds who were very prominent and broad between the eyes,' the writer contended, since 'they were supposed, and it appears correctly, to be better able than others to distinguish the different sheep.' Mair's cast - surprisingly enough - showed just such a markedly broad forehead, vindicating perhaps the Earl of Selkirk's decision to place him in charge of his valuable Canadian flock. Other traits prominently represented on the plaster cast were 'individuality', 'combativeness' and 'a tendency to vagabondism' - all clearly connected with what was known of Mair's character and personal history, but it is hard to shake off a niggling suspicion that the research might have carried more weight had its author not had prior knowledge of his subject's life-story and heavily-publicised recent departure. Today the 'science' of phrenology is viewed by most as nothing more than a curio of the past, and, while it is all too easy to pass judgment from a modern-day standpoint, it seems puzzling to say the least why its exponents appeared never at any point to consider the possibility that Allan Mair had been mentally ill.

James McWheelan : October 1848

By all accounts, the Dudsday fair of May 1848 was a particularly busy one with both shopkeepers and public-houses reporting a brisk trade as country people and their families converged on Kilmarnock. As well as providing farm-workers who were disgruntled with their current lot an opportunity to negotiate a better position for the forthcoming term, those content to stay put likewise benefited from the day's holiday, and many put it to good use by travelling to town and treating themselves to a new suit of clothes - hence, it has been suggested, the name *Duds-day*. It was for this very reason that James Young, a sixteen-year-old local farm worker, made his way into Kilmarnock on Friday 26 May 1848.

We know that, in common with many others, James bought himself various new articles of clothing. Later in the day, in the company of his father, John Young, he visited his married sister's new home - she had flitted that very day - following which the two men made their way to where John lived at Knowehead farm, Riccarton, stopping off briefly at a friend's house where John accepted the offer of a dram and James a glass of ginger beer. After finishing their refreshments, they continued to Knowehead where James intended to leave his new purchases. Because of the lateness of the hour, his mother suggested that her son should perhaps stay the night but, keen to get back to his workplace, James left at around eleven o'clock to cover the couple of miles or so to Fortyacres farm. Sadly, as events turned out, the young man would never arrive at his destination and, when his parents bade him goodbye at Knowehead, it would be the last time that John Young and his wife would ever see their son alive.

Some hours later - between three and four o'clock in the morning of Saturday 27 May - John Gebbie, a Kilmarnock weaver, and his companion, John Scott, a calico printer, were walking near Fortyacres Toll when to their horror they stumbled across a lifeless body, sprawled in a pool of blood. Shocked, the men rushed to rouse Robert Hendry, the toll-keeper, and Joseph Smith, the farmer of Fortyacres, who instantly recognised the dead boy as his employee, James Young. Shortly before seven o'clock, James's father arrived on the scene where he was faced with the unenviable task of identifying his son's body. Ironically, when fate caught up with James that night, he was easily within hailing distance of his destination.

Later in the morning, Police Superintendent Thomas Penny arrived at the crime scene, followed shortly afterwards by Sheriff-Substitute James Robison and the local Procurator-Fiscal, James Murdoch. The cause of death wasn't hard to see. An injury to the back of James Young's head appeared to have been caused by a heavy stone which was lying close by - the size, it was reported, of a large potato. A bloody chisel, retrieved from an adjacent field, appeared to have been responsible for a savage gash on the side of the boy's neck from which a large quantity of blood had spouted. His pockets had been rifled and, knocked from his head, his cap lay not far away. Closer inspection revealed that his pocket-watch, a gift from his older brother, was missing, in addition to fifteen shillings in silver. A post-mortem investigation, carried out later that day by doctors Haldane of Ayr and Paxton of Kilmarnock, revealed no possible clue to the attacker's identity.

Remarkably, although no witness to the crime ever came forward, within a few short days a suspect had been identified, apprehended, charged with murder and placed under lock and key at Ayr, largely as the result of a series of fortunate events. On the morning of Sunday 28 May, a toll-house at Lochwinnoch - some fifteen miles north of the crime scene - was found to have been broken into overnight and £35 in cash removed, in addition to a watch. The day before the burglary a stranger's odd behaviour had aroused the suspicions of a local farmer, William Orr, so he saddled up his horse and set off in pursuit, eventually catching up with his suspect some five or six miles away in the town of Johnstone where he succeeded in pinning the man down until a local police constable, Alexander Davidson, could arrive to effect his arrest. When searched, the man was found to have in his possession a sum of nearly £35 as well as the watch that was missing from the toll-house. Charged with theft and housebreaking, by Sunday night he was securely locked up in Paisley Jail.

The following morning, Monday 29 May, a police officer in Dalry successfully added the next piece of the jigsaw. Descriptions of James Young's stolen pocket-watch had been circulated fairly widely and, when Constable Hutchison examined a watch pawned two days previously at William Lowry's establishment in New Street, Beith, he was able to verify from its serial number - 908 - that it was indeed the one which had been taken from the murder victim. From his records, Lowry was able to advise police that the watch had been deposited (through a third party, as it transpired) in the name of one James McWheelan, an Irishman who had previously been employed in the nearby Glengarnock Iron Works. When it emerged that McWheelan had caught a train for Johnstone but had failed to complete his journey, disembarking at Lochwinnoch instead, the penny must very definitely have dropped.

At Paisley Jail police soon identified the individual charged with the Lochwinnoch burglary as one and the same as James McWheelan, the man in whose name the stolen watch had been pawned at Beith. Denying all knowledge of the watch, the Irishman was nonetheless unable to offer any credible explanation and quickly found himself sucked into far deeper trouble than a simple charge of housebreaking. The following day, Tuesday 30 May, he was escorted by train to Ayr where he was charged with the murder of the farm-servant, James Young. The fact that less than four days had passed since James's death was a tribute both to meticulous policing and, in particular, to the plucky efforts of the Lochwinnoch farmer, William Orr.

It would be another four months before the McWheelan case came before the Circuit Court of Justiciary in Ayr - on Wednesday 4 October - and, although the accused man showed no hesitation in pleading not guilty, it soon became clear that he had an uphill struggle on his hands. One of a total of 93 witnesses called by the Crown, a Kilmarnock labourer,

Robert Thom, described how in the early hours of Saturday 27 May he had been having a drink with a stranger in Andrew Anderson's public-house in Waterloo Street when he noticed bloodstains on the man's clothing. 'You have surely been murdering somebody, or killing somebody's swine,' Robert Thom had quipped. His drinking-companion, whom he was able to identify as James McWheelan, replied that he had been involved in 'a skite' over a girl, then drained his glass and abruptly departed. The testimony of successive further witnesses allowed the accused's route towards Beith to be traced. One man, John Marshall, recounted how an agitated McWheelan had accused him of insulting him and had proceeded to assault him on the roadside near Stewarton. A barber in Beith, John Crawford, told the court how the Irishman had attempted to skip the queue in his urgency to have his beard shaved off in what looked suspiciously like an attempt to disguise his appearance. In a development that seems to owe more to detective fiction than to real life, it emerged that a distinctive, pink-patterned handkerchief, recovered from the vicinity of the murder scene, could be reliably linked with the prisoner who persisted nonetheless in maintaining that he had never at any time set foot in the parish of Dundonald, where Fortyacres Farm was situated. In an effort to explain away his bloodstained clothing, he claimed to have taken a lift some time earlier in a farm cart which was transporting slaughtered calves - a story, perhaps surprisingly, that the cart's driver, Hugh Allan of Dalry, was prepared to corroborate.

But at the end of the day it wasn't enough. After hearing a summing up by both Crown and defence lawyers and the concluding remarks of the presiding judge, Lord Mackenzie, the members of the jury took a mere fifteen minutes to reach a unanimous verdict of guilty on charges both of robbery and murder. Turning to the convicted man, Lord Mackenzie advised him that in a case of murder Scots law permitted no discretion, and that he should hold out no hope of a reprieve. 'You must,' he told McWheelan bluntly, 'consider your life in this world at an end.' The judge then concluded by informing the prisoner that he would be sustained by bread and water alone until he faced execution in three weeks' time, on Thursday 26 October. McWheelan cried out at this, still denying the murder but admitting for the first time an association with James Young's pocket-watch. 'I got the watch, although I never said it before,' he confessed, 'from a man named Hall in Kilmarnock.' Of course, his outburst sounded exactly like what it was most likely to have been - a last, lame attempt to stave off what was inevitable.

McWheelan was not a model prisoner. Hostile and suspicious, he was easily roused to anger if pressed to confess his crimes. In discussion with two local clergymen, he stated that, Protestant by birth, he had attended church during his childhood years but had long ago fallen by the wayside. To the ministers' horror, he claimed no knowledge of the existence of God and was happy to ridicule the notion of hell. His lapse into crime, he insisted, was the result of his lowly position in society and he candidly admitted to having served a number of spells of imprisonment. It seems likely that the two clergymen's eyebrows shot skywards when McWheelan inquired of them whether the punishment to be suffered by a triple-murderer in hell would be subject to proportionate increase. Of course, it is quite possible that he was simply mischief-making. Then again, perhaps not.

For all his bluster, McWheelan was a deeply troubled man. While awaiting trial he had already attempted suicide - a small blade from a pair of weaver's scissors had been found, secreted in a corner of his cell - and he made a second attempt shortly after being sentenced. When a bent nail, sharpened to a point, was discovered, concealed among his bedclothes, he was kept thereafter under close watch. He was obliged to wear handcuffs at night which were permitted to be removed during daytime. Although barely able to read, the condemned man impressed his visitors by his ability to repeat virtually verbatim extended passages of any book which had been read to him. Perhaps surprisingly, the person to whom he appeared most responsive was Prison Governor McKissock and in the weeks leading up to his execution the two men spent many hours in private conversation. Bit by bit the prisoner began to relax, to sleep better, even - it was noted - to put on a little weight. We might wonder whether it might have been the first and only time in McWheelan's life that he was free to benefit from a spell of leisure. Gradually his trust grew and he started to open up concerning his own personal circumstances. Since he was unable to write, this information was noted down at his dictation.

McWheelan stated that he had been born in Dublin, maybe thirty years earlier - maybe 32. He was led to believe that his father had died before he was born. While he was still small, his mother relocated from

Dublin to Belfast where she had friends and, in what must have been a fairly hand-to-mouth existence, she and her young son subsisted on what income she could glean from selling small items out of a basket. When McWheelan was around seven years old, his mother left Belfast on a return visit to Dublin and that was the last he saw of her. After what must surely have been a time of excruciating uncertainty, it was finally concluded that she had either died or been murdered. For a while he was cared for by his mother's friends in Belfast but, when they died, he was sent to live in a household of three unmarried brothers and a sister who put him to work herding cattle. His new guardians, he recalled, treated him kindly enough, but from that time on he received no education whatsoever and very soon he forgot the rudiments of reading which he had learned from his mother.

In an effort to improve his prospects, McWheelan left Ireland in his early twenties and sailed to Glasgow where he took up a gardening job. His memory of his subsequent employment history was somewhat hazy, but sometime later he had started work with a contractor in Ardrossan whom he named as Mr King. Here he remained for a number of years and, during this settled spell, it looked for a time as though things might just turn around for James McWheelan when he became romantically involved with a servant in his employer's household to whom he promised marriage. But by this time excessive drinking had started to exert a grip on him and the girl, he recalled, warned him repeatedly against its dangers but, sadly, to no avail. In recent years alcohol-consumption had taken a devastating toll on him. There is no question that, when it suited him, McWheelan could be an inveterate and accomplished liar but, somehow or other, his sad tale has a ring of truth about it. As a child, he had no father's hand to steady him and it seems possible that in the person of Governor McKissock he may have belatedly discovered the father figure that he had never previously known.

On Tuesday 24 October - 48 hours before the scheduled time of his execution - McWheelan received a visit in his prison cell from a distressed young woman who arrived in the company of his former employer, Mr King. The condemned man made repeated efforts to distract the girl from her grief, declaring himself happy and resigned to the fate that awaited him but, for reasons that were entirely understandable, he was unsuccessful. The old McWheelan resurfaced, however, when she tearfully urged him to confess to his crimes. 'Ay!' he is said to have snapped. 'Who learned you to come with that story? It's strange that everyone wants me to go to the scaffold with a lie in my mouth.' It seems likely that his words, spoken in anger, were ones that he would later regret.

The following day - Wednesday 25 October - McWheelan finally appeared to crack, confessing his guilt for the first time, then immediately recanted, only to repeat his confession in the presence of Governor McKissock. He went on to give his startled listeners an account of events which he maintained had taken place on the night after James Young's murder which he had spent alone in a rented room at Lochwinnoch. A single, solitary candle on the table before him, he told them, had suddenly blazed out with the light of a dozen candles and illuminated one of the room's two doors. Overcome by fear, he made a vow before God that he would desist from leaving by that particular door, yet immediately found himself passing through it nonetheless. The most likely explanation, of course, was that the overwrought McWheelan had mistaken dreams for daytime reality, but what a Freudian might make of it all, who can say? He went on to ask that the girl who had visited him the previous day be sent for but sadly this proved impossible. She had returned home to Ardrossan and was unable to be contacted in time. McWheelan later confessed that, while working with Mr King, the contractor had provided him with a sum of money to allow him to marry his sweetheart, but that he had failed to do so. The chances are, we might suspect, that the money was spent on drink.

Whether the ministers' persistence finally paid off or, what is possibly more likely, imminent death served to focus his mind, for whatever reason McWheelan's attitude to religion mellowed somewhat, on the surface at least. He made what Rev. Graham believed to be a full and frank confession, during the course of which he admitted to his involvement in James Young's killing but for the first time implicated a partner-in-crime. On Dudsday evening, he recalled, his accomplice and he had sized up an earlier possible victim but in the event had taken pity on the man when he revealed that he had an elderly mother who depended on him. A short time later they had overheard James Young and his father bid one another goodnight on the doorstep at Knowehead and had subsequently shadowed James as he made his way down the Fortyacres road where they had launched the now infamous attack.

McWheelan's own intention, he insisted, was purely robbery, never murder, and his accomplice had been the one who had struck the fatal blow. Though he confessed to having previously considered highway robbery as a means of obtaining money for alcohol, McWheelan maintained that, until allying himself with his accomplice, his nerve had always failed him. After listening to the condemned man's confession, Rev. Graham was convinced that he had at last come clean, almost at the eleventh hour. McWheelan's story, however, spectacularly unravelled when the first potential victim - the man with a dependent mother - was identified and revealed that he had been approached on Dudsday by one man alone whose description answered remarkably closely to that of James McWheelan. As for the shadowy accomplice, it is tempting to see him as some sort of alter-ego - a Gil-Martin-type figure as in James Hogg's *Justified Sinner*, published some 24 years earlier - though the chances of McWheelan's having been familiar with Hogg's disturbing novel are surely virtually nil.

On the morning of the execution - Thursday 26 October - proceedings began when the magistrates and authorities met just after seven o'clock. The condemned man arrived shortly after, accompanied by the Revs. Knox and Graham whom he requested to say a prayer for him. His appearance, it was said, made a strong impression on the large crowd of men, women and children who had assembled to witness his final moments. Roughly five feet ten inches in height and of a muscular build, McWheelan was described as having jet-black hair and bushy whiskers, with the dark eyes and complexion of a man of foreign birth. He walked upright and with apparent total composure. When he addressed the crowd, those who were within earshot described his voice as deep and resonant. 'I bear anger at no man,' McWheelan announced. 'I owe no man any ill will. Fare-ye-well.' At that, he turned to ascend the scaffold which was surrounded by a guard of Special Constables and local Yeomanry. All the while McWheelan was heard to be uttering prayers - 'Lord, take me to thyself. O Lord, do not let my guilty soul die in sin' - words that did not perhaps qualify quite as remorse, but at the very least were an admission of wrongdoing. Once the prisoner was in place, the executioner - the octogenarian John Murdoch of Glasgow - drew a cap down over his face.

The crowd and assembled officials waited expectantly while McWheelan remained unmoving on the scaffold - a full thirty minutes during which the tension mounted unbearably, and still the condemned man did not release the handkerchief which would act as the signal that he was ready to die. Finally, it was left to the magistrates to prompt the executioner who, on receiving his cue, drew back the bolt and sent the prisoner plummeting to his death. Several minutes passed while his dangling body convulsed repeatedly until finally all signs of life departed and the corpse was able to be cut down for burial within the precincts of the prison. It was noted that throughout the entire procedure only one single, solitary groan was emitted by the crowd. Once the grisly proceedings were complete they filed out - quietly, it was said - and proceeded to disperse. A crude old couplet, composed by an unknown rhymester, commemorated the sorry occasion for many years afterwards:

'Twas on Kilmarnock Fast and Glasgow Fair,
Was the day McWheelan was hanged at Ayr.

The tangle of truth and deceptions that James McWheelan wove around him, his confessions and immediate retractions, untruths, half-truths and evasions, all hinder our ability to take a balanced view of the man he was and the life he chose to lead. That he was an alcoholic and a murderer seems beyond doubt, but his claim that poverty and social exclusion were what determined his descent into crime was not, perhaps, a notion that the family of James Young might have felt disposed to accept. One thing seems certain. On 26 October 1848, when the trapdoor was released and McWheelan plunged out of this world and into the next, he must surely have carried many of his secrets along with him.

James Robb : October 1849

James Robb was only 22 years old when he ascended the gallows in October 1849. Onlookers commented on his pallid complexion, and his intense anxiety was clear to see. When asked by Aberdeen's Lord Provost whether he had any final words to say, a statement was read on his behalf by the prison chaplain, Rev. Strahan. 'Lust, drink, and Sabbath-breaking have brought me to a shameful and untimely death,' he had written, before going on to advise others not to follow his example. 'I cast myself entirely on the mercy of God, through Christ,' he concluded, 'whose blood cleanseth all sin. God pity, pardon, sanctify and save me, for Christ's sake - Amen, and Amen.' All perfectly laudable, you might think, for a condemned man to direct his final thoughts to the afterlife, though some might suggest that his attention should have focused more on his victim and the ordeal he had put her through during her final moments of life. If he felt any guilt in connection with the death of the quiet 63-year-old spinster, Mary Smith, then he chose not to mention it.

Since Robb's return to Aberdeenshire after a spell of absence, he had wasted no time in acquiring a bad name for himself. In February 1849 he had followed a local woman, Jean Gammie, on her way home and somewhere along the way had pulled her into the roadside shadows with unmistakeable intent, but was forced to release her when she drew her nails across his face and threatened to scream. Whether she detected a whiff of alcohol on his breath she failed to mention. Overhearing the commotion, a group of nearby farm-workers later confirmed Jean's story and reported that when she left the scene they had been obliged to restrain Robb from setting off in pursuit. She later explained that she chose not to report the incident to police since at the end of the day she had emerged from the distressing incident unhurt, on top of which she did not want to cause her attacker's parents any embarrassment. Had Jean chosen differently, Mary Smith might well have been spared her cruel fate some two months later. In a small rural community, word of Robb's misbehaviour soon leaked out and was a matter that Mary Smith discussed with her sister, Mrs Fraser. Sometimes he would stop off at her isolated cottage, Mary told her, under the pretext of obtaining a light for his pipe. On one occasion she had felt distinctly uneasy when, glancing towards the roof of the house, he had observed that, although there were no windows, it would be a matter of no great difficulty for any would-be intruder to enter the cottage via the *lum*.

Employed as a labourer at the Tillymorgan slate quarries, James Robb spent Monday 9 April drinking and carousing with his cronies at Badenscoth Fair, an occasion infamous in the locality for its boisterous shenanigans. During the course of the day he misplaced his walking-stick but promptly replaced it with a distinctive substitute: a circumstance, fairly trivial on the face of it but whose significance would become clear at a later point. In the evening as he was preparing to depart, Robb was heard boasting - reputedly in the coarsest of terms - of his intention to gratify his lust on any unfortunate female whose path he might cross as he made his way home that night. How seriously his offensive remarks were taken is impossible to say, but it seems likely that his associates assumed - mistakenly, as it turned out - that his talk was no more than idle bravado and that it was drink that was doing the talking. Unfortunately for poor Mary Smith, his boasting proved a good deal more than empty bluster. 'Never married, or a mother' - a clear euphemism for virginity - the elderly spinster lived alone in her one-room cottage at Redhill, mid-way between Badenscoth and Robb's home at Fisherford, a mile or so farther south. Under no illusions regarding his dubious character, she had recently remarked to a neighbour that she was 'not afraid of anybody, except that lad Jamie Robb.' Her fears, as it transpired, were well founded. After leaving the fair, Robb turned up at her cottage sometime after ten o'clock and cried out that he needed a light for his pipe. Mindful of his unsavoury reputation, she declined to let him in but, not to be outdone, he immediately proceeded to climb on to the roof of the cottage and make his way down through the chimney. Mary's terror must surely have been extreme as she watched a burly, soot-begrimed figure - a satanic parody of Santa Claus - as he clambered from her chimney and drew himself upright. Strangely for a man who could squirm his way down a lum, Robb would later be described by Lord Cockburn, one of the two judges who presided at his subsequent trial, as 'stout' though undoubtedly the job he carried out at Tillymorgan quarry was one that required great strength. Poor Mary just didn't have a chance and tragically there was no-one within reach whom she could call upon for help.

The following morning local people noticed that there was no sign of activity at her cottage and, seeing the front door gaping wide, they were concerned for Mary's welfare and stepped inside. A dreadful sight awaited them. What they found was her dead body lying obliquely across her broken bed with the bedclothes soiled and disordered. Her expression was wild, it was said, and her hair in a state of dishevelment. Her clothing was rucked up around her waist, leaving her lower body naked, and her legs were thrust apart and bloodstained. Clues as to who might have perpetrated such an appalling crime were quick to surface. A metal button, torn from the attacker's clothing, was found nestled in a lirk - or fold - in the bedclothes while propped against an outside wall was a highly distinctive walking-stick, identified later as the property of James Robb. The intruder's means of entry was ascertained when streaks, such as might be made by corduroy clothing, were discovered in the soot inside the chimney as well as on Mary's bedclothes. Robb turned up late for work that day, around one o'clock in the afternoon. Noticing that his coat was marked with traces of soot, some of his colleagues at the quarry were prompted to quip that he had 'surely been doon someone's lum.' After what appears to have been a series of blunders on the part of the authorities, he was eventually arrested late that night by Geordie Webster, a local sheriff's officer, by which time Robb had returned to his father's house and retired to bed. A pair of soot-marked corduroy breeches was found by his bedside and a coat that was missing a button. Questioned by a local magistrate, he claimed in all apparent seriousness that when his knocking at Mary Smith's door went unanswered, he had descended her chimney in order to obtain a light for his pipe.

The exact details of what took place in Mary Smith's cottage can never be known for sure but when her injuries were examined they told a horrifying tale. They were described some time later by Dr Francis Ogston of Marischal College, Aberdeen, one of three medics who conducted an examination of her body in the Badenscoth Inn in the immediate aftermath of the murder. The doctor's initial comments concerned James Robb whom he described as 'a stout young man of about 22 years of age ... who was in custody on suspicion of having violated and afterwards taken away the life of Mary Smith, aged 63, an unmarried pauper living by herself.' On Robb's breeches were found 'dark brownish' marks whose carbon content led Ogston to identify them as traces of peat soot. His face had been badly scratched, as though raked by ragged fingernails, and in places his clothing was found to be bloodstained. The doctors then turned their attention to the dead woman. 'Bloody fluid', Ogston noted, had leaked from her mouth which gaped wide open with her tongue protruding. The lower part of her body was marked by 'partly-clotted' blood which had seeped down to stain the bedding beneath, and the appearance of the genitals indicated 'a forced sexual connection'. Despite the level of violence to which Mary appeared to have been subjected, it was, the men believed, insufficient to account for her death while the fact that her body displayed no sign of disease effectively ruled out any possibility - a formality surely - that death had arisen from natural causes. This apparent contradiction was explained, however, when examination of Mary's heart revealed signs of 'organic disease'. While the right cavities were 'distended with dark fluid blood', those on the left contained virtually none with the result that 'the heart was morbidly thickened on one side and morbidly thinned on the other.' Though candidly admitting that they could not be categorically certain, the doctors concluded that 'death in this case had been occasioned by primary or direct arrest of the respiration, or in other words, by ordinary asphyxia.' What it meant, in point of fact, was that when a hand was clamped over Mary's mouth and nostrils and the weight of a man was placed upon her chest her unknown condition would have ensured that she died more quickly and easily than would a person with a healthy heart. What was beyond doubt was that Mary had met a distressing and gratuitously violent end.

Six months later James Robb was tried for rape and murder before Lords Cockburn and Moncrieff in Aberdeen where, owing to the nature of the charges, proceedings took place behind closed doors. In what looked like an attempt at plea bargaining, he indicated that he willing to plead guilty to rape but his proposal was rejected and the case against him duly went ahead. What exchanges might have taken place between the Crown lawyer, E. F. Maitland, and Robb's defence, C. F. Shand, was never made public but it became known that Shand had made great play of a similar case in Glasgow, some 23 years earlier, in which the victim's death was shown to be unintentional which had resulted in the convicted murderer being sentenced to lifetime transportation rather than facing execution. In relation to the case in hand, once the evidence of more than forty witnesses had been heard and the members of the jury retired to consider their decision, the public and press were admitted to the courtroom and, following an absence of half an hour, the jury returned to announce their verdict of guilty as charged on cases both of rape and murder, but they attached as an unexpected addendum their recommendation to mercy on the grounds that 'they did not think that [Robb] had any intention of committing the crime of murder' - a consequence, perhaps, of the persuasiveness of the defence's analogy. In summing up, Shand addressed this point once again, arguing that his client's sentence should reflect his lack of intent but, when the time came for the Crown to counter, Mr Maitland maintained that the prisoner 'had committed an act criminal and dangerous, the natural effect of which was the loss of life.' Unconvinced by the defence's line of argument, Lord Moncrieff at the bench pointed out that Robb had been convicted of, not one, but two capital crimes and, given that the case was a particularly dreadful one, a death sentence was the inevitable outcome. All that was left was for Lord Cockburn to don the black cap and address the guilty man, telling him that the crimes of which he had been convicted were 'the two very worst offences for a man to commit', and reiterating the expressed view of Lord Moncrieff that there was no alternative to a sentence of death. The prisoner would be 'taken from the bar to the jail of this city,' he stated, 'there to be fed upon bread and water till the 16th of October, and on that day, between the hours of eight and ten, to be led forth to the public place of execution, and hung by the neck upon a gibbet till ... dead.' 'This is pronounced for doom,' the judge concluded, 'and may God Almighty have mercy on your soul.' The condemned man, it was said, showed little or no reaction and, after occupying a total of eleven hours, the court proceedings were finally wound up.

Given the particularly brutal circumstances surrounding Mary Smith's rape and murder, the jury's recommendation to mercy was a surprising one but no more so than a petition that was subsequently got up in support of the condemned man though, in line with expectation, it was unsuccessful in obtaining a reprieve. Prior to being tried, Robb had shown little interest in spiritual matters but after his fate was settled he devoted himself for the first time to contemplation of religion, guided by Rev. Strahan, the prison chaplain, and two Episcopalian ministers - Revs. Cheyne and Wagstaff - in whose church he had been brought up. On Saturday 13 October he received a visit in prison from his brother and the day immediately prior to his execution he took a final farewell of his father. During his last night, it was said, he slept no more than half an hour and devoted what little time he had left to religious devotion. Shortly after eight o'clock the following morning he was pinioned by the hangman, William Calcraft of London, and transferred into the custody of the Aberdeen city magistrates. The words of his statement were read aloud by Rev. Strahan: 'I hereby confess that I entered the house of Mary Smith, when I was under the influence of drink, with the intention of ravishing her; that, while struggling with her in order to accomplish my purpose, she coughed twice or thrice, and then ceased to breathe; and I hereby declare that the crime of rape was not committed.' This, of course, was at odds with his initial plea to the court as well as in direct contravention to the medical evidence. When the chaplain fell silent, Robb was accompanied to the scaffold by the three clergyman who had attended him during his final days in prison. By this stage a large crowd of spectators had gathered to witness the grisly event - mostly, it was reported, representatives of the lower orders with a disproportionately large number of young females in evidence. After the noose was placed around Robb's neck the drop fell within two minutes and it was reported that he slipped from this life with no apparent struggle.

A fortnight after his execution Robb's case cropped up in discussions relating to the selection of potential candidates for election to Aberdeen town council. During the course of a public meeting nominees were invited to express their views in relation to capital punishment and, perhaps surprisingly in the light of recent publicity regarding the brutal nature of Robb's crimes, two of the four men in contention voiced their complete opposition to the death penalty on the grounds that it was 'inconsistent with God's law and with humanity', while the remaining two opposed capital punishment for all offences other than murder. It would appear, however, that during the course of his lifetime Lord Cockburn experienced no weakening of his resolve. Penning his memoirs forty years later, he recalled the outrage he had felt on hearing the jury's unexpected recommendation to mercy on behalf of a man whom he described as 'a known reprobate'. 'It is difficult to drive the horrors of that scene out of one's imagination,' Lord Cockburn continued. 'The solitary old woman in the solitary house, the descent through the chimney, the beastly attack, the death struggle, all that going on within this lonely room, amidst silent fields, and under a still, dark sky. It is a fragment of hell which it is both difficult to endure and to quit. Yet a jury, though clear of both crimes, *recommended the brute to mercy* because he did not *intend* to commit the murder! Neither does the highwayman, who only means to wound, in order to get the purse, but kills.' Lord Cockburn, quite clearly, had experienced no change of heart over the years and perhaps for perfectly sound reasons. James Robb was a hefty 22-year-old man who had shown no mercy towards his victim, a vulnerable maiden lady in her sixties.

In nineteenth-century rural Aberdeenshire the shockwaves caused by Mary Smith's brutal death would have spread quickly and widely, but James Robb's relatives appear not to have become tainted through association with the black sheep of their family and there is no suggestion that they were in any way shunned by the local community. On a frosty Friday in December 1849, a mere two months after his son's execution, innkeeper George Robb provided a splendid meal for the competitors in a ploughing match on the farm of Mains of Rothmaise, immediately south of Fisherford, a practice that he again repeated in subsequent years. In January 1850 George was involved as a competitor himself and was reported as taking eleventh place out of a field of 42 ploughs. The message it sends is possibly this: that an individual must be responsible for his or her own actions and that family members and associates, however closely connected, are not to be held accountable.

William Bennison : August 1850

In the middle years of the nineteenth century the sight of Sandy Milne and his dog was a familiar one to the residents of Edinburgh's Leith Walk. Disabled since early childhood, Sandy relied heavily on his pet which he harnessed each day to a small cart which the creature pulled in order to let him get about. Allowing the dog out for a run one April afternoon in 1850, his distress can easily be imagined when it returned that evening in a sickly state and, after a night of retching and vomiting, died the following morning. The dog, it transpired, had been spotted scavenging on waste which one of Milne's neighbours, William Bennison, had given to a serving-girl to be disposed of in the street and, when it emerged that the creature's fatal final dinner had been vomited some time earlier by Bennison's dying wife, alarm bells started to ring. Suspicions thus aroused, the body of the dead dog was removed to Surgeons' Hall to allow the contents of its stomach to be analysed.

An Irishman in his early thirties, William Bennison had left his native Portadown just over ten years earlier with plans to establish a new life in Scotland. Born into a family of rural peasants, his background was undeniably modest and, owing to a perceived eye weakness, he received no education whatsoever and never gained mastery of the skills of reading and writing. That, however, did nothing to prevent him from becoming known in Methodist circles for his religious fervour, but finally the abject poverty of life as a landless labourer compelled him to abandon his native heath in search of a better life on the far side of the North Channel. Settling first at Maybole in Ayrshire, Bennison initially experienced some difficulty in adapting to his new home but when he moved some time later to Paisley things began to look up. On 5 December 1839 he married a local woman, Jean Hamilton - some six or seven years his senior - in the town's Wesleyan Methodist chapel and the newlyweds set up home together nearby. Some months later, he left his new wife behind while making a return trip to Ireland but when he reappeared in Paisley, dressed in mourning, he had an unhappy tale to tell. Accompanying him back from Ireland, Bennison's sister, Mary, had been travelling to the town of Airdrie where she had previously been employed. During the crossing she had suffered from what appeared to be acute seasickness but on reaching dry land her symptoms had failed to ease until, considerably weakened, she had finally passed away at her destination. Bennison brought back with him from Airdrie a bundle of his sister's clothing which he handed over for use by his wife. Among the various items was a blue mantle or shawl, the significance of which did not surface until some considerable time later.

Not long after his return from Ireland, a rather unsettling encounter took place one Sunday outside Paisley's Wesleyan chapel when Bennison was approached by a man unknown to him who indicated that he thought he recognised his face. The stranger went on to ask, 'Was it not you who buried your wife in Airdrie?' Visibly shaken, Bennison replied with an abrupt 'No' before quickly moving off in what looked like a determined effort to stall the conversation. As it happened, Jean was not present to overhear the exchange, but a visit that she made with her husband to Ireland soon after must undoubtedly have provided her with considerable food for thought. Her shock is easy to imagine when it came to her notice during the trip that William's sister, Mary - supposedly dead and buried in Airdrie - was, in fact, alive and well and living in her mother's home. When questioned, Bennison attempted to make light of the matter, suggesting that some kind of misunderstanding must have taken place, but, in spite of Jean's purported naivety, a seed of suspicion had taken root in her mind which refused to be dispelled. Sometime later, when her husband planned another visit to Ireland - this time by himself - she parcelled up his sister's clothes and insisted that he take them with him as she no longer felt entitled to wear them. Not long after this episode, Bennison moved from Paisley to Edinburgh and, despite Jean's misgivings about her husband's past, it appeared that they were insufficient to deter her from joining him in the capital a little later. As things turned out, her decision to do so was one that would cost her dearly.

But the skeletons inhabiting William Bennison's closet were not destined to emerge for some time yet and, as Jean and he settled down to new lives in the Edinburgh area, he appears to have been leading a curious double-life. Through his Methodist church connections, he was successful in obtaining employment in the town of Dalkeith but it is on record that he had to be reprimanded repeatedly for vices such as gambling, drunkenness and even stealing from his neighbours and, for all his professed Christian principles, his misconduct ultimately lost him his job. Obliged to decamp once again, this time to Leith where he found employment as a 'moulder' - making moulds for casting iron - in the Shotts Iron Foundry where, in spite of her tender years, his six-year-old daughter laboured alongside him and earned a small pittance. His wife's sister, Ellen Glass, was in service at Mound Place, Edinburgh, and when she paid the Bennisons a visit during the spring of 1850 she quickly became aware that all was not well. Jean, she discovered, had suffered through much of the preceding winter with a persistent cough and Ellen could not help noticing an 'apparent coolness' in her brother-in-law's attitude towards his ailing wife. Jean confided in her sister that William was in the habit of spending a good deal of his free time away from home but, when Ellen broached the subject with him, Bennison replied to the effect that he worked hard by day and felt that he was entitled to attend Methodist services during the evening. Ellen smelled a rat, however, when she spotted him several times in the company of a local girl, Margaret Robertson, whom he had met in a singing class they both attended and who, as it so happened, attended the same evening prayer meetings as he did where the two were known to be in the habit of sitting together. Ellen took the decision to say nothing to her sister at this point regarding her suspicions for fear of the possible effect upon spirits that were already subdued.

Despite Bennison's gloomy assessment of his wife's health, Ellen, by contrast, was heartened by certain positive signs which she interpreted as an indication that Jean had turned the corner at last and was finally on the mend. She was taken by surprise, therefore, when a few short days after returning to Mound Place she received a visit from her highly agitated brother-in-law who blurted out that the previous day - Saturday 13 April - his wife's health had taken a sudden dip and that he believed she 'could not last many hours.' When she arrived at Stead's Place, Ellen found a family friend, Agnes Turnbull, already in attendance and when she set eyes on her sister she was shocked by the deterioration in her condition. Jean, she was told, had been retching and vomiting for more than 24 hours until powders, obtained from a local dispensary - comprising ammonia, ginger and pepper - had provided a degree of relief. (It would later emerge that Bennison had taken it upon himself to disregard the chemist, William McDonald's, accompanying advice that he should also consult a doctor.) Unable to account for his wife's rapid downturn, Bennison told Ellen Glass that the last food that Jean had taken had been a small portion of porridge some two days earlier: harmless enough, you might think. Although her vomiting had now ceased, it was plain to Ellen, as she bathed her sister's hands and face, that her condition remained far from stable. Tormented by a raging thirst and suffering from severe internal pain, her tongue was badly swollen, her mouth parched and dry, yet she had the greatest difficulty when attempting to swallow. Acutely aware of the gravity of the situation, Ellen and Agnes Turnbull remained by Jean's bedside throughout the night as, shivering uncontrollably, she could not be made to feel comfortable. In spite of the pain and distress she was suffering, Jean was under no illusions regarding her situation and was at pains to request that her 'dead clothes' be got ready and letters written in preparation for her funeral. Throughout this whole time, Ellen could not help but notice that Bennison seldom approached his dying wife and that never on any occasion did he speak to her. When Agnes Turnbull offered to run for a doctor, he rejected the idea out of hand, saying - 'It's of no use. She is going home, she is going home to glory.'

It is a sad irony of the situation that by the time that Jean received professional medical attention her condition had deteriorated to the point where she was beyond saving. By Bennison's own account, he had gone out to find a doctor around midday on the previous day - Saturday - but his search, he later stated, proved fruitless. During the course of the afternoon he made a second attempt (against his wife's wishes, so he said) but the outcome on this occasion was no different. The following morning around eleven o'clock he met a Dr Gillespie in the street, apparently by chance, and brought him back to Stead's Place where the physician gave Jean an examination and suggested that she be given a little wine to drink - though, speaking privately with Bennison, he expressed little optimism regarding any prospect of recovery. When exactly Jean breathed her last that night is not entirely clear but it appears that Bennison was out of the room at the time and, when told of his wife's death, he reacted by uttering the words - 'Thank God, she's gone home.' Despite his sister-in-law's expressed wish that a post-mortem examination be conducted, his obvious reluctance and the haste with which he set about organising the burial (coupled, no doubt, with the unexplained death of Sandy Milne's dog) was sufficient to set tongues wagging.

Given its sudden and unexpected nature, it should have come as no surprise when the authorities took a keen interest in the circumstances relating to Jean's death. As the weight of suspicion mounted steadily against him, William Bennison found himself under arrest and charged with his wife's murder - with an additional charge relating to the crime of bigamy. Police investigations revealed that, a few days after his wife's death, Bennison had paid a return visit to the chemist, William McDonald, and the exchange that took place on this second occasion was a revealing one. Bennison started off by requesting confirmation in writing of the contents of the powders which the chemist had supplied him with but, wary of so doing, McDonald declined to put pen to paper. He did, however, go so far as to reassure his visitor that, if questioned, he would personally vouch for the powders' innocuous ingredients. All well and good, it might have seemed, but Bennison was not finished yet. Referring to moves currently afoot to exhume his late wife's body, he asked the chemist whether he would be likely to face arrest if traces of poison were detected during a post-mortem investigation. If it hadn't already done so, the penny must have well and truly dropped when Bennison reminded McDonald of a previous visit that he had made to his shop, some two months earlier, when he had been served by the chemist's wife. His purchase on that occasion had been a 'pennyworth' of white arsenic powder.

The reason Bennison gave at the time was not unusual. His wife, he explained, had grown nervous about fetching coal from the cellar of their home for fear of a large population of rats which had recently taken up residence there. Initially hesitant about handing over such a lethal substance, Jane McDonald had finally given in to persuasion and agreed to Bennison's request. When he returned to the chemist's shop following the death of his wife, Bennison made no bones about the main reason for his visit, namely his hope that William McDonald might be persuaded to remain silent about his earlier purchase, adding that 'As I got [the arsenic] from your wife, you could easily say I did not get it from *you*.' Overhearing the men's conversation, Jane interrupted to say that this would not be possible and her husband brought the conversation to a close by advising Bennison not to deny that he had acquired poison as 'it might otherwise go hard with him.' Visibly agitated, Bennison asked for, and was given, wine to drink and the meeting ended with his statement that 'God had carried him through many difficulties and would carry him through this too.' What passed between McDonald and his wife after Bennison's departure we can only conjecture. When a few days later Jean's body was exhumed - with a 'much agitated' William Bennison in attendance - the post-mortem examination subsequently carried out did indeed detect arsenic in her stomach and liver in quantities that the doctors involved deemed 'sufficient to account for her death.' The wooden tub which had been used to contain the dying woman's vomit likewise showed traces of the poison.

When Bennison's court case was heard two months later, in July 1850, it quickly became clear that he had an uphill struggle ahead of him. The representative of two insurance companies, Andrew Carr, confirmed that he was a fully paid-up member of both and stood to benefit to the tune of £5 in the event of the death of his wife. Eyebrows must surely have been raised when it emerged that he had joined the second scheme a mere fortnight before Jean's death and had, in fact, handed over no more than one shilling and fivepence in premiums. William Fairgrieve, a fellow-employee of the Shotts Iron Foundry, testified that Bennison had told him that he expected to take in some £11 in total from a variety of such policies that he held. His neighbours at Stead's Place did his cause no favours when, with one solitary exception, none would confess to having been troubled by rats for a considerable number of years and it emerged that a sheriff-officer, George Fergusson, had paid a visit to Stead's Place on Friday 19 April where he made a thorough inspection of the coal cellar but nowhere was he able to pinpoint a spot where rats might have effected entry. Perhaps the most dramatic revelation of the entire trial came about when Rev. John Meneely, Presbyterian minister at Ballymacarret, County Down, testified that Bennison had previously been married in Ireland and three Irish ladies confirmed that in 1838 he had taken as his wife a local girl by the name of Mary Mullen (or McMullen) whom he deserted soon after when he took himself off to Scotland. He had reappeared some eighteen months later, the ladies recalled, and when he departed once again for Scotland this time Mary had accompanied her husband - with some considerable reluctance, according to the witnesses, since it was known that he had been in the habit of beating her. As Mary Mullen took her final farewells, they recalled that she had been wearing a blue cape.

Bennison's own version of events was laid out in a series of three written declarations in the first of which, dated Friday 19 April, he admitted having acquired a quantity of arsenic for the purpose of eradicating rats from his home. He claimed that he had handed the poison over to his wife one evening shortly before leaving for a religious service and that he had specifically advised her to handle the poison with care and to ensure that it was placed beyond their daughter's reach. And that, he insisted, was the last he saw of it. Regarding the traces found in Jean's stomach after death, for that he could offer no explanation. His second statement, given some two months later, was categorical in its denial that he had ever previously been married, a claim that he chose to overturn within days in his third and final declaration. Now for the first time Bennison admitted his earlier marriage to Mary Mullen. Unemployed at home, he said that he had taken his new wife's advice to come to Scotland in search of work, leaving her behind in Ireland, but six months later news had reached him of her death - by what channel he omitted to say - and, having no reason to doubt that he was now a widower, he had gone on in 1839 to marry Jean Hamilton. By a very odd coincidence, Bennison continued, the very day after his marriage in Paisley he had received a letter from Ireland which indicated that his first wife was still living. By a strange irony, the letter had apparently been delayed in the post, having been delivered first to another Paisley family by the name of Bennison before subsequently being redirected. For entirely understandable reasons the news that the letter contained prompted a rift between Jean and himself and they had thereafter lived apart for a month. During that time, Bennison stated that he had arranged for one William Wilson to write a letter on his behalf to Ireland, seeking to place his marital status beyond doubt. When the reply arrived, its contents were sufficient to effect a reconciliation between Jean and himself but, some months later when he returned to Ireland to visit his parents, Bennison was shocked to find that his first wife, Mary, was still alive. Travelling via Belfast and Glasgow, she had returned with him to Scotland but, following a bout of seasickness during the crossing, she finally passed away at Airdrie. Penniless himself, Bennison declared that her coffin had to be provided by 'the people of the house' - presumably Mary's former employers - and he himself was the one and only mourner to attend her funeral service. Returning to Paisley, he made a clean breast of what had occurred to Jean who warned him never again to mention his earlier marriage - not even to her sister, she specifically added. When push came to shove, the final declaration sounded rather desperate and the chances of Bennison's garbled tale convincing anyone were probably highly unlikely. Despite various manoeuvres attempted by the defence, in the event it took the twelve-man jury a mere twenty minutes to return a unanimous verdict of guilty as charged both of bigamy and murder. Reports at the time suggested that the prisoner showed no emotion in response, his sole reaction being to murmur quietly to a court officer at his side - 'It is of both the charges.' It sounds very much as though the verdict hadn't yet quite sunk in.

It certainly appeared to do so a few minutes later, however, when Lord Moncrieff embarked on his summing up and Bennison bent forward as he listened while resting his forehead on the railing in front of him in what many construed as an attitude of despair. Making clear his belief that the jury had 'no alternative' but to find him guilty, His Lordship made little effort to mince his words: 'I must say,' he informed the court, 'that I have never seen any [trial] in which deeper criminality was involved.' When he ended his remarks, the Lord Justice-Clerk took over and continued in a similar vein, choosing to highlight Bennison's religious hypocrisy: 'You had the professions of sanctity upon your mouth', he stated, 'even at the time your unhappy wife was dying before your eyes from the effects of the poison you administered.' The culmination of the two-day trial then followed when, donning the black cap, the Lord Justice-Clerk proceeded to pass sentence on the convicted man, ordering that he be detained during the next month in prison where he would be fed on bread and water alone until the morning of Friday 16 August between eight and ten o'clock when he would be taken to Edinburgh's common place of execution and hanged upon a gibbet until dead. 'And,' said his Lordship in conclusion, 'may Almighty God have mercy upon your soul.' Matters, however, did not rest there when Bennison asked for, and was granted, leave to address the court. Speaking in a distinct Irish brogue, he said, 'I do not blame the Court or the Jury for their verdict; but I say that I can here solemnly declare before God, and before all present, that of the murder of my wife I am innocent.' He went on to suggest that certain of the witnesses had been guilty of perjury, concluding in the grand Biblical style for which he was known - 'I do solemnly forgive them this day, and they know themselves what they have done.' He was led immediately after from the court.

It was only a matter of days, however, before Bennison changed his tune yet again. He was regularly ministered to in Calton Jail by Rev. John Hay of Leith Methodist Church and it was to this dedicated gentleman that he finally chose to disburden himself. In conversation with the minister, Bennison confessed that on Friday 12 April he had laced a bowl of porridge with arsenic which he had subsequently served to his wife. Careful to wait until his young daughter was in bed and out of harm's way, he himself had feigned illness in order to explain his own failure to eat. Of his motives he appears to have said nothing: to do so might simply have duplicated those revelations that had already been made during the course of his trial. Beyond this confession, he would go no farther and he persisted with his story that he had had no hand in his first wife, Mary's, demise. Such was his apparent sincerity, it seems, that the Rev. Hay resolved to press him no further on this matter - though perhaps the kindly clergyman left himself open to a charge of naivety in this connection, having apparently wiped from his memory Bennison's 'heartfelt' proclamation at the close of his trial which subsequently proved to be entirely untrue. Around this same time a letter was received in Edinburgh from a resident of Airdrie who recollected an individual by the name of Bennison who had lived in that town for a short time in 1842. During the time of his residence the man's wife was taken suddenly ill and died under what were viewed as highly suspicious circumstances. Strangely, no further investigation of this matter appears to have taken place, perhaps because it had been ascertained during Bennison's trial that Mary Mullen died two years earlier in 1840. The possibility of the Airdrieonian gentleman's memory being rather less than perfect seems not to have been considered. When Ellen Glass saw Bennison in prison their meeting was described at the time as being 'as satisfactory as could be expected' and he was said to have begged his sister-in-law for forgiveness. Also permitted to visit him in jail was his young daughter who had reportedly been kept in ignorance of his forthcoming ordeal. In what must surely have been a highly affecting scene, the little girl sang a hymn at her father's request and, understandably, Bennison showed great difficulty in controlling his emotions when her visit drew to an end. A letter received soon after from the Home Secretary, Sir George Grey, extinguished what little hope there might have been of a reprieve and confirmed Bennison's fate beyond doubt.

The day prior to his execution he was transferred from Calton Jail to one of the cells located within the High Court, a short distance from where the scaffold would soon be erected. Onlookers gathered to watch him pass and the consensus was that he came across as troubled and anxious - keen, it was thought, to avoid the public eye. Around midnight bands of revellers, both men and women, began to occupy the surrounding streets and 'laughter, shouts, yells and ribald jests' filled the air as something of a party atmosphere developed during the early hours of the morning. The scaffold was constructed behind a substantial wooden stockade with a strong body of policemen, commanded by Chief Superintendent Richard Moxey, in attendance to maintain order. Meanwhile, as the crowd reached an estimated 20,000, some spectators were obliged to take up positions on surrounding rooftops in order to be assured of a clear and uninterrupted view. A few short paces from the fun and merrymaking, the mood in the condemned cell was rather more sombre as Bennison spent much of his final night engaged in prayer. Somewhere between five and six o'clock Rev. Hay and a second clergyman, Rev. Hislop, arrived on the scene, followed sometime later by two magistrates, Bailies Fyfe and Law, who were charged with responsibility for overseeing proceedings on behalf of the Edinburgh authorities. Shortly after their arrival, Rev. Hay announced the singing of a hymn - chosen from John Wesley's collection, popular with Methodist congregations - and it was noted by those present that Bennison participated fully in the singing. He kneeled during the prayer that followed and only once did his emotions appear briefly to get the better of him.

Shortly after eight o'clock a small procession emerged from the court building led by Town Officers bearing halberds who were followed in turn by the two magistrates, Fyfe and Law; then the condemned man himself, supported on either side by the accompanying clergymen. At the tail end came the octogenarian hangman, John Murdoch of Glasgow, and the executioner's assistant. Despite having his wrists bound, Bennison made his way toward the gallows steadily and without any sign of faltering, though it was noted that he appeared pale and to have lost weight in the months since his court appearance. An audible gasp arose from the crowd when he reached the top of the scaffold where, dressed in a frock coat, coloured vest and white neckcloth, he removed his hat and stood for some considerable time gazing out at the sea of faces before him. After Rev. Hislop had offered up a final prayer, all that was left was for the executioner to place a hood over the prisoner's head and face and the rope around his neck - a task that Murdoch undertook with such unfeeling roughness as to prompt the intervention of Bailie Law. The signal - a white handkerchief - was then placed in Bennison's hand which he thrust away from him as though with distaste while uttering the words - 'Lord Jesus, have mercy on my soul.' The bolt was immediately withdrawn, the prisoner plunged from the scaffold and, following a violent struggle that lasted some two minutes - due, it was reckoned, to the rope's being improperly adjusted - life finally departed and all sign of movement ceased.

So - as William Bennison paid the ultimate price for his crimes, his story drew to a close. Well, not quite yet. Such was the level of public interest that his case had aroused that various ballads were composed in connection with his crimes which did the rounds for some time afterwards within the local area. Some made a fairly obvious effort to depict the murderer's character:

Farewell this vain world and all its delusions,
In which I have acted a hypocrite's part;
Under guise of religion I have join'd in devotion,
While the devil triumphant did reign in my heart.

Others, however, took a rather blunter approach:

Great was the throng to see him hung
For crimes that were so vile.
To Edinburgh upon that day
They tramped for many a mile.
They led him out all clad in black -
Black coat and vest so white -
A mocking smile was on his lips,
He wore a nosegay bright.

Probably the latter verse's gleeful tone shouldn't come as too much of a surprise. For all his church connections and for fairly obvious reasons, Bennison's case had never been one to generate much by way of sympathy and during his final days behind bars it could hardly have escaped him that friends and allies were thin on the ground. When a petition was circulated in support of him among the 160 employees of the Shotts Iron Foundry, no more than 23 of his co-workers could be prevailed upon to sign. That must surely have spoken for itself.

Helen Blackwood & Hans MacFarlane : August 1853

It all began on the morning of Saturday 11 June 1853 when two ship's carpenters, Alexander Boyd, and his friend, James Law, embarked on a day-long drinking session in Glasgow. Though Scottish by birth, Boyd was a long-time resident of Valparaiso, Chile, from where he had recently returned to wind up his late mother's estate. With around £2 in silver in his pocket he proved an open-handed companion, treating his friend in style to the extent that Law would later remember nothing after the early afternoon when the men were comfortably settled in their third establishment of the day - John Gray's public house in Broomielaw Street. Later that evening they were still on the spree when they teamed up in Exchange Square with two ladies of the night, Mary Hamilton and Ann Marshall, and all four retired to a hostelry in Ingram Street where the drinking continued. Shortly before midnight they left to walk a short distance to the New Vennel where they climbed the stairs to the tiny top-floor flat where Mary Hamilton lodged with a couple, Hans Smith Macfarlane and Helen Blackwood. After a full day's drinking the two carpenters were very drunk indeed - Law incapably so, and as soon as they entered the tiny apartment he lay down on the floor and promptly fell asleep. In the light of what lay ahead, he turned out to be the lucky one.

Sometime later two local policemen, Robert Campbell and David Henderson, were patrolling their beat in the New Vennel when they heard a strange, muffled thud at the back of a tall building known as Croiley's Land. Hurrying to investigate, they found the near-naked body of a man lying spread-eagled on the ground and bleeding profusely from a gash on the back of his head. Neighbours and passers-by gathered to watch as the two officers carried out a quick examination but there were no signs of life to be seen. Throughout this whole time, raised voices could be heard coming through the open window of a flat directly overhead, and seconds later fragments of pottery crashed to the ground close to where the onlookers were standing. Constable Henderson left to investigate but it was not long before he was back. After quickly talking things over, the two officers decided that Campbell would return to the police station for assistance while Henderson waited alongside the dead man who, it later emerged, was Alexander Boyd. The police had a fair idea of who they were looking for. Constable Duncan McInnes was the man given the job of finding and arresting the tenants of the third-floor flat, Macfarlane and Blackwood, whose descriptions he studied closely. After leaving the police office, within a remarkably short time he located the two suspects whom he found walking a short distance apart in Reid Street, a mile or so from the New Vennel.

When questioned, Macfarlane offered the explanation that he was simply 'going for a walk' - an early morning stroll for sure - and he gave the impression that he was puzzled at being stopped, while, for her part, Helen Blackwood claimed that Macfarlane was a total stranger whom she had never met before. Constable McInnes, however, was not to be taken in quite so easily and, in line with his instructions, he brought the two in for questioning. During his interview Macfarlane began by stating that he was a miner to trade and that his current lodgings were in New Dalmarnock Road, Bridgeton. Some months earlier, he explained, he had rented a one-room flat on the third floor of Croiley's Land for his lover, Helen Blackwood, where occasionally he would spend the night. At around six o'clock the previous evening he had called at Blackwood's flat and spent an hour or so there before moving on to Glasgow Green for a performance at the Queen's Theatre which had lasted until 11 p.m. Afterwards, in the company of two fellow-colliers whom he had met in the theatre, John Nixon and John Clifford, he had gone on to visit a number of public houses in the Gallowgate area - he could not remember which ones - until around one o'clock in the morning. At that point he had accompanied his friends as far as Barrowfield Toll before turning around and making his way back to the New Vennel, 'to see how [Helen Blackwood] and her friends were getting on.' Arriving at Croiley's Land, however, he had heard about Boyd's accident and, wary of becoming implicated, he had remade his plans accordingly. After paying a brief visit to one of the neighbours, he had left to return to Bridgeton and, at an area known as 'the Butts', he had fallen in with Helen Blackwood. It was as the two were making for Bridgeton that they were intercepted by PC McInnes close to the Rutherglen Bridge. Questioned separately, Helen Blackwood was able to fill in a few of the gaps, explaining how a disagreement had flared in her flat between Ann Marshall and Mary Hamilton over the question of money. James Law - currently comatose - had planned to borrow cash from his friend in order to pay for Hamilton's professional services, and now that her client was out of commission she felt entitled to a share of Marshall's earnings. Roused by the women's 'loud words', Boyd had got up from where he had been dozing in bed, stepped across to the window 'to make water', somehow had lost his balance and took a fatal tumble. It was as simple as that, or so Helen Blackwood said. By this time Mary Hamilton and Ann Marshall had also both been arrested.

It turned out, however, that Blackwood's account was not one that was borne out by the evidence. A post-mortem examination of Alexander Boyd's body was carried out by Dr Robert McGregor, lately physician to Glasgow Royal Infirmary, and Dr J. A. Easton of Anderson's Institution - the forerunner of Strathclyde University. Their report began by stating categorically that Boyd had been 'a strong muscular man' who had died as a result of violence, not natural causes. The temporal and parietal bones of his skull had been fractured, thus allowing blood to escape and apply pressure to the brain, interrupting its normal functions. In the belly they found a large quantity of blood whose source was a wound in the liver, more than one inch long and half an inch in depth. All of these injuries, the doctors believed, were consistent with a fall from a considerable height, and death could have resulted from either the brain injury or the laceration of the liver, or indeed a combination of the two. But there was more. On each of Boyd's testicles the doctors found 'a deeply livid mark of a recently inflicted bruise, an inch in length, perpendicular in direction, and oblong in form.' From their situation and appearance, the doctors were in no doubt that these were recent bruises which 'had not been occasioned by a fall, or even by a kick', and could not have been 'the result of friction or chafing.' This led them to conclude that Boyd's testicular bruising 'had been caused by the parts having been rudely grasped by an adult hand', most likely during an attempt to overpower him.

There was more bad news for the four individuals involved. What none of them had reckoned on was the fact that two of their neighbours, Jane Leitch and Mary Kelland, had been spying on their activities that night through a crack in the door and had witnessed Boyd's final moments. Earlier in the evening, it transpired, the two girls had seen him in the company of Blackwood and Hamilton who appeared to be acting in the role of the decoys in a honeytrap, the latter taking him by the arm. Macfarlane, they noted, was keeping an eye on things from a short distance behind. There was no doubt at this stage that Boyd was already a good deal inebriated and, as they entered Croiley's Land and climbed the staircase, Jane Leitch overheard Blackwood say, 'It's a good chance', and Hamilton agreeing in response. Sensing that something was afoot, Mary whispered to Jane a suggestion that they follow them, and, on reaching the top floor, the two girls knelt and peered through a crack in Helen Blackwood's door. Strange though it may seem, Jane and Mary were not the only witnesses to what took place in the candlelit flat. Astonishingly, in addition to the six adults in that cramped and crowded room - little more than eight feet by six - there were also two small boys whose father was dead and their mother absent. Pupils at the 'Ragged School' - a charitable institution whose object was to provide destitute street children with a basic education - William and James Shillinglaw were in the habit of sleeping on the floor beneath Macfarlane and Blackwood's bed-frame.

Once all six adults were comfortably settled, Alexander Boyd gave Helen Blackwood a half-crown and sent her out for a jug of whisky, saying 'he would make them happy for the night.' On her return, she handed him a shilling in change and filled up a dram glass - the only one in the house - which was then passed around from person to person. Everyone took their turn to drink, with the single exception of James Law who was lying insensible on the floor. It was not long before Boyd was leaning forward, his head slumped blearily over his chest, too drunk to be aware of what was going on around him. As Jane and Mary watched agog, Blackwood furtively slipped her hand into her pocket, withdrew a small paper packet and quickly upended its contents into the whisky glass which she then passed on to Boyd. As soon as he had drained the cup of its contents - whisky, contaminated with snuff - he immediately started gasping, and became 'stupid-like', as if he were choking. With great effort he managed to struggle to his feet, fearful probably of being robbed, and lashed out at Blackwood who was standing at the end of the bed. She in response lifted up a chamber pot and, standing directly in front of him, struck him a fearful blow to the side of his head which shattered the earthenware pot while at the same time knocking him backwards full length to the floor where his head made contact with a large block of stone that served as a footstool. Groggy and disorientated, Boyd was easily overpowered and as he lay groaning in agony, William Shillinglaw heard one of the women say, 'Oh! What'll we dae wi' him?' followed by Macfarlane's grim reply - 'It's dark, naebody will see, heave him owre the windae.' Before doing so, however, they stripped him down to his underwear and socks at Blackwood's suggestion. 'We'll get a shilling [from the pawnbroker] on the man's umbrella on Monday morning,' Jane Leitch heard her saying, 'beside what we'll get on the clothes.' Visibly shaking as she went through Boyd's pockets, Blackwood drew out a handful of coins, bending to retrieve a stray 'copper' which fell to the floor and secreting it within her clothing. Then, as Mary Hamilton looked on, Macfarlane and she took an arm each while Marshall grabbed hold of his feet and, lifting Boyd from the floor, they 'hove' him head first out of the window. As his body hit the ground a second or two later, William Shillinglaw distinctly heard the sound of a sickening thump.

Then the pantomime began. Ann Marshall started wringing her hands, crying, 'Oh! my man's deid! My man's deid! He went to the windae to make his watter, and fell owre.' In an effort to lend a degree of plausibility to her charade, one of the other women gathered up the fragments of pottery that lay scattered about the floor and tossed them out of the window after him. Then, before the authorities could be summoned, all four miscreants slipped away from the crime scene, Blackwood blowing out the 'ha'penny candle' and locking the door behind her, apparently having forgotten the two small boys inside. James Law, still lying across the fireplace, remained totally oblivious. After leaving the top floor, Macfarlane went straight to the door of a downstairs neighbour, a bone gatherer named Charles Scott, rapping loudly and crying, 'Open, Charles!' Entering in a state of tremendous agitation, he blurted out his version of events, presenting Boyd's death as purely accidental. 'What am I to do?' he asked in obvious despair. 'What are Helen and I to do?' When police arrived at the door a few minutes later he remained out of sight, listening quietly by the fireside as Scott told the officers that he had not been involved in what had taken place. When the policemen left to climb to the top floor, Macfarlane seized the opportunity to slip out of the building and flee into the night. Upstairs, the two small boys heard cries of 'Police!' and a few seconds later officers broke down the door and entered the flat. Along with James Law, they were conveyed to the police station at around three o'clock in the morning where Boyd's battered corpse had preceded them.

Six weeks later on Thursday 21 July 1853 Blackwood, Hamilton, Marshall and Macfarlane appeared at the High Court in Edinburgh, charged with having 'wickedly and feloniously administer[ed] to Alexander Boyd a quantity of whisky, mixed with snuff', following which 'with a chamber pot [they] did strike him one or more severe blows about the head, did grasp or violently compress his testicles and did throw him out of a window, whereby he fell from a height of 23 feet [and] soon thereafter died.' When his turn came to take the stand, eleven-year-old William Shillinglaw recounted how on the evening of Saturday 11 June he and his brother, James, age nine, had bedded down for the night at around nine o'clock. At that time the only other person at home was Helen Blackwood. When he awakened sometime later Mary Hamilton had appeared on the scene in the company of a drunk man, James Law. Five minutes later Blackwood, Marshall and Macfarlane had arrived with a second drunk man, Alexander Boyd, in tow. Complimented at the time of the trial as 'an intelligent little boy', William gave a lucid account of what he and his brother had seen. After the arrests, the boys had spent the following six weeks in prison but, under cross-examination by Hamilton's lawyer, William stated with simple dignity, 'I was not in jail for any offence. I was put there because I had no home. I have never been charged with any offence.' A number of other witnesses were called to the stand: Jane Leitch, Mary Kelland and other neighbours for the most part, as well as police officers including Assistant-Superintendent George Mackay who reported on exhaustive inquiries he had carried out into Macfarlane's alleged companions on the evening of 11 June, John Nixon and John Clifford, colliers at Baillieston. Of the two men in question he had found nary a trace.

During the course of the trial Hans Macfarlane alone betrayed any emotion, leaning his head on his hands from time to time and showing clear signs of distress. The women, by contrast, remained stony-faced, stoical and silent. In summing up for the prosecution, the Solicitor-General, Robert Handyside, suggested that, as the only man on trial, Hans Macfarlane's guilt was impossible to ignore. Of the three women, he continued, one had drugged Alexander Boyd's drink, another had helped strip his body, while the third had assisted in ejecting him through the window. But, the Solicitor-General suggested, in the case of the female prisoners extenuating circumstances might be found 'if [members of the jury] thought that without the aid and concurrence of Macfarlane this diabolical occurrence would not have taken place.' In conclusion, he called for a guilty verdict against all of those accused, but pointed out to the jury the possibility of appending a recommendation to mercy on behalf of the women. The strongest argument that the defence could muster was to suggest that, when they threw Boyd's body from the window, the four accused had been unaware that he was still alive at the time, and that their sole motive in so doing had been to rid themselves of incriminating evidence. When arguments for both prosecution and defence had all been heard, the members of the jury withdrew to consider their verdict. It did not take them long. Returning within the space of twenty minutes, they announced that they found Macfarlane and Blackwood guilty of murder as charged. Marshall likewise they found guilty but added in her case a recommendation to mercy: inexplicable, since to all intents and purposes her involvement had been identical to that of the others. Finally, the case against Mary Hamilton they found not proven, and she was thus dismissed from the court. In his address to the three convicted prisoners, the Solicitor-General advised them that 'the verdict which has been returned in your case ... admits of but one sentence.' Turning specifically to Ann Marshall, he urged her 'not to indulge hopes which may be disappointed' in relation to the jury's recommendation to mercy. Then, assuming the black cap, he advised all three that they would be executed at Glasgow three weeks hence, on Thursday 11 August. As he was led from the dock, Hans Macfarlane made an attempt to address the court, but he was overcome by nerves and the words became stifled in his throat. No such difficulty was faced by Helen Blackwood, however, who maintained her composure throughout. 'We have not got justice!' she exclaimed. 'There is a higher judge for us! We are innocent!'

In spite of her deep involvement in Boyd's death and Lord Handyside's words of warning - as well as the absence of any popular petition in her favour - a royal reprieve for Ann Marshall, signed by Home Secretary, Lord Palmerston, was received in Glasgow on Sunday 7 August, less than a week before the proposed date of her execution. Her gender, some believed, had been Marshall's salvation and, rather than face the death penalty, she would instead be transported overseas for life. No such relief was available to the other condemned prisoners, Macfarlane and Blackwood. Following conviction, they were housed separately in the North Prison where they were sustained on bread and water alone, though out of common humanity the water was sweetened at times with treacle and the bread moistened in weak tea. In contrast to this meagre diet, the hangman, William Calcraft, recently arrived once again from London, was said to have routinely feasted on roast beef and port wine. The two prisoners, it was said, responded well to the ministrations of the prison chaplain, Rev. Reid, but, despite irrefutable evidence against them, they remained resolute in protesting their innocence. Despite this, Macfarlane admitted to having lived a low existence and revealed an unexpectedly poetical turn of phrase when he was quoted as saying, 'I have often wondered that the earth did not open up and swallow up myself and the other inhabitants of Croiley's Land.' He was candid in acknowledging that 'his sins had found him out.' With what was believed to be Helen Blackwood's consent, the day after the couple's return to Glasgow following their conviction at Edinburgh he made a request to the Governor of the North Prison for permission to allow them to be married, but for such a ceremony to take place in the condemned cell was viewed as inconceivable and his application was flatly refused.

A number of details emerged concerning Macfarlane and Blackwood's respective lives and backgrounds. Now aged 25, Macfarlane had been born of Irish parents in Partick - still described as a village then. At the time of his conviction his mother alone was still alive. Of a similar age, Blackwood had been born of Scottish parents in the Gorbals district of the city. Largely neglected by her father, her mother was said to have been a chronic alcoholic. Neither one of the two had ever learned to read or write and Macfarlane, 'could not go beyond words of a single syllable.' Viewed as shocking in mid-Victorian Britain, it was suggested that Helen Blackwood had never during the course of her existence passed through the door of a church. When her lineage is considered, it surely should have come as no surprise to anyone that she went badly off the rails. In a case of history repeating itself, the greater part of the money that she and Macfarlane acquired, whether by honest or other means, was spent on the purchase of alcohol. For all the difficulty and debauchery of their lives, the genuine fondness that existed between the two was obvious to all.

In the early hours of Wednesday 11 August - while the city streets were still quiet - Blackwood and Macfarlane were removed from the North to the South Prison. Attended by two female warders, Blackwood's final night was said to have been virtually sleepless. Slightly more fortunate, Macfarlane snatched a few hours' sleep before spending what was left of the night listening to readings from the scriptures and making what were said to be faltering attempts to read the Bible for himself. At around six o'clock each of the prisoners was given tea and a glass of wine and, following the arrival of Rev. Reid, Macfarlane was conducted to Blackwood's cell where the two met for the first time since their trial and were joined together in prayer. Shortly before 8 a.m. the hangman, Calcraft, entered and pinioned the prisoners' arms, following which the couple exchanged their final affectionate farewells. Meanwhile outside the prison, even before day had dawned, large numbers of onlookers had started to gather with a view to reserving for themselves places that offered an unobstructed view, while workmen set about erecting the scaffold. By around seven o'clock something approaching 600 policemen were on duty, and what was said to be the largest crowd for any similar event in living memory - an estimated 40,000 - stretched in a sea of faces as far as the eye could see. Those assembled, it was noted, were drawn not only from the lower rungs of society, but there were also many in attendance who were of a more prosperous appearance.

Working the crowds were hawkers of 'broadside ballads' - doggerel poems, printed on a single sheet and sold at a modest cost. Like the ghost of Hamlet's father, or the figure of Banquo in Macbeth, in one such ballad Alexander Boyd returns from beyond the grave to point an accusatory finger:

> In our gloomy cells, when 'tis midnight,
> His dying groans we hear,
> And no rest here can we find,
> For his murdered form appears,
> Pointing unto us with scorn,
> Which makes us quake and pale,
> As he with solemn words does cry
> For vengeance on us all.

Not lines, we may be sure, that Shakespeare would have been terribly proud of. In the light of Helen Blackwood's dysfunctional family background, the irony of the second ballad is rich:

> If by our parents we'd been ruled,
> We now might happy be.

And anyone living in the cramped squalor of Croiley's Land would scarcely have recognised the idealised world depicted in the poem:

> Had we but remained in the bright paths of virtue,
> Our lives might have ended in comfort and joy.

Alongside the balladeers, of course, there were others among the crowd who took advantage of the opportunity to relieve gentlemen of such items as their wallets and pocket watches.

At eight o'clock the prisoners were led from the South Prison along an underground passage which linked with the courthouse where they were permitted to sit for a few moments and fortified by a glass of wine. In accordance with city tradition the Lord Provost remained absent.

When asked by the prison governor, Captain Mullen, whether he had any final statement to address to those magistrates in attendance, Macfarlane replied, 'None, but what I have already made' - a reference, quite clearly, to his consistent claim of innocence. Blackwood offered a similar response. Both prisoners were then escorted to the scaffold and, though he was noticeably pale and weary, Macfarlane appeared composed as he climbed to the platform and took up his position. Blackwood by contrast required support. As the ropes were given a final adjustment, a white handkerchief was handed to Macfarlane for use as a signal, and with a hand that was visibly trembling he waited for perhaps a minute before allowing it to be released, prompting the hangman to draw back the bolt immediately and launch the two prisoners into the air. Macfarlane died almost instantly and suffered very little, but Blackwood, a good deal lighter in weight, was much less fortunate and was forced to endure severe, protracted struggles that lasted some two to three minutes before all traces of life finally departed. In line with custom, the prisoners' bodies were left to hang for 45 minutes or so before being cut down and placed in coffins for burial later that day within the precincts of the prison. The scaffold was dismantled immediately and, the morbid spectacle now at an end, the vast crowd melted away quickly and without fuss.

The question that many must surely have been asking at the time was how did two small boys - William and James Shillinglaw - end up sleeping on the floor of a den of vice in one of Glasgow's poorest districts? Sadly, a catalogue of family disasters had brought them to this point. A Shetlander by birth, the boys' father, Joseph, had worked as an engraver in Edinburgh before moving west to Glasgow, and when he died in 1844 he left behind a widow and three sons, the eldest of an age to enlist in the army and be self-supporting. A native of Haddington, East Lothian, and a former lady's maid, the boys' mother did her best to raise her two younger sons in decent circumstances, and in 1851 she married a Glasgow pastry baker, George Blackwood - father of the murderess - but, following his death a year or so later, she was left in a worse position than ever with a tiny infant to support in addition to William and James. For three weeks she was granted Parish Relief payments of one shilling and sixpence, but the allowance dried up when she declined a place in the city Poor's House, aiming instead to find lodgings and employment which would allow her to be independent. Despite her skills as a needle-woman and willingness to work, however, she fell behind with the rent and was evicted in late May 1853 - a fortnight before the death of Alexander Boyd - and the only accommodation she could subsequently find was in the house of a friend in College Street where she and her tiny infant slept on bare boards. Instructed by their mother to seek refuge at the Night Asylum for the Houseless, William and James went instead to the home of their step-sister, Helen Blackwood, who showed a charitable streak when she provided the boys with accommodation, however primitive. The family tragedy was complete when William and James's baby step-brother died at ten months old in early July.

The boys' appearance at such a high-profile trial alerted the public to their plight and, following a successful appeal, they were provided with more appropriate accommodation as well as clothing and bedding. Notably intelligent and comparatively well-educated, they were set to work at learning a respectable trade. By early September the appeal for their betterment had attracted donations amounting to nearly £20 which was viewed at the time as a singular success. At the end of the day, it was probably the only glimmer of a silver lining to emerge from what had undoubtedly been a very dark cloud indeed.

A strange little story has been told and retold over the years concerning a brief exchange between Macfarlane and Blackwood as the lovers stood on the brink of eternity. 'Helen Blackwood,' Macfarlane is supposed to have said, 'before God and in the presence of these witnesses, I take you to be my wife. Do you consent?' 'I do,' came Helen's reply. 'Then,' Macfarlane eloquently continued, 'before these witnesses I declare you to be what you have always been to me, a true and faithful wife, and you die an honest woman.' The chaplain, Rev. Reid, had barely time to utter the word 'Amen', so we are told, before the drop fell and the newly-wed couple plunged to their deaths. It is a poignant tale, to be sure, but also a doubtful one. The marriage was apparently never formally recorded, and otherwise detailed press reports at the time failed even to mention it.

Mary Timney : April 1862

At first glance the single-storey house at Carsfad, with its small adjoining byre and stable, might have seemed much like any other modest Galloway farmstead but, on closer scrutiny, its neatly-whitewashed walls and securely-slated roof were inclined to set it apart and hinted perhaps at a higher than usual degree of prosperity. In the new year of 1862 its hardworking tenant, William Hannah, had recently expanded operations when he took on the lease of a second local farm, a clear marker of his industry and ambition. Living with William were his brother, Lockhart, and forty-year-old sister, Ann, and the family's only immediate neighbour was an Irish roadman by the name of Francis Timney who occupied a nearby cottage with his 27-year-old wife, Mary, and the couple's four young children. Relations between the two households were, it must be said, not consistently cordial.

What lay at the root of the problem was money. For some considerable time, Mary Timney (née Reid) had been in the habit of 'borrowing' from various local people, including the Hannahs' elderly mother at Carsfad. After the old lady's death, she continued the practice, calling regularly at the farmhouse and appealing for items such as tea, perhaps, or a little sugar until finally Ann Hannah's patience ran out and she started to refuse. That Mary took offence was entirely predictable and the resentment she felt was compounded in December 1861 when she was reprimanded by Ann who had found her collecting firewood on her brothers' land and accused her, by Mary's account, of stealing turnips. When approached by Mary, William had no hesitation in backing his sister up and he in turn refused her permission to gather sticks. Tensions escalated as a result to the extent that on one occasion Mary was said to have arrived at Carsfad in high dudgeon and gone so far as to threaten Ann with violence. In the sparsely-populated Glenkens valley, the Timneys' money problems could hardly be hidden away but, despite the thorny nature of relations with his neighbours, William Hannah was not completely stony-hearted. When informed by Francis Timney on the morning of Monday 13 January 1862 that he was due to depart for a week's work at Corsock and had no money to leave behind for the upkeep of his family at home, William duly obliged and handed over two shillings and sixpence by way of a loan. An hour or so later, as William and his brother set out for their newly-acquired farm of Greenloop where they had chores awaiting, the two men could have had no inkling about what the day would bring. A group of children saw nothing out of the ordinary when they passed Carsfad around half past nine, greeting Ann on their way to school and inquiring of her the time. A few short hours later, however, by the time that Agnes McLellan called at the Hannahs' farmhouse during the early afternoon, disaster had already forestalled her.

The daughter of a neighbouring farmer, Agnes was known to both households at Carsfad. That Monday she had been at her father's house at Hannayston, about to sit down to her midday meal, when she was interrupted by Mary Timney's nine-year-old daughter, Susan, bearing a message to the effect that the child's mother was unwell and hoped that Agnes might be willing to come and bake bread for her family. It was nearly one o'clock, Agnes later recalled, before she tidied up after dinner and set out on her walk of a mile to Carsfad, her direct route passing within a few paces of the Hannahs' front door. Having known the family throughout most of her life and conscious of Ann's recent bereavement, it was only natural that Agnes should have called in on her in passing. The shocking scene that confronted her was one never likely to be forgotten.

Agnes found the door of the farmhouse partly open, but if she called out before entering she certainly received no reply. The reason became clear when, stepping inside the kitchen, she found Ann Hannah, lying face down and apparently unconscious with her head resting on her hands. Her hair was dishevelled and matted with blood which, welling from various head-wounds, had gathered in pools on the uneven flagstone floor. Not far away, her cap lay beside her, as well as a large, bloodstained knife and an iron rod with blood and hair adhering to it which Agnes recognised as the Hannahs' poker. From the washing tub beside the window, it looked as though Ann had been in the act of attending to her laundry when catastrophe struck, and there were various articles of wet clothing strewn across the floor. 'Oh dear, what's ado?' gasped Agnes, unsure at this stage whether her friend was dead or alive. What she did next might seem a little odd when, instead of raising the alarm with Ann's nearest neighbour Mary Timney, little more than fifty yards away, Agnes chose instead to retrace her steps the best part of a quarter of a mile to the lodge-house at Knocknalling where she blurted out news of her horrific discovery to Elizabeth Coats. Accompanied by John McAdam, a Knocknalling estate employee, the two women returned to Carsfad, running as fast as their legs would carry them, followed soon after by Elizabeth's husband, Robert Coats, who, when he arrived, turned Ann over in an effort to see whether her throat might have been cut. Once this was ruled out, an effort was made to make her more comfortable by lifting her on to her bed and, while the operation was taking place, she was heard twice to mutter the words 'Oh dear' - words, as it turned out, that were to be her last. From that point on Ann Hannah said nothing and failed to respond when spoken to.

Under no illusions concerning the gravity of Ann's situation, Elizabeth Coats dispatched her son to Dalry to summon a doctor. In the meantime, presumably alerted by the ongoing commotion, Mary Timney had appeared at her neighbour's house with an infant in her arms and, on being informed of recent events, was heard to comment - 'O this is an unco job!' and, addressing Agnes - 'Dear me, Nanny, I think the like of this was never here before.' Finding it curious that neither Mary nor any of her children had heard anything out of the ordinary, Elizabeth Coats questioned her, asking whether she hadn't noticed any strangers in the vicinity. Mary replied that, owing to illness, she had not stepped outside her house at any time since seeing her husband off to work that morning. In the meantime, William Hannah had got wind of the tragedy and hurried back from Greenloop, reaching Carsfad sometime after one o'clock with his brother, Lockhart, left in charge of the horse and cart, following on a little later. Suspecting a motive of theft, William searched the house and discovered that his sister's purse and its contents were missing. The sugar-bowl appeared to have been stolen and there was no tea to be seen. It looked very much as though he had already formed his suspicions when he ejected Mary Timney and her fretful child from the house. When the doctor, Andrew Jackson, arrived from Dalry around half past two he found Ann Hannah unconscious but still breathing. So heavily 'clotted with blood' was her head that he took steps to remove her hair before embarking on dressing her wounds - as many as seven on her head, he noted, as well as a further three on her face. Concerned about the possibility of bodily injury, he proceeded to remove part of her clothing but, as it turned out, no significant further damage was evident. Jackson remained at Carsfad and attended to Ann for some seven hours, during which time he attempted - without success - to induce her to swallow a little wine and to restore heat to her body by applying hot water bottles. But all to no effect. His patient remained in a coma-like state, until finally, around half past nine, all signs of breathing finally ceased and her life slipped away.

A post-mortem examination, carried out by Jackson and two fellow-physicians in the days that followed, confirmed what had seemed fairly obvious from the outset - namely, that Ann Hannah had unquestionably died as a result of her injuries. The doctors' joint-report makes for grim reading. Ann's death, they declared, had been 'caused by the effects of extensive wounds of the head and face and compound comminuted fractures of the skull.' Confirming Andrew Jackson's initial reckoning, they identified a total of ten wounds, varying between one and seven inches in length. 'On removing the scalp,' their report continued, 'a line of fracture was found to have conjoined all of the individual fractures.' Interestingly, the medical men were careful to rule out any possibility that the fatal injuries might have been self-inflicted or sustained as the result of a fall, even if accompanied by a violent push. The smaller wounds were thought to have been caused by the iron poker found alongside the body, and the knife, also recovered from the kitchen floor, was judged likely to have been responsible for the wounds on the face. Chillingly, Andrew Jackson would later suggest that these facial injuries were possibly inflicted, not during the initial onslaught, but rather sometime later, after Ann had lapsed into unconsciousness. The most severe of her wounds, the doctors believed, had been inflicted by 'a blunt weapon.'

But even as the ink on the post-mortem report was still drying, police investigations were proceeding apace and just such a blunt instrument as the doctors' report described had already been identified. Alerted by Lockhart Hannah, Constable John Robson of New Galloway arrived at Carsfad around six o'clock on the evening of the murder and within a very few minutes he turned his attention to those living closest to the scene of the crime. Visiting Mary Timney's cottage, he found her resting in bed, still fully dressed, with her four children around her. Noticing spots of blood on her clothing, Robson conducted a search of the house - no hard task, you might imagine, when the family's accommodation comprised one single room - where he quickly located various items of interest. Secreted inside a glove he found a sum of money amounting to seven shillings and seven pence in change and, recalling what he had been told by the Hannah brothers, his attention was drawn to a quantity of tea and sugar, mixed together and wrapped in a cloth. Behind a meal barrel beside the fireplace, he noticed a heavy, wooden mallet - known as a beetle, routinely used for kitchen tasks such as mashing potatoes. Although it appeared recently washed, curiously Robson failed until two days later to connect the mallet with the crime he was investigating. By standing on a barrel and levering himself up between the joists, the policeman went on to examine the loft-space and, on a loosely-floored area immediately beneath the turf roof, he discovered a bundle of clothing wrapped up in a woman's tartan dress, still wet from having been washed but displaying nonetheless unmistakeable traces of blood. His findings were reason enough for Robson to arrest Mary Timney on the spot, and at around ten o'clock she was taken into custody at New Galloway and moved on the following day to the county town, Kirkcudbright. At little more than a year old, her youngest child, John, was permitted to accompany her, while her three older offspring were left in the care of her mother, Margaret Good (née Corson), in Dalry.

In her subsequent statements to the authorities, Mary Timney's stance was consistently one of flat denial. Owing to illness, she repeated, she had not stepped out of doors throughout the entire morning of 13 January and she categorically stated that at no point on that day had she worn her tartan dress. There was, she explained, an innocent explanation for the tea and sugar found by Constable Robson, the items in question having been purchased two days earlier from William Smith's grocery store in Dalry by her eldest daughter, Susan. The bloodstains on her clothing, she continued, dated from a fortnight earlier and were of menstrual origin. Referring to the wooden *beetle* - on which traces of blood and human hair had by now been detected - she denied ever previously having set eyes on it - though her husband, Francis, contradicted her when he stated that the mallet had been used in their home for some considerable time. But it was Mary's final declaration, made on Tuesday 4 February, that brought the authorities up short.

In this statement Mary started off by admitting that, in order to protect another person, up till that point she had deliberately suppressed the facts. Now, however, she had resolved to bite the bullet and finally come clean, stating that 'It was my own mother, Margaret Corson, who murdered Ann Hannah.' Having dropped that bombshell, she then proceeded to fill in the details. On the morning of 13 January Margaret Corson had arrived from Dalry, she recounted, with a view to assisting her daughter in attending to her laundry. Because Margaret was wearing 'her good frock' she decided to change into a tartan dress belonging to her daughter before rolling up her sleeves and getting down to work. At some point during the morning Margaret spotted Ann Hannah, going about her business at Carsfad, and muttered that she would dearly like to repay her daughter's neighbour for 'setting your man against you when you were taken to Kirkcudbright.' (The background for this grievance was never subsequently explained.) By her own account, Mary did her best to diffuse the situation, warning her mother that 'Ann Hannah is stronger than you, and she'll fell you.' But Margaret was not to be dissuaded and left the cottage, and a few seconds later Mary watched her enter Ann Hannah's farmhouse. Some ten to twenty minutes later, by Mary's reckoning, Margaret arrived back, dripping with blood and crowing that she thought she had 'near killed her.' Quickly she changed back into her own clothes and, conscious of the need for haste, prepared to leave for home. Incongruously, Mary recalled suggesting to her mother that she might like to 'put on the kettle and have a cup of tea' before she left. Presumably for practical reasons, Margaret declined and departed shortly before noon.

For all its dramatic content, when all was said and done the chances of Mary's final declaration convincing anyone must surely have been virtually nil. When her trial got underway in Dumfries on Tuesday 8 April it didn't take long for her version of events to unravel under the glare of courtroom scrutiny. William Smith, grocer in Dalry, stated that no member of the Timney household had visited his premises in the week prior to Ann Hannah's death, either to purchase tea, sugar or for that matter anything else. Passing schoolchildren testified to the fact that they had seen Mary wearing her tartan dress, later found bloodstained, on the day of the murder and even her own daughter, Susan, admitted to seeing her wearing it that morning as she went out to feed the pigs. Visibly holding back, the nine-year-old finally cracked under pressure and tearfully confessed that her mother had left the house later that forenoon to visit Ann Hannah. As far as the matter of Margaret Corson's possible involvement was concerned, that was easily cleared up. Her husband, Samuel Good, stated that she had never left home that day and the couple's sixteen-year-old daughter, Jane, and several of their neighbours in Dalry were in a position to confirm this. As the weight of evidence piled up, not a single witness was called in Mary's defence and the outcome of the trial looked increasingly like a foregone conclusion. During the course of his summing up, the presiding judge, Lord Deas - known darkly as Lord *Death* - highlighted a number of inconsistencies in Mary's evidence and focused the jurymen's attention on the part in proceedings played by the *beetle*, inviting them to assess the medical evidence and judge whether this instrument was, in fact, the murder weapon. If the answer was yes, he told them, then the fact that Mary had deliberately armed herself before entering Ann Hannah's house was highly significant, revealing as it did a clear intention on her part to commit murder. The question of her mother, Margaret Corson's, involvement he dismissed out of hand. When the judge's voice fell silent and the jury retired to consider their verdict, it was a mere twenty minutes before they filed back into the courtroom, their deliberations complete. There were to be no surprises. 'The Jury are unanimous,' their spokesman announced, 'in finding the prisoner guilty of murder.'

This was the cue for Lord Deas to turn his attention now to the newly-convicted murderess. 'The time for all of us in this world is short,' he told her. 'In your case your days are numbered.' Calm up till now, Mary cried out at that - 'No, sir!' and 'No, my Lord!' - but the judge was not to be deflected. 'You will have access to ministers of religion,' he continued, 'and I recommend you to use the short time which you have still in the world in making peace with God.' Famously bluff and plain-speaking, he held out little hope of a reprieve: 'I should betray my duty were I to hold out to you false hopes, for I have not the least hope that the sentence will be otherwise but carried into effect.' Donning the black cap, he prepared to pass sentence. Mary would be held in Dumfries prison, he told her, where she would be sustained by bread and water alone until some three weeks hence when she would be taken to the place of execution on 29 April and 'hanged by the neck upon a gibbet until dead.' Her body would subsequently be interred within the precincts of the prison. Unsurprisingly, it was all too much for Mary. As she was removed from the court, her anguished cries rang out - 'O my Lord! O dinnae dae that! O dinnae dae that, my Lord! O my weans! O my weans!' It must surely have been heartrending for all who heard.

It took several days for Mary to settle down in Dumfries prison and start eating and sleeping well - buoyed up, it was suggested, by hopes of a reprieve. During this time, she faced being examined by the government's forthrightly-titled 'Commissioner in Lunacy', Dr William Browne, who concluded - hugely patronisingly - that she possessed the 'average intellect of her class' but appeared 'destitute of moral training.' The prison chaplain, Rev. Cowans, called on her twice daily and, during one of his visits, Mary offered yet another version of what had taken place on the day Ann Hannah died. She had left her cottage that morning, she told him, with the intention of gathering sticks for the fire when she was accosted by Ann who accused her once again of thieving. Voices were raised, it seems, and on this occasion hard blows exchanged. Returning home, Mary found herself burning with desire for revenge and left home a second time, meaning 'to give [her neighbour] a beating.' When she entered the farmhouse kitchen, Ann launched an immediate attack, delivering a violent kick to her leg, the impact of which left a two-inch scar still visible when she was in prison. As Mary crumpled, Ann struck her on the back with a wooden *beetle* which then fell from her grasp and clattered to the floor. From Ann's point of view, letting go of the wooden implement was a careless error and one which would be tragic in its consequences. Quickly recovering herself, Mary wasted no time in laying hold of the beetle and made use of it to strike Ann a violent blow to the head. Such was her temper, she admitted, that she followed this up with several other similar blows - though she had, she insisted, 'no intent to kill.' Leaving her neighbour bleeding and unconscious, Mary returned once again to her own home, carrying the *beetle* with her. Why her husband had identified it as his own possession Mary did not explain, nor why indeed she had chosen to remove it from the farmhouse.

During this time various petitions were circulating throughout Dumfries and district - signed in the end by well over 5,000 people - whose objective was to halt the town's first execution for some 35 years, but the Home Secretary, Sir George Grey, in whose gift any possibility of a reprieve lay, remained stubbornly silent. The cause was taken up by two local ladies, Mrs and Miss McCulloch of Castle Street, who made a round trip of nearly three hundred miles to pay a personal visit to Grey's private residence at Falloden Hall, Northumberland, where they were reportedly received with great courtesy. Gratified at the Home Secretary's detailed knowledge of Mary Timney's case, they failed nonetheless to elicit from him a categorical answer to their petition and, some days after returning to Dumfries, Mrs McCulloch received a letter in which Sir George laid out his reasons for failing to grant a reprieve. Not yet defeated, however, the redoubtable Mrs McCulloch now wrote directly to Queen Victoria but, at the end of the day, the monarch did not deign to intervene. No further avenues remained open to Mary's supporters and on Saturday 26 April it fell to the prison chaplain, Rev. Cowans, to break to her the news that all hope of a reprieve was now extinguished. On hearing this, Mary immediately suffered a brief convulsive seizure but, when finally she regained her composure, she appeared - on the surface at least - to have become resigned to her fate.

During her last few days Mary spoke often of her children. She was visited in jail by her husband and her second-youngest child and, before the couple parted, she urged him to 'remember the weans' and bring them up 'in a godly manner.' Their final farewell was said to have been calmer than might have been expected. That same day her sister and mother came to say goodbye, the family's recent differences presumably set aside. On Monday 29 April - the last day before the execution - the hangman, William Calcraft once again, arrived in Dumfries and for his own safety was accommodated within the prison. It was reported that Mary had risen early that morning in a state of some confusion, convinced in her mind that her final day was upon her, and had to be reassured. During her midday meal she remarked that this would be the last food she would taste on earth, a prediction that in the event proved entirely accurate. During the afternoon a great exhaustion descended on her and if her execution had not been scheduled for the following day, Dr Scott, the prison medical officer, was said to have been doubtful of her ability to survive much longer. One of Mary's final tasks was to dictate a number of letters, some to members of her family and one to Mrs and Miss McCulloch, thanking the ladies for their efforts on her behalf and which she concluded by stating that her intention had never been to take Ann Hannah's life. During the course of transcribing the letter into her own handwriting, Mary suffered a meltdown of some sort, moaning loudly and periodically uttering 'Oh, Jesus!' Prescribed a sedative by Dr Scott, she gradually became calm and subsequently slept all night until between five and six o'clock the following morning. Around seven o'clock she was paid a final visit by Rev. Cowans but she showed no appetite for breakfast.

The morning of Tuesday 30 April was dismal and gloomy, with the town of Dumfries enshrouded in a dense mist. Sent specifically from Edinburgh, the scaffold had been erected under cover of darkness in a location within the precincts of the prison, higher than the top of the boundary wall so as to be visible from the street. Two hundred special constables, sworn in for the occasion, were posted outside and various barricades erected for maintaining order among the expected crowds. Inside the prison formalities relating to the death warrant required to be completed before the provost and town bailies could emerge in order to attend a short religious service, conducted by a local minister, in which psalms were sung and prayers offered up. Not yet present, Mary's anguished cries could already be heard, emanating from within the prison, and when she finally appeared, modestly attired in a lilac robe, tartan shawl and with a small cotton mutch covering her head, she wept and wailed incessantly as she was escorted on her short journey to the scaffold. Her arms were pinioned to her sides. At first sight of the gallows, her distress visibly intensified and she hung back, saying 'Let me stand a minute, I'm weak.' A few moments later she was assisted in mounting the scaffold - averting her eyes the whole time and calling out 'Oh, my puir weans! My weans! My puir weans!' Just as she finished climbing the steps a moment of high drama occurred. When a letter bearing a London postmark was handed in apparent haste to the prison governor, James Stewart, standing at the foot of the gallows, proceedings were immediately suspended and a hush descended. It was known that Mrs McCulloch had recently written to London in a final last-ditch attempt to stop the execution and, as the governor tore open the envelope and read what lay within, the sense of anticipation was palpable. But no - it was not to be. The ill-timed letter, it transpired, was from the representative of a London newspaper, the Evening Herald, requesting that a telegraphed account of the execution be dispatched to London in time for his afternoon edition. 'Go on!' Governor Stewart instructed the hangman who immediately resumed his grisly preparations. For her part, Mary seemed to have been oblivious to the letter's arrival and mercifully it looked as though no false hopes had been raised.

Standing atop the scaffold, she needed to be supported by the executioner's assistant while having her ankles bound. During her last few minutes of life Mary gazed out towards the crowd with what was described poignantly at the time as 'a pitiful yearning look, as if she were looking to see whether there were none who would pity her or save her.' Unsurprisingly her final thoughts appeared to focus on the children she would never see again and her piteous moaning - 'My puir weans! Oh, my fower weans!' - was highly affecting to those who heard. As her ordeal approached its climax, Mary's moaning became a scream, more muffled after the white cap was drawn down over her face. Her final cry was stifled midway when, at precisely twenty-three minutes past eight, the hangman, Calcraft, drew back the bolt and she dropped from the scaffold. Things, however, did not end there. As her body swung in the air, Mary's arms continued to jerk spasmodically for some minutes until they eventually came to rest, quivering by her side. For a full minute she remained motionless and tension in the crowd was just starting to subside when her body gave one last convulsive judder which finally brought her agony to an end. Calcraft's work complete, it was less of a botched job, people said, than on other occasions for which he became known. Chastened perhaps by what they had witnessed, the members of the crowd - estimated at some 2,500 - proceeded to disperse quietly through the town and it was noted that very few women formed part of the throng. Mary's body was left hanging for a short time before being cut down and laid to rest within the prison grounds later that afternoon. No-one could doubt for a second that she had paid in full the price for her crime - the last woman in Scotland, as it turned out, to do so in a public arena.

At the end of the day, what was it, we might ask, that prompted Mary Timney to commit such an atrocious crime? Why did a young wife and mother take it upon herself to batter and subsequently mutilate her near neighbour, Ann Hannah, a woman held in high regard throughout the local area and who had in the past been generous to Mary? In the words of Lord Deas, she had 'very small motive.' In her own statements Mary was never totally candid but, during one of her conversations with the prison chaplain, she let slip a significant detail - namely, that she was jealous of Ann Hannah. The chances are that Mary's revelation came as no surprise to Rev. Cowans. In relative terms her neighbour was living in what looked like affluent circumstances, she was free of dependants and her brothers had sufficient funds to have recently assumed the tenancy of a second farm. With four small children at her knee and with her entire family confined to a single room, Mary, by contrast, was reduced to surviving through what was tantamount to begging. In the days immediately prior to Ann Hannah's death, she had faced a number of setbacks. She had been refused credit by the grocer, David Cowan, in Dalry. She had turned up at the big house at Knocknalling in hopes of borrowing a little tea but was prevented from even approaching the housekeeper. She had even waylaid a passing police constable, James Richardson, at Carsfad, telling him she had 'neither meat nor money in the house' and had unsuccessfully attempted to cadge a sixpence from him. The very morning of the murder Mary's husband, Francis, had been forced to borrow half-a-crown from their neighbour, William Hannah. It seems likely that repeated refusals had a cumulative effect upon Mary and, when an apparently trivial dispute concerning sticks for kindling blew up, it came as the final straw, acting as a trigger and causing something within her to snap. As it turned out, two deaths and incalculable suffering were to follow as a result.

John Reilly : May 1864

It was a cold, blustery morning on Tuesday 8 December 1863, still pitch-black at five o'clock when William Buchanan set out for work. From his home at Chapelhall, near Airdrie, he had three miles to walk along the Biggar Road towards Newarthill where he was employed as a miner. After a mile or so, he reached the Cross Roads junction where he continued directly ahead, but a couple of hundred yards farther on there was something he spied that brought him up short. Lying face-down in a ditch running parallel to the road was the form of a woman, snugly dressed and to all intents and purposes incapably drunk. 'Woman,' said Buchanan, bending down to give her a shake, 'rise, or you'll be lost with the cold.' When she failed to respond, he simply shrugged and went on his way, but when he reached Newarthill at around half past five the matter was still preying on his mind so he reported what he had seen to the pit watchman, John McLachlan. Hearing the story, McLachlan went to investigate and located the woman, just as Buchanan had described, lying in the 'sheugh' near the entrance to a field at a stretch of the road known as Scobie's Brae. When he probed more closely, however, and detected no signs of life, McLachlan quickly realised that the situation was a good deal more serious than a routine case of drunkenness. The woman's body, he found, was cold to the touch, her clothing wet through, and when he drew back her shawl he saw a nasty cut on the left side of her face. Leaving her for the time being where she lay, he hurried on to Cross

Roads where he met two men, John Summers and his son, and told them that there was 'a dead or murdered woman' in the ditch. Led to the spot, Summers recognised her instantly. 'I knew her,' he said. 'Her name was Nancy Laffy.'

Back at Newarthill, McLachlan reported his grisly find to the local policeman, Constable David Carnachan, who accompanied him back to the scene and arranged for a cart to be sent to uplift the woman's body. As McLachlan had indicated, Carnachan could see that her left cheek was badly gashed and her face stained with blood. Her head was bare and her hair hanging loose, but lying underneath her he found a cap. Looking around for possible weapons, he picked up a large stone which was lying close to the woman's left side and took it with him when he returned to the police station where he secured her body in a locked outhouse. When word reached him that she had been seen the previous evening in the company of one of her neighbours, a miner named Patrick Doyle, he arrested the man on suspicion and locked him up at Newarthill. Between nine and ten o'clock he returned to Scobie's Brae and conducted a thorough search which turned up a number of items, including lucifer matches, some cotton cloth, and a small stone to which Nancy's hair was still adhering. A hundred yards or so farther up the road he noticed that the ground was bloodstained, and a trail could be seen through the wet grass along which he guessed that the woman's body had been dragged. There was no bag, purse or money to be seen. A post-mortem examination, carried out the following day, revealed multiple head and body wounds which had led to copious bleeding. Four upper teeth had been dislodged and the woman's neck appeared to have been compressed by her attacker's hands. If a single assailant was responsible, the examining doctors believed that a protracted struggle was likely to have taken place.

Nancy Laffy, née Stevens, was a sturdy, strongly-built woman in her early fifties and was married to Thomas Laffy. The couple lived at Legbrannock, a small settlement of coal-miners and their families near Holytown, Lanarkshire. During the course of her lifetime she had given birth to a total of fourteen children, eight of whom survived. Bit by bit Nancy's movements on Monday 7 December were established. The day before her body was found, Nancy's husband had been due to appear at the local Police Court, facing a charge of breach of the peace. Thinking a fine was the likeliest outcome, Nancy left before Thomas, planning to pawn his overcoat and make enough money to cover any payment required. Halfway to the town, she dropped in on a friend at Calderbank, Agnes Mooney, who gave her six shillings and sixpence of 'aliment' - the most recent instalment of poor relief due to Nancy's elderly mother which Agnes was in the habit of collecting for her and which Nancy was apparently prepared to divert for her husband's benefit. Leaving Calderbank, she carried on to Henry Cowan's pawnbrokers in Airdrie where she was attended to by an assistant, Hugh Allan, who advanced her the sum of ten shillings against Thomas's coat. Confident now that she had rustled up enough money - something approaching £1 - she entered the courtroom and took her place on the public benches just in time to see her husband found guilty as charged. What came as a surprise, however, was when Thomas was sentenced to twenty days' imprisonment without being offered the alternative of a fine. Before he was led away to the cells, Nancy was able to speak to him briefly, and he handed over to her an ounce of tobacco plus two shillings and sixpence in cash.

This was the point where the suspect, Patrick Doyle, entered the story. He had also been in Airdrie on Monday 7 December and attended Laffy's trial, after which he and Nancy were both part of a group which headed for McAulay's public house. She drank relatively little - a glass of wine, perhaps, and maybe two of ale - and late in the afternoon Doyle and she left to walk back to Legbrannock together. Part-way home, they stopped off at Adams' pub at Chapelhall where they sat down to another drink. As Nancy ordered whisky for Doyle and gin for herself, the barmaid, Isabella Ney, could not help but notice that she had a considerable sum of money - four half-crowns, she thought, plus smaller change in silver - in a purse which she wore on a string around her neck. A short time later Doyle and Nancy were joined in the pub by two women they knew - Catherine Murray, a millworker, and her mother. Nancy wanted to continue drinking but Doyle told her that, given her state of inebriation, she was unlikely to be served, so at about eight o'clock they left Adams' premises and moved on to the Murrays' house. Nancy was now 'kind o' drunk' and Catherine and her mother tried to persuade her to stay the night, but when it was suggested that she was 'the worse of a glass' she became annoyed and somewhere between nine and ten o'clock insisted on leaving for home. The night was blustery and Catherine and her mother left to accompany her for part for of the way, while Doyle stayed put for another half-hour or so before returning once again to Adams' hostelry where he met a friend, Hugh Dillon, and drank with him until closing time. Calling back briefly at Mrs Murray's, he left for home at last, following the road as far as Cross Roads where he made a right turn for Legbrannock. By now it was very late, the road was deserted and he had no reason to doubt that Nancy had reached Legbrannock ahead of him and was safe and secure at home. He could not have known that, not far from where he turned at Cross Roads, in a few hours' time Nancy's body would be found in a ditch. Initially suspicion fell upon Doyle but it wasn't long before another suspect came under the spotlight and, much to his relief, he was eliminated by the police from their inquiries.

Patrick Doyle had not, in fact, been the only one out late that night. A maid at Bellshill, fourteen-year-old Hannah Ewart, had finished work for the day when she set out to walk the four and a half miles to her father's home at Newhouse, immediately east of Cross Roads. As she was passing Holytown schoolhouse a man emerged from Reid's public house and waylaid her, asking in an unmistakeably Irish accent for directions to Legbrannock. Although he spoke fairly coherently she could see that he was staggering a little on his feet and she was in no doubt that he had been drinking. The stranger had a peculiar, dark cloth tied about his head, and there was something about him that made the teenager uneasy. Even though she was going towards Legbrannock herself, she felt apprehensive at the prospect of walking with him so she told him that she was uncertain of the way.

Less than a week before, the stranger, John Reilly, had moved into lodgings near Newarthill in a two-room house occupied by William O'Donnell and his wife, Helen. Employed as a labourer on a new stretch of railway track near Clelland, the Irishman's day had not gone well. Clearly in need of cash, first thing in the morning he had offered to sell a shirt to his landlady, but when she refused to take him up on it he had gone instead to the Newarthill pawnbroker, Henry McCary, who had advanced him one shilling for the article in question. That he was short of money was surely confirmed when he returned to McCary's shop later in the day, explaining that he had no plans to redeem his shirt at any point in the future and offering, therefore, to sell back the receipt. Aware that Reilly had been drinking, the pawnbroker agreed to the arrangement nonetheless and paid him an additional threepence in exchange for the receipt. By the time that Reilly turned up at William Johnston's public house in Holytown that evening, however, it was obvious that he had already had enough and the publican's wife, Catherine, accordingly refused to serve him any more alcohol. Reluctant to leave with nothing, he told her that his cap had been blown away by the wind and wheedled that 'Reilly would be lost' if he had nothing to cover his head. In an effort to appease him, Catherine handed him a piece of black cotton cloth which he wound around his head before leaving. She also gave him a clay pipe which he managed to light but which somehow slipped out of his fingers on the way out, leaving fragments scattered on the floor. Somehow or other, he had acquired a replacement by the time he entered Reid's public house, directly across the road, where he stopped off briefly to ask for a match. He paused at the bar to light the pipe, then stepped out into the night just as fourteen-year-old Hannah happened to be passing.

After Hannah's brief initial exchange with Reilly, he set off ahead of her but to her dismay it did not take long before she caught up with him again, at a place where the railway line crossed the Legbrannock road. As previously, he tried to engage her in conversation. Once again, he told her, he had managed to lose his pipe and he asked if she knew where he might get hold of another. She suggested that he try one of the cottages alongside the railway, then, taking advantage when his back was turned, she ran on ahead, hoping to outpace him. Unfortunately, he soon caught up with her at the gateway to Lauchope House where he informed her that he still had no pipe. 'That's a pity,' she awkwardly replied. In an uneasy silence they continued along a quiet stretch of the road until, to Hannah's intense relief, they reached the house of a friend of hers, a miner named James Keir, where she turned aside and knocked on the door. Reilly, she was careful to note, did not stop but kept on walking. By this time, it was after eleven o'clock and Keir had already retired to bed but, seeing Hannah, he got up and opened the door to her. Stepping into the lobby, she told him that she had been pursued by a strange man, so Keir closed the door firmly behind her and turned the key in the lock. It was a few moments later that things took a distinctly creepy turn.

There was no light in Keir's house except for a glow from the fire in the grate and, as Hannah recounted her story, they heard the sound of a footstep outside the window, as though her strange companion had turned back upon himself. A shadow fell across the blind, the shape of a man's head, as though he were trying to see inside. There the shadow waited for a full two minutes before finally moving away, only to reappear a short time later. At last the stranger appeared to give up, and both Keir and Hannah breathed a sigh of relief as they listened to his footsteps fading. For entirely understandable reasons, Hannah was afraid to continue alone and she stayed on for more than an hour until, shortly before midnight, Keir arranged for a young neighbour, Isaac Allan, to see her safely home. Out on the road the stranger appeared to have vanished.

Much around the same time a pit-worker from Newarthill, James Russell, was walking along the Biggar Road in the direction of Chapelhall where he was planning to spend the night before visiting Shotts Fair the following day. As he approached the foot of Scobie's Brae, he encountered a man he did not recognise who was standing, looking towards the hedge that ran alongside the road. From closer up Russell made out the form of a woman, lying on her back with her head 'at the root of the thorns.' She neither moved nor spoke. The stranger turned toward Russell and explained that the woman had been assaulted and robbed. Russell decided against stopping. Describing the encounter later, he said that he thought it was most likely to be a case where a husband and wife had had too much to drink but, he admitted, he had felt a little afraid. 'I didnae ken the man,' he said, 'and I didnae want to hae ony traffic with him. I kent by his tongue he was an Irishman.' He kept on walking, put the matter from his mind and was in bed at Chapelhall by the time the clock struck midnight. He did not realise at the time that the stranger had been John Reilly and that he had just passed by the scene of a murder.

Sometime after midnight, Reilly's fellow-lodger at Newarthill, Joseph Connolly, was disturbed by a loud rapping at the window of his room, and when he got out of bed he found Reilly outside, asking for admittance. Connolly may well have grumbled, but he let him in nonetheless and thought no more about it before falling asleep once again. Reilly was in the habit of sleeping in the kitchen, in a bed directly opposite his landlady's, and a short time after his late arrival his odd behaviour aroused her suspicions. Somewhere between two and three o'clock in the morning, Helen awoke and saw him seated on a low stool in front of the fire, partially hidden by wet clothes that he had hung up to dry. As she continued to watch, he counted a number of coins from one hand to the other, but in the low light she could not tell whether they were coppers or silver. After slipping the coins into his pocket, Reilly became conscious that he was being watched and, turning to his landlady, he asked where he might find a washing bowl. A suitable bowl was pointed out to him which he filled with warm water from the kettle, but thereafter Helen saw nothing when she drifted back to sleep. In the morning Reilly did not get up till ten o'clock, and he asked Helen if she would mend a tear on his shirt. Stretching from the wrist to the 'oxter', the damage had been done the previous evening, he explained, during the course of a tussle with two miners and the quarrel, he added, accounted for scratches that were visible on his face. While Helen was carrying out the repair he slipped out of the house and returned sometime later with no explanation - a gap in time he would be required to account for at a later date. When Helen broached the subject of his drinking, he replied light-heartedly, saying that 'he was always doing something when he was drinking.' 'Worst of all,' he quipped, this time 'he had sold his drawers.' He told a workmate, Michael McIntyre, a similar story, adding the extra detail that he had benefited from the transaction to the tune of a sixpence. Whatever Reilly might have expected, the matter of his lost underwear did not end there, and a few months later it would, we might say, return to haunt him.

When Reilly vanished from the area a day after the murder, suspicions were certainly awakened. He had lodged with the O'Donnells for little more than a week and, even though he was owed wages, he did not wait until pay-day. It was well known for labouring men to come and go as a matter of course but, even despite that, the level of suspicion was sufficient for notices to be placed in the *Police Gazette* nationwide, seeking information about his whereabouts. Some weeks after his disappearance, police in Lanarkshire received a tip-off that Reilly might be working at Redesdale, Northumberland, and consequently a hint was dropped to Superintendent John Gillespie of the local constabulary. As a result, the police chief immediately made a point of instructing his officers to keep their eyes peeled and, in an example of outstandingly sharp policing, Reilly was identified that very day in the small market town of Kirkwhelpington. When questioned, he gave his name as Bryans but that went for nothing: 'You are wanted for murder at Newarthill, in Lanarkshire,' he was told firmly. On the way to Morpeth Jail, Reilly dropped his guard a little when he mentioned to his escort, Constable

John Hurles, the murder of a woman. 'Who said so?' the officer asked him. 'Didn't you say so?' Reilly replied. 'No,' said Hurles, 'you are charged with murder but there was no person mentioned.' And, right enough, the advertisement in the *Police Gazette* had not, in fact, given any details relating to the murder victim. Sergeant Edward Connelly was dispatched from Lanarkshire to accompany the prisoner back across the border, and at some point during the journey Reilly asked whether there were many witnesses against him. At least, he told the policeman, nobody could say that they had seen him carry out the murder. His unguarded remark spoke volumes and Sergeant Connelly, we may be sure, would have drawn his own conclusions.

While Reilly was locked up in Hamilton awaiting trial, there was an unexpected development. On Friday 25 March 1864 a couple of Newarthill lads, James Donald and Hugh Philip, were rooting around in a patch of woodland when something unusual caught James's eye. Half-submerged in a watery ditch was what looked like a scrap of material which he promptly hoicked out on the end of a stick. It was, he quickly realised, no great find - nothing but a pair of old drawers - but when Hugh's father, Michael, heard of the boys' discovery he immediately connected it with Nancy Laffy's supposed murderer and informed the local policeman - Constable David Carnachan, once again - and showed him where the garment had been found. Strange though it may seem, the soggy underwear was to feature prominently in Reilly's official declaration, and also when his case was heard at Glasgow Circuit Court on Saturday 23 April with Lords Deas and Neaves at the bench. In two formal declarations to the authorities, Reilly claimed that on Monday 7 December he had been assaulted by three men at Holytown, one of whom had knocked him to the ground and kicked him, cutting his knee and bloodying his nose. On the way back to Newarthill he had not met anyone, he said, and he was emphatic that he had seen no-one lying by the roadside. In connection with the question of why he had chosen to wash his underwear in the dead of night, his explanation was a little unsavoury. 'I was taken short when I was knocked down,' he said, 'and eased myself into my drawers.' As well as that, the garment, he claimed, was stained with blood from a wound on his knee (whose scab he still bore) and more blood, he thought, had dripped down from the scratches on his face. Even after being washed, the drawers retained a lingering unpleasant smell, so the following morning he had decided to dispose of them in a nearby plantation. When he returned to the same wood some two hours later - no reason given - he found that the underpants had been torn to pieces and he had tramped the shredded material down into the mud with his heel. A dog he saw scavenging nearby he thought the likely culprit. He had left the area the day after the murder, he said, since his railway work at Clelland had dried up and, as he headed south towards Biggar, he had no more than a penny and a farthing to his name.

There were, however, a number of flaws in Reilly's story. For one thing, his boss, Richard Bell, told the court that railway construction remained ongoing and - contrary to Reilly's declaration - he had been free, had he so wished, to continue working. Secondly, while he was being held at Hamilton, Hannah Ewart had positively identified him as her menacing late-night companion. On top of that, there was also the matter of his bizarre nocturnal laundry for the jury to consider, plus the controversial question of whose blood it was that had stained his underwear. On the other side of the coin, there were various aspects of the case which remained uncertain. First, no-one had actually seen him in Nancy Laffy's company on the night she was murdered; and, secondly, it seems a little odd that it took Hannah Ewart three separate visits to Hamilton before she finally was sure enough in her own mind to swear to Reilly's identity. Thirdly, as regards the coins that Helen O'Donnell watched him counting by her fireside, her uncertainty as to whether they were copper or silver was a matter of considerable importance because, if the former, they might possibly have been the balance of the shilling he had received from Henry McCary for his pawned shirt, and not therefore acquired by dishonest means. And lastly, it was impossible to know for sure whether the traces of blood on his underwear had come from his own cut knee or from elsewhere. Reading between the lines, the judge, Lord Deas', opinion was pretty clear, something that would hardly have been lost on the members of the jury when they retired shortly after midnight to consider their decision - a full fourteen hours since the start of the trial. A little over an hour later they trooped back into the courtroom, and their spokesman announced that by a majority verdict - reportedly nine to six - they found the prisoner guilty. As throughout most of the trial, Reilly displayed no obvious emotion. Thanking the jury for their 'trouble and attention', Lord Deas then closed proceedings for the day by stating that, owing to the lateness of the hour, he proposed to postpone sentencing until the following morning.

What Reilly's feelings might have been during the intervening 24 hours we can only guess, but certainly he appeared to show no sign of anxiety when he returned to the dock the following morning. In addressing him, Lord Deas made much of his statement to Sergeant Connolly during their journey back to Scotland to the effect that no-one had witnessed Nancy Laffy's murder. 'If you imagined that you might commit such a crime as this with impunity because nobody saw you do it,' Lord Deas told him, 'you were labouring under a delusion. If any other persons working through the country or moving through the country as you were, imagine that because they are not much known or known at all in the district, and because there is no eye but the eye of God upon them, they may commit murder with impunity, I trust that the result of this case will be a warning to them.' The sentence he would shortly pronounce, he stated, was one set down in law, in relation to which he was permitted no discretion. He then gave instructions for the prisoner 'to be removed from the bar to the prison of Glasgow, therein to be detained, and fed on bread and water, until the 16th day of May next, and upon that day, between the hours of eight and ten o'clock forenoon, to be taken from the said prison to the common place of execution, and there, by the hands of the common executioner, to be hanged by the neck upon a gibbet until he be dead.' 'And,' the judge concluded, 'may Almighty God have mercy upon your soul.' A profound hush in the courtroom was eventually broken by Reilly himself, when he spoke out, saying, 'My Lord, I am innocent of the crime.' With that, he stepped down from the dock.

Following his conviction, details gradually emerged relating to Reilly's previous existence. A native of Annamullen, County Monaghan, Ireland, he had been born in 1832 into a respectable working-class family. At the age of eighteen he had enlisted in the 60th Regiment under what appears to have been his original name of John Bryans (the name, it may be recalled, that he gave when arrested in Northumberland) and he had spent the following six years serving in India before being discharged on health grounds. The fact that he drew a pension of sixpence per day for the following nine months suggested that his conduct in the army had been satisfactory. Since returning from overseas he appeared to have led a nomadic existence, labouring on various railway projects and moving from job to job when the work was completed or alternatively if lured by better prospects. In Northumberland, it was said, he went under the surname of Bryans, while in Scotland he quickly became known as 'Sodger Reilly'. Married but without children, despite living apart from his wife in Ireland he was believed to be on good terms and in regular contact with her. Following his trial in Glasgow, a strange little story circulated concerning his recent past. Alleged to have assaulted a woman he was involved with somewhere in the border country, for whatever reason he was never brought to book. During his flight from Newarthill, he apparently entered a lodging-house in Biggar where, by pure chance, he encountered this same woman. He removed himself from the scene, it was said, with the utmost alacrity.

Following his murder conviction, it became clear that Reilly was not without support in Glasgow. On Thursday 5 May a well-attended public meeting was held in the City Hall where grave doubts were expressed regarding the security of his conviction. The fact that as many as six jury members were dissatisfied with the evidence against Reilly was sufficient to convince many of those present that a 'not proven' verdict would have been more appropriate. The result was a petition submitted to the Home Office and appealing for the Royal Prerogative. But, as it turned out, all to no avail. Reilly remained quiet and composed during his final days in prison where he was attended on a daily basis by a Roman Catholic priest, Rev. Black, and visited on two separate occasions by Bishop John Murdoch. In accordance with his wishes, neither his wife back in Ireland nor any other relative was to be made aware of his plight. Though he was said to have dropped hints to the effect that he was guilty of Nancy Laffy's murder, never at any point did he make an official confession. On Friday 13 May - an inauspicious date, for sure - William Calcraft arrived from London and the following day Reilly was moved from the North to the South Prison. There appeared to be some difficulty in enlisting the services of an assistant hangman, but this was finally resolved when a suitable candidate came forward in Edinburgh who was willing to undertake the duty. Having reportedly served in the army during the Indian Rebellion of 1857, the unnamed individual was said to have been accustomed to presiding over the execution of a dozen men at a time.

During the early hours of Sunday morning the scaffold was put together in front of the South Prison and surrounded by a black screen, a recent innovation from south of the border whose object was to conceal part of Reilly's body from the gaze of the public at the moment of the drop. A timber barricade was also put in place, ten or twelve feet from the scaffold, and a larger space marked out to be kept clear of spectators and manned by a strong cordon of police. Estimates of the crowd varied between 20,000 and 30,000, somewhat fewer, it was noted, than on previous similar occasions, a circumstance that was possibly explained by local Roman Catholic churches' exhortations to their congregations to boycott the execution. That said, spectators gathered at every possible vantage point, some even on the opposite bank of the River Clyde, and a high proportion were reportedly youths and women, some of surprisingly tender years. For the most part, the crowd was well-behaved and any minor instances of disorder were swiftly quashed, so it was said, by 'a few harmless strokes of the baton.' There was nothing in the air to suggest any feeling of sympathy for the condemned man.

Reilly was reported to have remained calm throughout his final night, and during the early hours he received visits from Rev. Black and Bishop Murdoch from whom he received his final communion. At half past five he drank tea, but showed no appetite for food. Entering the condemned cell at around eight o'clock, the executioner, Calcraft, pinioned the prisoner's arms and conducted him to the Court House where he was received by city magistrates. Dressed in a decent black suit - said to have been donated by friends - Reilly was visibly pale and drawn, but it was noted that his bearing gave the impression of a deep underlying resolution. Bishop Murdoch spoke on his behalf, intimating to the magistrates that the prisoner had nothing that he wished to say. As he was led to the gallows, the clergymen remained by his side and the bishop kept a firm hold of his left arm. He ascended the staircase with a firm step and knelt down on the drop where, flanked by the two priests, he bowed his head in a final prayer. When his devotions were complete, he rose to his feet and the executioner approached to give the rope a final adjustment, place the white hood over his head and bind his legs together with a strap. The clergymen took turns to shake him by the hand, and then - with no time wasted - the bolt was drawn, the drop fell and a spontaneous groan was heard, arising from the crowd. Suspended on the end of the rope, Reilly's body was racked by convulsions for an excruciating three minutes, then for several minutes more a quivering was visible through various parts of his body - a harrowing sight that most spectators were prevented from seeing by the surrounding black screen. When all signs of movement finally ceased, his body was left to hang for thirty minutes or so before being cut down for burial within the prison grounds later that day. It then took less than an hour for the scaffold to be dismantled and removed, by which time the great majority of the crowd had melted away and dispersed through the city streets. Only a few small groups remained to mingle and ponder the dismal fate of Sodger Reilly.

Edward Pritchard : July 1865

While carrying out his duties during the early hours of Tuesday 5 May 1863, a sharp-eyed Glasgow constable became conscious of an alarming circumstance. Observing that the attic window of the house at 11 Berkeley Terrace was lit up by a fiery glow, the officer hurried to the front door, rang the bell and was admitted almost immediately by the householder, Dr Edward Pritchard, who, it transpired, was already aware that fire had broken out in his home, having been alerted some moments earlier by the cries of his two young sons. Pritchard recounted how, emerging from his own bedroom, he had entered the boys' room where they told him that their sleep had been interrupted by the sound of cracking glass and the smell of smoke. Leaving his children downstairs, the doctor had rushed to the top floor where his 25-year-old housemaid, Elizabeth McGirn, was in the habit of sleeping in the attic bedroom. Calling out her name, he had received no answer in return until, defeated by smoke and fumes, he had been forced to retreat, arriving on the ground floor just as the vigilant local constable stepped up to his doorstep. The two men made a second attempt to reach the maid's bedroom but once again smoke and flames barred their progress and prevented them from entering the burning attic.

Powerless to do more, they then set about raising the alarm, initially contacting Anderston Police Station where officers in turn made use of modern telegraph technology to alert the local fire services. Quick off the mark, firefighters arrived soon after at Berkeley Terrace where they wasted no time in bringing the blaze under control and, once the flames were sufficiently doused, those firemen who climbed to the top floor of the building were confronted with a harrowing sight. Entering the attic bedroom, they found the housemaid, Elizabeth McGirn, dead in her bed, her body dreadfully charred to the extent that her face was totally destroyed and her right arm had been almost entirely consumed by the flames. Certain of the young woman's ribs were exposed to view. It was known that Elizabeth had been in the habit of reading in bed and the conclusion was drawn that she had perhaps failed to extinguish the gas lighting before falling asleep and the 'bed-hangings' which routinely formed a part of Victorian bedroom furniture had some time later caught light. When questioned, her employer, Dr Prichard, stated that when he had arrived home around eleven o'clock the previous evening he had noticed that a light was still burning in the attic bedroom. Contrary to his usual practice, he explained, he had not spoken with Elizabeth McGirn before checking on his young sons and retiring to his own bed around midnight. As it happened, a second servant who normally shared the attic bedroom had been out of town that night - accompanying Mrs Pritchard - and, left alone in the attic, the unfortunate Elizabeth was deemed likely to have died as a result of smoke inhalation, thus perhaps explaining why no effort appeared to have been made to escape the flames. When all was said and done, the housemaid's death was put down to a tragic accident, dreadful but not uncommon, the consequence of carelessness and human frailty.

That said, a number of uncomfortable questions remained unanswered. Why, it was asked, had the vigilant police officer found Dr Pritchard fully dressed in his daytime clothing at three o'clock in the morning? After all, he had by his own account only just been wakened by his two young sons a few minutes earlier. Why too was no trace of the jewellery for which he submitted a hefty insurance claim to be located among the ashes? And why did the body of poor Elizabeth McGirn display no indication whatsoever of any kind of distress? And if all that wasn't suspicious enough, there were some who regarded it as an odd coincidence that fire should choose to break out on the very night that Pritchard's wife and his second household servant happened to be absent from home. But even if tongues wagged - and, if nowhere else, eyebrows were undoubtedly raised in the offices of the doctor's home insurance company - the law concluded its investigations in due course and promptly washed its hands of the matter. Suspicions in the community, however, were not allayed and within the space of a few short years a further series of fatal events, also involving Edward Pritchard, reignited speculation about the circumstances surrounding the blaze at Berkeley Terrace.

Dr Edward William Pritchard was not a native-born Glaswegian. Born in 1825 into a distinguished seafaring family on the south coast of England, he was apprenticed in his mid-teens to a surgeon in nearby Portsmouth and continued his medical studies in London before following family tradition and going to sea in 1846, initially aboard HMS *Victory*, Lord Nelson's former flagship at the Battle of Trafalgar. While at home on leave from HMS *Hecate* during 1850, he attended a social event where he was introduced to Mary Jane Taylor, the daughter of a prosperous Edinburgh silk merchant who happened at the time to be a guest in the home of his uncle, a retired naval surgeon, Dr David Cowan. It would appear that love blossomed, for later that same year Edward and Mary Jane were duly wed with the blessing of the bride's parents. Sometime later Edward left the navy and, with the financial assistance of his parents-in-law, he set himself up in a small medical practice in Hunmanby, Yorkshire, which proved sufficiently successful for him to extend operations to nearby Filey in an effort to target those wealthy visitors who descended on the coastal town in numbers in order to avail themselves of the local spa facilities. During those same years he became an active Freemason, as well as finding sufficient time and energy to publish a series of articles, both on medical topics and based around his experiences at sea, and to pen a guidebook - *Antiquities of Filey* - detailing the attractions of the local area. No less industrious, his wife, Mary Jane, gave birth to no fewer than five children at this time - three daughters and two sons - before matters in Yorkshire took a turn for the worse and Pritchard deemed it prudent to uproot his family and move on - under a cloud, so it was said, as rumours piled up concerning financial irregularities and the doctor's dubious relations with certain of his female patients. Crossing north of the border, the Pritchards lodged for a time with Mary Jane's parents in Edinburgh and, after a spell of medical work in the Middle East, Edward moved his family west to take up residence in their new home in Berkeley Terrace, Glasgow.

Arriving in the city, it could hardly be said that Pritchard made an attempt to blend in quietly but he appeared, on the contrary, to go out of his way to draw attention to himself. In what was viewed as an obvious effort to impress, he became known for spinning fanciful tales about his illustrious brother, the Governor of Ceylon, and was frequently heard to claim a close personal friendship with the famous Italian statesman, Giuseppe Garibaldi, producing as evidence a walking stick whose silver band was inscribed with the words - *Presented by General Garibaldi to Edward William Pritchard.* (Some, however, were inclined to the view that the impressive lettering was a late addition, engraved suspiciously recently.) Around the six-foot mark in height in an age when most Scotsmen were noticeably shorter than today and sporting an opulent, flowing beard, Pritchard presented a figure that was hard to ignore as he perambulated around the city streets - distributing photographic postcards of himself to those individuals whom he encountered along the way whom he deemed worthy of such an honour. Perhaps unsurprisingly, the majority of those so favoured were said to have been female. During this same time, he delivered a series of public lectures based on his far-flung adventures during which he boasted memorably that he had 'plucked eaglets from their eyries in the deserts of Arabia and hunted the Nubian lion on the prairies of North America' - an impressive claim (if geographically a little muddled) though it was noted that, for similar reasons, a good many of his yarns would not stand too close a scrutiny. At the end of the day, however, Pritchard's efforts to ingratiate himself with Glasgow society were destined to fail. In some quarters his insinuating, southern tones were met with a degree of resentment and a whiff of the bogus that persistently clung to him proved hard to shake off. His attempt to join a professional body, the Faculty of Physicians and Surgeons, fell flat when no existing member could be found who was willing to sponsor his application, and his efforts at securing the Chair of Surgery at the Andersonian College when it became vacant hit a similar brick wall. Glaswegians' reservations, it is true, were in large part justified. Though claiming to have studied at King's College, London, it would emerge in the fullness of time that his medical degree had been purchased in 1857 *in absentia* from a university in Germany. For its part, King's

College claimed no knowledge whatsoever of Edward Pritchard's existence.

There is one Glasgow connection, however, that it seems likely that he would have made at this time. Edward Pritchard's fellow-countryman, John Henry Greatrex, was a professional photographer of similar age who joined the Glasgow Photographic Association in 1863, the year prior to Pritchard's being made a committee member of the same society. Both men, it appears, had been sponsored by the same member, John Rex Young. At the time Greatrex was an active member of the Plymouth Brethren community and was regularly to be found preaching on Glasgow Green, but a few years later it emerged that he had apparently failed to live up to his Christian principles when he fell under suspicion of having turned his photographic skills to his advantage by forging Union Bank of Scotland notes. A warrant was issued for his arrest and he was eventually apprehended in the city of New York, thanks to the ingenuity of a dogged Glasgow detective, Alexander McCall, who had followed him across the Atlantic. On being escorted back to Scotland, he was convicted at Edinburgh and duly sentenced to twenty years' penal servitude in England. But, prior to Greatrex's ignominious exit from the Scottish scene, his path would cross with that of Edward Pritchard on at least one further occasion.

So, with the possible exception of Glasgow's future forger, it seems that Pritchard was successful in establishing few connections in the city and life, it transpired, did not go exactly to plan. By the autumn of 1864 he and his family were installed in new accommodation at 131 Sauchiehall Street, in a property purchased partly through the generosity of his Edinburgh in-laws. When Mary Jane Pritchard fell violently ill that October, relations between husband and wife had been showing signs of strain for some time - ever since, in fact, she had caught her husband in a clinch with their new housemaid, a fifteen-year-old girl from Islay named Mary McLeod. When she labelled her husband a 'a nasty, dirty man', Mary Jane's enraged reaction was entirely understandable but, had she only known it, he had in fact been conducting an affair with the teenager since during the summer months when she and her children were absent from home while holidaying on the coast near Dunoon. Diagnosed by Pritchard as gastric fever, Mary Jane's bout of sickness was followed in quick succession by several others but by late November she had recovered sufficiently to make the journey to her parents' home in a leafy district of Edinburgh where she planned to stay until Christmas in an attempt to recover her health. At Lauder Road she picked up almost immediately and started to regain some of the weight that she had lost during her illness. She became well enough to dine out with friends, prompting her daughter, Jane Frances (who lived at that time with her grandparents in Edinburgh) to report back that 'Ma is very well, all fat and blooming.' It was not, perhaps, what her father wanted to hear.

As it turned out, the improvement in Mary Jane's condition was to be short-lived and, back in Glasgow, she suffered a further relapse early in the new year of 1865. By this time, it had become clear that eating was inclined to aggravate matters so Mary Jane resorted to having her meals sent to her bedroom where she developed the habit of dining alone. A few weeks later, in early February, her malaise flared up with a vengeance. When the family's cook, Catherine Lattimer, overheard her mistress retching, she rushed to her bedside where she found her suffering cruelly from cramp. 'Catherine,' Mary Jane gasped, 'I have lost my senses. I was never so bad as this before.' The following day Pritchard wrote to his wife's second cousin, Dr James Cowan, recently retired from practising medicine in Edinburgh, and invited him to come to Glasgow to give the benefit of his opinion. For whatever reason, Dr Cowan's examination of Mary Jane led him to conclude that her condition was not overly serious and he suggested that small quantities of champagne and ice might prove beneficial with possibly the application in addition of a mustard poultice. At the end of the day, Cowan's medical advice provided his patient with no benefit whatsoever but his parting recommendation was one that, in the fullness of time, would lead to grave repercussions. Mary Jane, he suggested, might benefit from the support of her mother and he went on to propose that the old lady might be brought from Edinburgh for a spell to keep her daughter company.

Within hours of James Cowan's departure - and before, of course, old Mrs Taylor had time to make the journey to Glasgow - Mary Jane suffered yet another attack. Sometime around midnight Catherine Lattimer was disturbed once again, this time by loud screaming, and when she hurried upstairs she found Pritchard already in attendance at his wife's bedside. He had administered chloroform but Mary Jane remained in an agitated state. 'Go for another doctor, Mary,' she urged Mary McLeod who was at her bedside. 'Be sure to go. Fetch Dr Gairdner.' Duly summoned from his home at Blythswood Square, when William Gairdner, Professor of Medicine at Glasgow University, arrived at the Pritchards' residence it didn't take him long to determine that his patient was under the influence of alcohol, the result, so he was told, of champagne dispensed by her husband in accordance with Dr Cowan's instructions. Mary Jane was not too far gone, however, to recognise the professor as a former classmate of her brother, Dr Michael Taylor of Penrith, but, even so, her anxiety remained intense and her mood volatile. When Gairdner turned his back, intending to warm his hands at the fire prior to examining her, she appeared to panic, crying out 'Don't leave me!' and her distress similarly resurfaced on any subsequent occasion that he made to step away from her bedside.

We might wonder what Gairdner made of Mary Jane's outburst when she turned to her husband and snapped, 'Don't cry, you hypocrite. If you cry, it was you that did it.' Could her words be attributed simply to the ravings of a sick woman, her mind befuddled by drink? Or did Gairdner entertain a niggling suspicion that there was possibly a bit more to it? Whatever his private thoughts, the professor restricted his advice to urging the patient's husband to avoid at all costs administering any further stimulants. (Conveniently, of course, Pritchard was able to lay the blame for this at Dr Cowan's door.) Having done what he could, Gairdner vanished into the night, saying he would return during daytime. By the time that he reappeared in the early afternoon Mary Jane's condition appeared to have stabilised somewhat, though the spasms that racked her body had not ceased altogether. The best that the professor could do now was to reiterate his advice regarding medication and - in marked contrast to Cowan's instructions - recommend that the patient be kept on a fairly bland diet of bread and milk with perhaps the occasional addition of a boiled egg. His work complete, there was nothing more for Gairdner to do but depart but his concerns were sufficiently strong for him to make contact with Mary Jane's brother in Cumberland and voice his reservations about the treatment his sister was receiving, suggesting in the same letter that she might benefit from spending time in her brother's home. On receiving Gairdner's letter, Michael Taylor duly wrote to his brother-in-law in Glasgow, offering to accommodate his sister, but all to no avail. Pritchard's reply, when it came, informed the Penrith physician that Mary Jane was not up to making the journey.

The very day after Professor Gairdner's visit Mary Jane's mother arrived from Edinburgh, a sprightly seventy-year-old who quickly got down to the task of caring for her daughter. Jane Taylor was a natural and efficient organiser and such was her level of vigilance that the two women immediately formed the habit of taking their meals together and, in order to provide round-the-clock care, the old lady and her daughter even shared a bedroom. Dr Pritchard slept separately. For a time, all went smoothly but, just as the invalid was starting to show encouraging signs of improvement, things took an unexpected turn. It began innocently enough when, to the delight of her mother, Mary Jane declared that her appetite had returned and she expressed a particular desire for some tapioca pudding. Her young son, Kenneth, was dispatched to purchase the article in question from the nearby grocery store of Burton and Henderson which, on his return, he placed on a table in the lobby, just outside Dr Pritchard's consulting room, where it remained sitting for the next half an hour or so before being taken up to be prepared by the cook. But, such being the whims of the sick, in the event Mary Jane found her tapioca pudding 'rather tasteless' and she changed her mind at the last moment, so, in preference to allowing the food to go to waste, she passed the plate over to her mother. No sooner had the old lady finished eating, however, than she became conscious of an unpleasant queasiness, the forerunner of much worse to come when some time later she was racked by a bout of vomiting and became violently ill. Once the worst of the sickness had passed and her stomach began to settle, Mrs Taylor found herself musing that whatever disorder she had been smitten by was very possibly one and the same as had recently afflicted her daughter. The old lady could scarcely have known just how accurate her instincts would prove to be.

But that wasn't the end of the matter. Rather than picking up, Jane Taylor's health dipped further in the days to come. A week or so after the old lady's first bout of illness, Catherine Lattimer left Pritchard's household staff after ten years' service ('too old' as the doctor bluntly put it) but that didn't mean that she vanished from the scene entirely. She returned periodically to Sauchiehall Street where she visited her former mistress and accompanied the children on various short outings. On the particular occasion when she arrived on Friday 24 February, it struck Catherine that old Mrs Taylor appeared utterly drained but she put her exhaustion down to the strain of nursing her daughter, the cause of whose condition remained no clearer. 'I don't understand her illness,' the old lady told Catherine. 'She is one day better and two worse.' Around nine o'clock that same evening Mrs Taylor went upstairs to check on her daughter and a short time later the servants' bell in the kitchen rang out. When Mary McLeod climbed the stairs in response, she found the old woman doubled over, retching and distressed. As she hurried back downstairs to fetch hot water, Mary encountered Pritchard and took the opportunity to tell him of Mrs Taylor's illness but he replied to the effect that he was not in a position to attend straight away as he was currently engaged in consultation with a patient. When some time later he did finally arrive upstairs, Prichard found his mother-in-law seated on a chair, apparently unconscious with her head lolling forwards over her breast. Her daughter was desperately rubbing her hand, saying repeatedly 'Mother, dear mother, can you not speak to me?', but all attempts to rouse Mrs Taylor appeared unavailing. When the new cook, Mary Patterson, placed her hand on the old woman's brow she found it cold. For whatever reason, Pritchard decided at this point to call on the assistance of a fellow medical practitioner, Dr James Paterson, who lived only a few minutes away. 'Edward, can you do nothing yourself?' implored his distraught wife. 'No,' came the callous response. 'What can I do for a dead woman? Can I recall life?' It was an odd reaction, to say the least, since at the time Mrs Taylor was still breathing.

It seems almost certain that for some considerable time now there must have been talk in the local area as gossip percolated out from the servants' quarters at 131 Sauchiehall Street into the wider community beyond. What with Dr Pritchard's taking responsibility for his wife's solitary meals, a clear connection between eating and illness had not gone unnoticed, not to mention Mary Jane's startling outburst that she directed at her husband - 'If you cry, you are a hypocrite!' - which must surely have provided Dr Gairdner with considerable food for thought. By the time of her mother's collapse, suspicion must surely have been rife but it would have been heightened yet further, we may be certain, had Pritchard's recent purchase history come to light. What had not yet become known was that, at regular intervals throughout the preceding months, the doctor had been stocking up on such life-threatening substances as antimony - a highly poisonous metallic element - and aconite - a vegetable toxin luridly dubbed the 'Queen of all Poisons' - until, ounce by ounce, he had amassed an extensive store of poisons - more, it was suggested, than the rest of Glasgow's doctors combined. In such frankly dubious circumstances, we might be puzzled that Pritchard chose to involve another doctor, James Paterson, following his mother-in-law's collapse. Perhaps by this stage in proceedings his state of mind was such that he felt himself completely invulnerable.

It did not take Paterson long to smell a rat. When he arrived around eleven o'clock, Pritchard took him to one side and laid out his version of the circumstances surrounding his mother-in-law's collapse, recounting how he had witnessed her drinking at suppertime in the company of her daughter (a not infrequent occurrence, he was careful to let slip) and how both had subsequently been sick, attributing their illness at the time to the unusually bitter taste of their beer. Sometime later, Pritchard went on, Mrs Taylor had been in the act of writing a letter when she slumped suddenly from her chair and required to be carried upstairs and put to bed in her daughter's room. Just how much credibility Dr Paterson placed in Pritchard's account of events - in point of fact, a total fabrication - it is impossible to say. On entering the bedroom, Paterson was presented with what must surely have been a fairly startling tableau. Lying unconscious on the bed, Jane Taylor was still fully dressed - wearing, he later recalled, a cap adorned with an artificial flower, while, underneath the covers alongside, her daughter, Mary Jane, looked strained and haggard, her face - by his account - 'thin and white' and her hair 'dishevelled'. On examining the old lady, Paterson formed the opinion that, while her health appeared generally sound, her breathing was slow and laboured and her pulse barely discernible. Gently prising her eyelids apart, he noticed immediately that the pupils appeared very much contracted, leading him to suggest to Pritchard that she might be under the influence of some kind of narcotic - opium, perhaps, which Mrs Taylor was, in fact, in the habit of taking to alleviate the pain of headaches in the form of a product known as Battley's Sedative Solution. Death, Paterson felt certain, was not far off. Rather than do nothing, however, he suggested applying mustard poultices and administering an enema. Pritchard indicated that Mrs Taylor had suffered similar attacks previously, though never as severe as at present, and, noticing that his mother-in-law had briefly recovered a degree of consciousness, he patted her on the shoulder with apparent affection while uttering the comforting words, 'You are getting better, darling.' Paterson, by contrast, was under no illusions about the old lady's prospects, believing more realistically that her case was 'utterly hopeless'. As if to confirm his fears, Mrs Taylor vomited up a quantity of 'frothy mucus' before lapsing again into unconsciousness. Unable to see how he could be of further assistance, Paterson left Pritchard's residence at around half past eleven and, as he made his way home along Sauchiehall Street, found himself pondering Mary Jane Pritchard's strange appearance. Based on his observations, he was of the opinion that she might well be suffering from the effects of antimony poisoning.

As he returned to his home in Windsor Place, Paterson's involvement in the matter had not yet ended. An hour after midnight he was awakened when Mary McLeod arrived at his front door with a request from Pritchard that he return once again to attend to Mrs Taylor. On this occasion, however, Paterson opted to stay put, believing that he could have no bearing on the inevitable outcome, but he did ask Mary to convey the message back that if Pritchard deemed his presence essential, he should send another message. In the event, Paterson heard nothing more and we must assume that he settled down for the night, untroubled by his conscience. Meanwhile, back at 131 Sauchiehall Street, Mrs Taylor's condition steadily deteriorated until, at some point during the early hours, her son-in-law emerged from her room with the news that the old lady had breathed her last. When the cook, Mary Patterson, entered the bedroom, she was met with the harrowing sight of Mary Jane kneeling on the bed, frantically rubbing her dead mother's hands and apparently incapable of accepting that she was irretrievably gone. The death certificate, completed by Pritchard himself (after Dr Paterson had declined to carry out the task) attributed his mother-in-law's demise to paralysis and apoplexy. The truth, as it would later emerge, was considerably different.

A few days after Jane Taylor's death, Pritchard happened to encounter James Paterson on Sauchiehall Street and he took the opportunity to ask if he might call on his wife the following day while he himself was out of town while attending his mother-in-law's funeral at Edinburgh (a lucrative visit, it emerged, when he learned that his wife had benefited from her mother's estate to the tune of £1,700 - nearly £200,000 today).

When Paterson duly arrived at Sauchiehall Street the following forenoon, he found Mary Jane in bed and, in an effort to visualise the overall picture, he set about questioning her concerning both her own but also her late mother's symptoms. In response to what he heard, he recommended that she restrict her diet to small quantities of mild and easily digestible foods, taken at regular intervals, with occasional sips of champagne or brandy to act as a tonic, and small pieces of ice to ease her persistent, raging thirst. For understandable reasons, Mary Jane remained deeply saddened by her mother's recent death and she asked whether Paterson had believed that Mrs Taylor was dying when he first saw her. His reply was unequivocal: that, yes, he had indeed formed this opinion and had straight away informed Mary Jane's husband, a response which prompted her to dissolve in tears while uttering the words - 'Good God, is it possible?' We can only speculate on what direction her thoughts had led her in. She did not elaborate further.

And if - as seemed to be the case - Mary Jane entertained suspicions about her husband, it is hard to imagine that the servants in the house could have been totally oblivious. When she invited Mary McLeod to taste a piece of cheese which Pritchard had sent up for her supper, the housemaid immediately experienced a burning sensation in her throat and, after she had eaten some of the leftovers the following morning, Mary Patterson became so unwell that she was forced to return to bed. On another occasion when Pritchard instructed the cook to put together some egg flip for his wife - an invigorating drink consisting of eggs, sugar and brandy - it did not escape her notice that he was careful to add the sugar himself. Before delivering it to her mistress, the cook risked a sip or two and commented to Mary McLeod about its bitter, unpleasant taste. She became sick shortly after and took several hours to recover. On drinking the egg flip, Mary Jane too experienced an adverse reaction and was forced to endure a restless night as a result. For the two servants, making the obvious connection must surely have been hard to avoid - all the more so after the cook spotted Pritchard visiting his consulting room immediately prior to contributing his 'sugar' to Mary Jane's drink. The fact that Mary Patterson remained silent is a reflection less of her suspicions, perhaps, than of the lowly position that her servant class occupied in nineteenth-century society. For her part, Mary McLeod had other reasons for keeping mum as would be revealed in due course.

A few days after returning from Edinburgh, Pritchard called on Dr Paterson to inform him of what he described as encouraging developments. Though Mary Jane remained weak, he reported, she had responded well to Paterson's suggested treatment and was now, as a result, a good deal more comfortable. It took less than a fortnight, however, for the story to change. Once again Pritchard visited Paterson's home to ask him to call on his wife but, when he arrived around eight o'clock that evening, the doctor was shocked by what he saw. Sitting up in bed, supported by pillows, Mary Jane recognised him and managed to muster a weak smile but Paterson could not help noticing 'a peculiarly wild expression' on her face. Her eyes, he observed, were 'fiery red and sunken' and her cheeks 'hollow, sharp [and] pinched-looking.' Examining her tongue, he found it badly discoloured and, most worryingly of all, her pulse had grown 'weak and exceedingly rapid.' In an effort to ease her unbearable thirst, Pritchard passed his wife a glass of water, adding solicitously as he did so, 'Here is some nice, cold water, darling.' When Paterson expressed alarm at the deterioration in Mary Jane's condition, Pritchard told him that, although she had not slept for several nights, she had nonetheless been strong enough the day before to spend time playing with her children. In an effort to ease the sick woman's distress, Paterson prescribed a solution of medicines that included morphine, to be repeated after four hours if required, and, that done, he departed for home.

In the event, Mary Jane experienced no improvement but, on the contrary, her condition slipped steadily downhill. Sometime after Paterson's departure, Pritchard prepared himself for bed, changing into his night-clothes before settling down alongside his wife. As a precaution, the decision was taken that the maid, Mary McLeod, would sleep on a couch in the same room in case any crisis should arise during the hours of darkness. It was, as it turned out, a prophetic move. At around one o'clock in the morning Mary Jane wakened her husband, saying 'Edward, don't sleep. I feel very faint.' Mary McLeod was dispatched to rouse the cook, Mary Patterson, who quickly made up a mustard poultice which was applied to the sick woman's stomach. Unfortunately, it afforded no relief. When Mary Patterson brought a second poultice into the bedroom, she was aware immediately that it was too late. A bizarre exchange then ensued. Drawing up his wife's nightdress, Pritchard instructed the cook to apply the second poultice. 'There's no use putting mustard on a dead body,' Mary told him bluntly. 'Is she dead, Patterson?' asked Pritchard. 'Doctor,' she replied, 'you should know that better than I.' Unconvinced, Pritchard sent Mary McLeod to fetch hot water but, once again, Mary Patterson pointed out to him the futility of the exercise. At this, reality appeared to sink in at last and Pritchard gave the impression of unravelling completely, sobbing, 'Come back, come back, my darling Mary Jane. Do not leave your dear Edward!' What came next was stranger still. 'What a brute! What a heathen!' he cried out before instructing Mary Patterson - in all apparent sincerity - to fetch a rifle and shoot him. To her credit, the cook remained level-headed. 'Don't provoke the Almighty with such expressions,' she told Pritchard. 'If God were to shut your mouth and mine, I don't know how we would be prepared to stand before a righteous God.' 'True, Patterson,' came his chastened response. 'You are the wisest and kindest woman I ever saw.' Oddly enough, a few hours later the distraught husband had pulled himself together sufficiently to attend to correspondence from the Clydesdale Bank in relation to his heavily overdrawn account.

Back at Windsor Place, Dr Paterson knew nothing of the night's events until he was awakened from sleep at around one o'clock when his doorbell rang. On the doorstep he found a breathless young man who blurted out a request for his attendance at 131 Sauchiehall Street as the mistress of the house, the boy reported, was very ill and thought to be close to death. Just as Paterson was in the act of dressing, his door bell was rung a second time, on this occasion by a girl who had been sent to relay the updated message that Mary Jane Pritchard had already departed this life and, thus, the doctor's presence was now no longer required. By his own account, Paterson would never again enter Edward Pritchard's home. At the end of the day, his role in the Pritchard case is a puzzling one which raises several unanswered questions - why, in particular, he failed to communicate to the authorities any inkling of his suspicions of antimony poisoning. Facing a barrage of adverse publicity later, he had no shortage of explanations: that to do so 'was not [his] duty'; that 'there was another doctor in the house'; put bluntly, that 'it was none of [his] business'; and - most oddly of all - that to report his suspicions would amount to 'a breach of the etiquette of [his] profession.' There were a great many, however, who took the alternative view that the preservation of life might have ranked rather higher in a medical man's list of priorities than mere professional loyalty.

Two days after Mary Jane's passing, on Monday 20 March, Pritchard completed her death certificate which specified gastric fever of two months' duration as the cause of her death. He then proceeded to accompany her body by train to Edinburgh for the purpose of organising her burial alongside her mother in the Grange Cemetery. Prior to the burial a strange little scene unfolded. At his parents-in-laws' home Pritchard requested that the coffin lid be unscrewed to permit his wife's relatives to take their final farewell and took advantage of the opportunity thus afforded to step forward himself and ostentatiously kiss his dead wife on the lips. On the train back to Glasgow, however, his sadness at her passing was not sufficiently overpowering to prevent him from donating a photograph of himself to a bemused fellow-passenger with whom he happened to have fallen into conversation. What he was unaware of at the time was that, the self-same morning as his journey to Edinburgh, an anonymous handwritten note had been received at the offices of Glasgow's Procurator Fiscal service which read as follows: *Dr Pritchard's mother-in-law died suddenly and unexpectedly about three weeks ago in his house in Sauchiehall Street, Glasgow, under circumstances at least very suspicious. His wife died today also suddenly and unexpectedly and under circumstances equally suspicious. We think it right to draw your attention to the above as the proper person to take action in the matter and see justice done.* The letter was concluded with the words 'Love of Justice', written in Latin. When its existence became known, it was widely believed to bear the hallmark of Dr James Paterson, though the gentleman in question was vehement in his denial that he had had any hand in the matter. Whether or not, the anonymous note was taken sufficiently seriously by the authorities for Pritchard, on his return from Edinburgh, to be intercepted on the platform at Queen Street railway station where he was placed under arrest by Superintendent Alexander McCall of the Glasgow police (the same officer who went on to arrest Greatrex a year later!) on suspicion of having been involved in the death of his wife. When word of his apprehension came out, many of those who knew him, including his in-laws, were unshakeable in their conviction that he was innocent and, while he was awaiting trial in the North Prison, those of his friends who visited made a point of leaving their calling cards.

An early police priority was to conduct a thorough search at 131 Sauchiehall Street, during the course of which a number of items of potential interest were seized, including various bottles and their contents as well as articles of clothing and bed linen with which Mary Jane was known to have been in close contact in the days immediately prior to her death. It did not take long for Pritchard's relationship with Mary McLeod to come under close scrutiny when she too was apprehended and quizzed by Sheriff Alison who was quick to dismiss any notion that the housemaid was implicated in any way in the murder of her mistress. When an examination of the accounts of local druggists was carried out - Murdoch Brothers and the Glasgow Apothecaries' Company in particular - things looked bad for Pritchard when his regular purchases of tartarised antimony, aconite and other poisons came to light: a far greater quantity, it was clear, than would normally be required for routine medical practice. Not surprisingly, the authorities were sufficiently suspicious that, when Mary Jane Pritchard was laid to rest on 22 March, samples of her body were required to be retained for subsequent chemical analysis. By the time that Pritchard appeared before Sir Archibald Alison, Sheriff of Lanarkshire, he had enlisted the services of lawyers, Galbraith and Maclay, to represent him and, ostensibly unruffled, he declared himself innocent of his wife's murder. Inevitably, his court appearance provoked an outburst of wild speculation and a plethora of sensational theories featured almost daily in the press but at this stage in proceedings public opinion remained largely in Pritchard's favour and those who took a different view were still in the minority. It didn't take long, however, for the tide to turn. Support quickly evaporated when the results of the chemical analysis of Mary Jane's body became known, revealing as they did intolerably high levels of antimony throughout her system. It didn't take long for a connection to be made with the death of her mother, only a few weeks earlier, and a warrant was duly issued for the exhumation of Jane Taylor's body from Grange Cemetery. Tests indicated similarly dangerous levels of antimony to those recently detected in her daughter's body and Edward Pritchard soon found himself facing charges on, not one, but two counts of murder.

In spite of the gravity of the situation in which he found himself, Pritchard remained notably calm during his early captivity, devoting part of each day to prayer. He went to considerable lengths to create a positive impression, hoping, we might suspect, to raise doubts that someone so devout and refined could possibly be responsible for the crime of double-murder - a line of defence his counsel would pursue during the course of his forthcoming trial. He chatted to visitors with every appearance of optimism about his plans to emigrate with his children and establish a new life overseas. His old vanity, however, bubbled to the surface when he voiced displeasure that no 'pomatum' - scented hair-oil - had been made available in the North Prison to assist in his personal grooming. Most likely it was his whiskers that were thus deprived, the hair on his crown being decidedly sparse. On Tuesday 26 June he was escorted by train from Glasgow to Edinburgh where he was accommodated in Calton Jail and delighted in showing the warders photographs of his family, identifying each individual by name. On the day of his trial - Monday 3 July - such was the level of public interest that his case had generated that the courtroom quickly filled to capacity and a substantial number of would-be spectators had to be turned away.

At ten o'clock Pritchard appeared before three judges, the most senior being John Inglis, Lord Glencorse. By special arrangement, the accused's brother was permitted to sit alongside him, a position he continued to occupy throughout most of the trial. When the charge of murder was read out, Pritchard replied with a firm 'Not guilty.' Taking the lead for the prosecution, the Solicitor General, George Young, based his case on the fact that, although no 'direct act' of poisoning could be attributed to the accused, there was no doubt that he had 'the means, opportunity and skill' to use poison to dispose of his wife and mother-in-law, on top of which his blatant dishonesty in registering their deaths hinted strongly at his guilt. Throughout most of the prosecution's three-day pitch Pritchard retained what looked like perfect composure but when the time came for his teenage housemaid, Mary McLeod, to face questioning under oath he was obliged to endure what were almost certainly his most uneasy moments.

From the witness-box, Mary confirmed that she had entered Dr Pritchard's service two years earlier, on Whitsunday 1863, when she was still only fourteen years old. When questioned about her relationship with her employer, Mary straight away showed signs of anxiety, frequently hesitating for long periods and replying at times with what looked like painful reluctance. Yes, she finally admitted, her mistress had caught Dr Pritchard in the act of kissing her in the bedroom but a good deal worse was to follow. During the course of their relationship, Mary told the court, she had become pregnant but before she was able to reach her full-term she had suffered a miscarriage. (At this point in proceedings the prosecution sought leave to ascertain whether Pritchard might have had any hand in the termination of the pregnancy but permission from the bench was not forthcoming.) Mary's miscarriage, however traumatic, did not put an end to her employer's attentions and he continued to lavish on her gifts of jewellery, including a ring, and - to no-one's surprise - photographs of himself. And if all that wasn't damning enough, near the close of her evidence Mary dropped an effective bombshell when she recounted, with unmistakable reluctance, how her employer had promised to marry her in the event of his wife's death. Shortly after Mary's testimony, Pritchard grew emotional as he watched from the dock while his daughter and son, aged fourteen and eleven respectively, described the happy relations that existed between their parents but whether his tears would be sufficient to claw back any lost ground remained at this stage to be seen.

Andrew Rutherfurd-Clark, defending, relied heavily on his client's education and social position and attempted to divert the blame for Mary Jane's death on to Mary McLeod - a fairly desperate line of argument, it might seem, which provoked a degree of censure from some quarters. As Pritchard openly wept, he went on to moot the possibility that his mother-in-law, Jane Taylor, might well have died as the result of an inadvertent, self-administered overdose but, significantly perhaps, he called upon no witness who was prepared to attest to his client's good character and, in marked contrast to the first three days of the trial which were fully taken up by submissions on behalf of the prosecution, the entire case for the defence was wound up by midday of the fourth day. On the fifth and final day of the trial the jury retired to consider its verdict but its members took no more than an hour to return to court where the outcome of their deliberations was delivered by their foreman, George Sim. 'The jury,' he announced, 'unanimously find the prisoner guilty of both charges as libelled.'

On learning the decision of the jury, initially Pritchard displayed no emotion, his only outward reaction to clasp his hands together. A few moments later, however, once the verdict had sunk in, he was seen to totter to one side and was obliged to lean for support on the shoulder of a nearby policeman. Only after being provided with a glass of water did he succeed in recovering his composure. During sentencing, Lord Glencorse addressed Pritchard directly, stating that the evidence by which he had been convicted 'leaves in the minds of no reasonable being the slightest doubt of your guilt.' He went on to urge him to repent of his crimes while Pritchard, standing upright in the dock, bowed from time to time as though to express his agreement. The judge then donned the traditional black cap prior to pronouncing sentence of death. The convicted man, he stated, would be returned to Calton Jail before being transferred under guard to prison in Glasgow where he would be fed 'on bread and water alone' until some three weeks hence when, between eight and ten o'clock on the forenoon of Friday 28 July, he would 'be taken furth of the said prison to the common place of execution of the burgh of Glasgow ... and there, by the hands of the common executioner, be hanged by the neck upon a gibbet until he be dead.' Before being led from the court, Pritchard once again bowed to the bench and also to the jury.

Back in Glasgow, the condemned man received a number of visitors in his cell in the North Prison including his brother, sister and his eldest daughter, Jane Frances, as well as his minister, Rev. Richard Oldham of St Mary's Episcopal Church, to whom he offered the first of the three confessions that he made during his final weeks. In it he admitted to the murder of his wife - carried out, he stated, through an overdose of chloroform - and went on to maintain that Mary McLeod had been present at the time and had been well aware all along that the meals she served up to her mistress had been laced with poison. His story changed somewhat by the time of the second confession, made some days later in the presence of other visiting clergymen, in which he claimed that during his relationship with Mary McLeod he had been 'living in a species of madness.' He went on to confess that, when she became pregnant, he had been instrumental in inducing a miscarriage. Once again, he acknowledged responsibility for the death of his wife but he remained resolute in his insistence that his mother-in-law had died as a result of a self-administered overdose of opium. In his third and final written confession, however, made just over a week later, Pritchard changed his tune yet again and appeared to come clean at last when he retracted his former allegation that Mary McLeod had been party to his crimes and, in words of high drama, finally admitted to the murder of his mother-in-law, Jane Taylor. The best explanation he could offer for his conduct was

- once again - a 'terrible madness' which had been exacerbated by his use of 'ardent spirits'. But, typical of the man, he left a significant loose end hanging: of the death of Elizabeth McGirn, mysteriously burned to a cinder in her attic bedroom two years previously, he made not a mention. Released to the press for publication, Pritchard's second and third statements were eagerly pored over by the reading public but his earliest confession was disregarded as not being sufficiently reliable to appear in the newspapers.

On Thursday 27 July Pritchard was moved from the North to the South Prison for more convenient access to Glasgow Green where his execution would be carried out. During his final 24 hours, he was said to have remained calm, sitting up late in the tiny condemned cell - a mere twelve feet by nine - and occupying himself with reading from the Bible in the company of the prison chaplain, Rev. Doran, and composing a number of farewell letters. Writing to Michael Taylor in Penrith, he predicted somewhat optimistically that 'Mary Jane, Darling Mother, and you, I will meet in happier circumstances', but how his letter was received by the murdered woman's brother is not on record. In relation to his forthcoming salvation Pritchard expressed similar confidence and declared himself ready to die - a fate which he now accepted, apparently, as no more than his just desserts. During the hours of darkness, while the condemned man presumably engaged in his final earthly slumbers, a crowd began to gather behind specially erected barriers on Glasgow Green, reserving their places for the morbid spectacle to come: 'the dregs of the very lowest classes', reported one sniffy commentator at the time - 'drunkards, thieves and vagabonds.' During the early hours the first appearance of the scaffold created a ripple of sensation and its subsequent erection was followed with close interest. There was a tangible shudder as the fatal rope was attached to the crossbeam and adjusted to the correct length to ensure - it was hoped - the rapid death of the victim. Clearly within view at the foot of the gallows, a plain, black coffin awaited the moment when it would be called into service.

As daylight steadily thickened the crowd grew more and more dense until an estimated 80,000 to 100,000 spectators jostled and rubbed shoulders in the Jail Yard and on the Green where they were addressed by a number of ministers and lay preachers - including, it is recorded, John Henry Greatrex. Others mingled among the crowds, sporting large boards bearing religious texts. Around half past seven the focus of attention turned to Calcraft, known as a bit of a bungler, who appeared on the scaffold with a faded rose in his buttonhole to be greeted with cheers and catcalls as he checked over his equipment to verify that all was in proper working order. As for the condemned man himself, after passing a peaceful night Pritchard was roused at half-past five and, despite appearing calm and resigned to his fate, for entirely understandable reasons displayed little appetite for food. Dressed in a black suit of mourning, he was visited in his cell by the prison governor, John Stirling, and three clergymen, including Rev. Oldham, who during the course of their discussions were successful in dissuading him from carrying out his intention of addressing the crowd from the scaffold. Shortly afterwards he was escorted by police officers to the courtroom where he was required to appear before city magistrates who inquired of him whether there was anything that he wished to say. 'I acknowledge the justice of the sentence,' Pritchard replied quietly before bowing to the bench. The protocol thus complete, all that was left now was for the magistrates to process to the gallows with the condemned man following on behind and the hangman bringing up the rear.

Near-silence descended as Prichard, outwardly calm at least, mounted the steps leading up to the scaffold. Approaching the drop, he was seen to stumble a little but quickly righted himself. At the forefront of the crowd one of those preaching was John Henry Greatrex who, in a sweeping, theatrical gesture, indicated the condemned man and thundered, 'Unless ye take heed, so also shall ye perish!' (Given his imminent fall from grace, Greatrex might have done better to concentrate on keeping his own house in order.) Adopting a more measured tone, Rev. Oldham offered up a quiet prayer before stepping down from the gallows while Calcraft carried out the next stage of his duties in placing the customary hood over the prisoner's head and face, moving his long hair and beard to one side to ensure that the noose was positioned correctly around his neck, and binding his legs securely together. A few tense moments later the condemned man gave the signal that he was ready to die, the hangman released the trapdoor and the whole sorry spectacle reached its conclusion as Pritchard plunged from the scaffold and paid for his crimes with his life.

Unfortunately, not quite yet. There were many in the crowd who averted their eyes while others wept at the unedifying spectacle that proceeded to unfold before them. For, swinging in circles at the end of the rope, Pritchard's body trembled and convulsed for some two to three excruciating minutes until finally his suffering was brought to an end when Calcraft added his extra weight by pulling on his legs from beneath. For the next thirty minutes or so the dead man was left hanging before the executioner, to an accompaniment of hoots and jeers from the crowd, re-ascended the scaffold and lowered his body so clumsily that the bottom fell out of the coffin, making a speedy repair necessary. This done, a medical doctor was brought forward to certify that the hanged man was indeed completely dead before his body was removed to a vault beneath the courthouse. Here his hair and beard were to be shaved off to allow a plaster cast to be made, for study later by phrenologists whose theory it was that Pritchard's tendency toward criminality might be discerned - like Alan Mair's 22 years previously - from detailed examination of the size and shape of his head. Later that afternoon his remains were interred in the prison burial ground.

For the murderer, Edward Pritchard, death had not come swiftly or easily but, that said, it was nowhere near as long drawn-out as the cruel, lingering ends that he had inflicted upon both of his victims. For others closely related to the case, life, of course, went on: for his unfortunate children, rendered parentless in the most harrowing of circumstances, their surname forever tainted by notoriety; and for the young girl from the islands, Mary McLeod, the stain of whose association with Pritchard would, we might imagine, mark her out for much of the rest of her life. And there is a curious postscript which requires to be added in order to complete Dr Pritchard's story. Long after the events of 1865, a local contractor was engaged to lay a new pipeline at Glasgow's South Prison which happened to cut across the site of the jail's old burial ground. Beneath a stone marked simply 'P', labourers turned up a skeleton whose leather boots had, by some freak of nature, remained in the same serviceable condition as on the day many years before when their owner, Edward Pritchard, had gone to the gallows. The boots were duly salvaged by one of the workers and subsequently sold but whether they were acquired by a curio-hunter or simply as articles for everyday wear is now impossible to determine.

Today Pritchard's old home is caught up in a bustling stretch of Glasgow's city centre, tramped each day by hundreds, if not thousands, of pairs of feet. But just how many of the shoppers and commuters, locals and visitors, have any inkling of the tragic history of the building they are passing? Few if any, we might suspect, and, given the dark events that took place there, then it is possibly just as well.

Andrew Brown : January 1866

When the schooner, *Nymph*, left Montrose harbour on Wednesday 6 September 1865 weather conditions at sea seemed to offer the prospect of a calm and uneventful voyage to come. With a cargo of wooden flooring in the hold and London as their final destination, the boat's four crewmen were well aware that they had a lengthy journey ahead of them but for the present they were happy to take full advantage of the relaxing interlude afforded by the current benign conditions. For the first few hours of her trip the *Nymph* hugged the Angus coastline, straying no farther than a mile or so from land, and a favourable sidewind meant that the only task required of the crew was to maintain the vessel's steady southward course. As she prepared to round Red Head, a conspicuous promontory some eight miles from Montrose, seaman John Pert was guiding at the helm while his skipper, John Greig - whose father was part-owner of the ship - sat nearby, chatting with him about various everyday matters. The third crew member, an older man named Alexander Raeburn, was busy elsewhere, occupied in one of the cabins, while the fourth seaman, Andrew Brown, passed his time by strolling leisurely on deck whilst smoking his pipe. Like the captain, Brown was a sailor in his mid-twenties.

With no demands on his attention for the time being, Captain Greig succumbed to the temptation to stretch out full-length on the deck, directly behind the tiller, where presently he fell asleep. Meanwhile Alexander Raeburn busied himself with the task of making tea and, handing a cup to Pert, he took control of the tiller for a spell. Still half asleep, the skipper declined Raeburn's offer, saying, 'Let me lie a bit and I'll get tea after', but by and by the sound of his gentle snoring resumed. Pert moved away to drink his tea in the company of the ship's mate, Brown, but returned a few minutes later to take charge of the tiller, thus freeing Raeburn to attend to washing up the dishes. To all intents and purposes the scene aboard ship was one of friendly cooperation but, as would soon become clear, the companionable atmosphere was set not to last when, a few short moments later, tragedy descended on the *Nymph* like a bolt from the blue.

From his station at the tiller, the first that John Pert knew of anything amiss was when he heard the sound of a heavy thump, directly behind him, followed in quick succession by a second similar blow. Turning to investigate, what he saw shocked him to the core. A few feet away, the ship's mate, Andrew Brown, was wielding an axe high in the air as he prepared to strike down at the motionless body of John Greig, still lying on the self-same spot where seconds earlier he had been snoozing peacefully. 'The master's head,' Pert later recalled, was 'lying in two halves.' Quickly recovering himself, he lunged forward and tackled Brown, successfully wresting the axe from his grip, but not before it had plunged down on the captain's head for a third time. With a quick motion of his arm, Pert hurled the offending article overboard, out of harm's way - and just as well, as it transpired, when Brown told him, 'Jack, it's a good thing you caught the axe, or else you would have got the same.' There was more to come. 'I have another man to kill before I die,' Brown continued, striking himself violently on the chest with his clenched fist. He went on to ask Pert to lend him a knife but mercifully Pert had no such article to give and, to his intense relief, Brown allowed the subject to drop. The ship's mate then calmly took control of the tiller, ordering Pert and Raeburn to trim the sails and set a new east-north-easterly course. His intention, he told them, was to pay a final visit to his mother in Stonehaven. 'I have done the deed and will have to suffer for it,' he observed and, turning to Pert, inquired matter-of-factly, 'Will you come and see me hung?' Pert replied that he would not.

Half an hour or so later a schooner hove into view which Pert identified as the *Union*, another Montrose-based vessel. Spying an opportunity, Alexander Raeburn scrambled up the rigging and waved his hat back and forth in an effort to attract attention but Brown was having none of it. His response was swift and ruthless. 'If you don't come out o' that,' he warned Raeburn, 'I'll heave you over the side.' From time to time other ships came and went but Brown was adamant that he would not deviate from the course he had set, and the three men each took turns at the tiller. Shortly before midnight, off Inverbervie, Brown requested his shipmates' assistance in throwing the dead man's body overboard but both of them flatly refused. They did, however, consent to help with washing away the blood that lay puddled on the deck. Throughout most of this time Brown appeared calm on the surface but his shipmates became aware of growing signs of anxiety. Were it not for his mother, he told them, he would 'go over the side' right now and bring his life to an end. When Pert ventured to ask the reason behind his actions, Brown replied that there was 'an old grudge' between himself and the skipper that had now been settled. As time went on, increasingly his composure showed signs of cracking. 'Jock,' he told Pert, 'I am going stark mad.'

As the *Nymph* drew closer to Stonehaven, Brown's mood darkened yet further. 'Can you lend me a shilling?' he asked Pert. 'It will be the last ... I will give my mother.' As she closed in on the harbour, the schooner was boarded by the pilot - a local guide who was familiar with the intricacies of the final approach and who was, as it happened, Andrew Brown's uncle. Initially incredulous, the pilot's shock at hearing what had happened was profound. Unwilling perhaps to face up to the consequences of his actions, Brown dropped the anchor prematurely but, in the event, it failed to secure a grip on the seabed and finally, at around one o'clock in the morning, the *Nymph* berthed at Stonehaven - but not before Alexander Raeburn had leapt from the still-moving vessel and hotfooted it along the pier in the direction of the local police station. Pert followed his example soon after, leaving Brown and his uncle on board, but by the time that officers of the law arrived on the scene they found that their bird had flown.

It wasn't as though he'd be hard to trace. Sure enough, in line with his stated aim Brown turned up a short time later on his mother's doorstep in an agitated state and apparently the worse for alcohol. Straight away he threw his arms around her neck, crying, 'Oh mother, I did not know what I had done till the Lord opened my eyes. It was drink that did it all.' He handed her a sum of money, telling her that it would be the last she would ever receive from him. It came as no surprise when Sergeant John Gartly arrived half an hour or so later and Brown received him calmly. Laying a hand on his shoulder, the policeman cautioned him and read out the charge of murder. 'Oh, Sergeant, it's all right,' Brown responded. 'It canna be helped noo; let me bide a while wi' my mother.' That, the sergeant explained, was not a possibility and, after putting up what seemed like no more than a token resistance, the suspect permitted himself to be handcuffed and frogmarched to the local police station where he proved to be a fairly garrulous prisoner. His late skipper he described as 'a bad bugger' who had introduced him to 'bad houses' in London and he went on to claim that a recent statement made by his mother - that she possessed 'neither money nor clothes to wear' - had provoked him to commit the crime. (In what way Greig might have been connected with these matters remained unexplained.) Now, he concluded, he and the skipper were 'quits'. On the receiving end of Brown's ranting, Sergeant Gartly attempted to silence him, warning him that anything he said now might well be used against him at a future date. During the rest of the night he looked in on the prisoner's cell from time to time and, on each occasion, found him fast asleep.

It seems safe to assume that Brown's peaceful night was a reflection less of a clear conscience than of his recent alcoholic intake. When his case came to court in Edinburgh four months later it was probably no surprise that a major focus of the trial was the place that drink might have occupied in what looked like an apparently motiveless crime. Under scrutiny, Brown's allegation of 'an auld grudge' was quick to crumble when he admitted that the story had been a total fabrication. Called to the stand, John Greig, senior, recounted how, an hour or so before the *Nymph* was due to sail, he had seen Brown in Collie's public-house in Wharf Street, Montrose, in the company of other seafaring men, Pert and Raeburn among them. Conscious of time passing, his two shipmates had finished their drinks and made for the door but, when Brown showed no signs of following, Greig had stepped across to remind him that, if he didn't budge soon, he might very well miss the boat. Brown took the hint, he continued, and departed from Collie's with a bottle of whisky under his arm which the publican's wife, Marjory Collie, had asked him to pass to his skipper. Summing up, Greig stated that, based on Brown's previous record, he had found him a reliable worker and habitually 'very sober aboard the ship' but, that said, he went on to indicate a darker, more sinister side to his character, recounting how, on receipt of his August wages - three pounds, nineteen shillings and sixpence in total - Brown had embarked on a prolonged three-day binge, during the course of which he had acquired two black eyes and ultimately found himself behind bars.

Following Greig at the stand, the accused man's uncle - also Andrew Brown - stated at the outset that his nephew was not under normal circumstances a heavy drinker, but on those rare occasions when he did overindulge 'he would be controlled by nobody' and became 'very quarrelsome'. He went on to recall that when, in his capacity as harbour pilot, he had boarded the *Nymph* at Stonehaven he had formed the rather ambiguous impression that his nephew 'was not sober, but he did not appear to be drunk.' Brown's uncle completed his evidence by recounting an incident which he had witnessed aboard the schooner when his nephew retrieved a bottle from where it appeared to have been concealed between two water-casks and proceeded to gulp down its contents. When questioned, Brown had claimed to be drinking merely water, but when his uncle detected the aroma of whisky he was highly sceptical. His nephew, he said, had wasted no time in casting the empty bottle overboard, never to be seen again.

When their turn came to take the stand, Brown's two shipmates testified that, when he caught up with them aboard the *Nymph*, his condition had given them no cause for alarm. Though Raeburn had also been in Collie's public-house, the elderly seaman maintained that '[Brown] was not drunk'; while, Pert, for his part, 'never noticed the effects of drink on him.' Even at the time of his murderous assault, Pert insisted that Brown had not given any indication of being under the influence of alcohol, and at no subsequent point in the voyage did he suspect him of drinking surreptitiously. Next to give evidence, Sergeant Gartly told the court how Brown had confessed to having sneaked a bottle of whisky aboard the *Nymph* (in all probability the self-same bottle that the publican's wife had intended for Captain Greig) but had refused to admit that he had drunk its contents. When push came to shove, the evidence supplied by those men closest to Brown on Wednesday 6 September was at best equivocal, at times inconsistent, and ultimately it did little to settle the question of whether or not alcohol had been a determining factor in relation to his actions.

Another matter that had still to be considered, however, was Brown's history and family background. His sister, Elizabeth, provided the court with fresh insights into his past which, from the account she gave, added up to quite a sorry tale. She recounted how, as a child of eight or nine, her brother had suffered an accident in which he fell into a ship's hold, bumping his head badly, which resulted thereafter in frequent headaches and a general decline in his health. Although not fully recovered, he was obliged to start work at the age of fifteen or sixteen, earning his living at sea for a number of years until, in his early twenties, he was involved in a second accident aboard the schooner, *Braes o' Moray* of Aberdeen, during which he received a grievous blow to the head from a heavy block of wood. Afterwards his speech was adversely affected, Elizabeth recalled, and for a time he was unable even to recognise his mother or other members of his family. In an effort to find a cure, he elected to undergo surgery at the hands of two local doctors - one, at least, without qualifications - and, although Elizabeth did not witness the operation, she described for the court her distress when she 'heard him scream.' Unfortunately, the unpleasant procedure failed to produce the desired outcome, and for some eight or nine months afterwards Brown remained 'weak in mind and body' and unable to return to work. His family members were conscious of a marked change in his personality and where previously he had been 'of a cheerful disposition', he now became morose and took to spending much of his time alone. Elizabeth recalled that during conversation he appeared incapable of looking anyone in the eye.

The testimony of other witnesses ran along similar lines. A second sister of the accused, Margaret Brown, stated that, after the accident aboard the *Braes o' Moray*, her brother had become 'silly', while a former neighbour in Stonehaven recalled that Brown 'spoke a great deal of nonsense' and was 'queer'. A local fisherman, Alexander Mackie, was someone else who noticed his change in his personality, stating that 'when he took any drink he was very violent.' Mackie also observed what might be seen as signs of paranoia when Brown fell 'under the delusion that people were taking the advantage of him.' Various other witnesses noted that his mood had become uncharacteristically 'dumpish' - downcast and gloomy. At no point, of course, was Brown entitled to testify in his own defence - a right not granted to the accused until well into the twentieth century - and as proceedings wound up it fell to his counsel, James Badenoch Nicolson, to sum up for the defence. Nicolson addressed the members of the jury, directing their attention to the testimony of the preceding witnesses. While making no attempt to absolve Brown of responsibility for his skipper's death - he had, in truth, no alternative - the main thrust of Nicolson's argument was an assertion that, at the time of the fatal assault, his client had been 'labouring under insanity', a condition which he attributed to the head injury he had sustained some years before. Nicolson stressed to the jury that there had been no prior history of acrimony between the accused and Captain Greig, and 'had the prisoner not been labouring under delusion,' he argued, 'he would not have acted as he had done.' In a moving conclusion, he closed his address by referring specifically to his client's mother and sisters, appealing to the jury to spare their son and brother 'the shame and agony of an ignominious death.'

Not everyone, of course, was in agreement. From the bench, one of the two presiding judges, Lord Ardmillan, clarified for the benefit of the jury the legal definition of insanity which could not, he advised, be based simply on a violent or aggressive personality, on low moral standards or on the influence of alcohol on criminal behaviour, but solely on the effect of some species of mental disorder which 'dethroned the reason.' He invited the jury to consider Brown's competence in taking command of the *Nymph*, plus the lucid admissions of guilt he had made to Sergeant Gartly at Stonehaven and, the following day, to the Sheriff-Substitute of Kincardineshire who had no doubt at the time that the man addressing him was 'in his sound and sober senses.' It looked very much as though Ardmillan's arguments had struck home when, after withdrawing to consider their verdict, the members of the jury took less than an hour to reach agreement. Their decision was duly announced by their spokesman, James Sinclair. 'The jury unanimously find the prisoner, Andrew Brown, guilty as libelled,' Sinclair informed the court, 'while the minority of the jury add the recommendation of mercy to the Crown.' On receipt of the guilty verdict, Lord Ardmillan intimated that in such circumstances only one outcome could now be expected but, in order to allow the location of Brown's execution to be settled, that he would postpone formal sentencing until the following day. Throughout these proceedings, the prisoner reportedly displayed no emotion whatsoever.

The next morning, shortly after ten o'clock, Brown was led into a courtroom that was full to bursting. He took his seat calmly, apparently oblivious to the ongoing hubbub and seemingly blasé about what lay ahead. His sentence, of course, was a foregone conclusion, and once the bureaucratic formalities had been completed by the two law lords, Neaves and Ardmillan, the latter turned his attention to the man in the dock, telling him in no uncertain terms that he had been guilty of 'a shocking and atrocious murder' and effectively putting paid to any hopes that he might have entertained of a possible reprieve. Assuming the black cap, the judge announced to the court that on the last day of January 1866, between the hours of two and four o'clock in the afternoon, Andrew Brown would be hanged at Montrose - 'which is pronounced for doom,' Ardmillan added, 'and may the Lord have mercy on your soul.' What little time the prisoner had left - a matter of some three weeks - the judge advised him to devote to 'unburdening [his] conscience' and to study of religion. Brown, it was said, remained stolidly impassive throughout, his eyes downcast, and the impression he gave was of total detachment from his surroundings. It was noted, however, that his sisters, by contrast, broke down and wept pitifully. Early the following morning the condemned man was taken by train to Forfar where he was secured under lock and key in the County Jail.

During his first few days of captivity Brown's demeanour remained sullen and morose, but as time went on he started to relax a little and open up. From his conversation with prison staff it was evident that he was deeply attached to the seafaring life as he recounted a multitude of anecdotes from his past and details of the many and varied places he had visited. Unsurprisingly for a seaman, he was an attentive observer of the weather and expressed great sadness on learning of the loss of a number of mariners during recent storms and voiced his concern for the welfare of those still at sea, including specifically his old shipmates. Ministered to by a kindly prison chaplain, Rev. Harry Stuart - often, it was said, for hours at a time - and by Rev. Richard Waterston of the Free Church in Forfar, Brown's contrition and hope for divine forgiveness struck the two visiting clergymen as genuine and sincere. When referring to his crime, he insisted that his actions had been spurred neither by hatred nor revenge and he explained that his invention of 'an auld grudge' had resulted simply from pressure he had felt to come up with some kind of an explanation for his conduct. He had hoped, he said, that citing a plausible motive might 'gie him a better chance.' In one of his lower moments he confessed to Rev. Stuart that he had reached the stage of having no wish to prolong his life any further.

Brown's hopes, however, were to some extent rekindled when he learned of a petition that had been raised in the towns of Forfar and Montrose to be submitted to the Home Secretary in London, Sir George Grey, with the object of securing for him a commutation of sentence. In an area with a strong seafaring tradition, however, collecting signatures proved tricky and Brown's crime - committed, as it was, against a local skipper - was widely viewed as particularly heinous. When the reply from London arrived it indicated that, having reviewed all circumstances relating to the case, the Home Secretary had concluded that there were insufficient grounds to justify his intervention in the legal process. Conscious of the faith that Brown had placed in the possibility of the petition's success, the unenviable task of breaking the bad news to him fell to Rev. Stuart. With his hopes now dashed once and for all, the prisoner's reaction was initially one of shock but he soon grew calm again and gave the impression of being resigned to the inevitability of what lay ahead.

Two days before his execution was due to take place a painful encounter took place in Forfar jail when a small group of Brown's relatives, including his brother and one of his sisters, paid him their final visit. For understandable reasons it was an emotional occasion for all concerned - the condemned man not least - and the pathos of Brown's situation was palpable when he made a final request of his departing guests that they be kind to his mother in Stonehaven. Though unaccustomed to the act of writing, he occupied much of the following day in penning to her a farewell letter that amounted to some ten pages of foolscap, as well as composing a short account of his life (never subsequently published) and an open letter in which he professed sincere repentance for the crime he had committed. Published verbatim in the press, the letter ran as follows:

Forfar Prison, January the 30, 1866.

Before I leave this world, I desire to acknowledge the Justice of my sentence. As God hath said, who so sheddeth man's blood, by man shall his blood be shed. I am looking for mercy from God, through the blood of Christ alone. I ask the forgiveness of my Captain's friends, for the great loss and sorrow I have caused them, I never meant to say that I did it because I had a grudge at him, although I was tempted to say it. [At this point several words have been carefully obliterated with ink.] It came into my head all at once, like the shot of a gun; but it was no sooner done than I would have given all the world to have gotten him to live again, and I have sincerely grieved for him ever since. I wish to die in peace with all men; what I may have said about my shipmates at any time I ask their forgiveness, as I hope for pardon myself. I want to thank everybody for their kindness to me, especially the Governor of the prison; and to Mr Stewart the Chaplain for the trouble He has taken for my soul's welfare. I finish with the earnestest of my heart, that this death of mine will be a warning to all, And especially to seamen, To avoid drink and bad company, and to think more of another world.

Andrew Brown.

For a good many of its readers, Brown's poignant message bore the hallmark of heartfelt sincerity.

At precisely the same time as the prisoner was committing his final thoughts to paper, William Calcraft arrived from England on the midday train and was met on the platform at Montrose by a gaggle of onlookers, all eager to catch a glimpse of the notorious hangman. Only with some difficulty did Calcraft succeed in struggling through the crowd to where Police Superintendent Brownlee and two of his constables were waiting to escort him to the Eagle Inn where his overnight accommodation had been arranged. The hangman remained indoors for the rest of the day, never at any time venturing outside. Naturally, of course, by no means everyone in Montrose had a prurient interest in the forthcoming fate of Andrew Brown, and on the day of the hanging itself a number of the more 'genteel' townsfolk took up the Scottish North-Eastern Railway Company's offer of return tickets to any other station on the line. They were fearful, it was suggested, that the day's unsavoury spectacle would attract to Montrose mobs of 'the blackguardism of Edinburgh, Glasgow and Dundee.' It would be their town's first execution for more than forty years.

On the morning of his final day - 31 January 1866 - Brown was roused at the unholy hour of three o'clock to be briefed concerning arrangements for the day ahead. He was provided with a breakfast of tea and toast but, with no appetite for food, he left the toast untouched. An hour later he was taken by horse-drawn cab to Forfar railway station where a specially commissioned train awaited his arrival on the platform. Throughout the hour-long journey to Montrose he was silent and subdued, in no mood to appreciate the comfort of the first-class carriage in which he, Rev. Stuart and other officials had been accommodated. The only other passenger compartment - third-class, as it happened - was occupied by a group of police constables. When the train reached Montrose shortly after five o'clock, there were few spectators on the streets to witness the handcuffed prisoner's arrival and his immediate transfer into the custody of the burgh authorities. Accompanied by the prison chaplain, he was taken by cab to the local police station by a coachman who had been specifically instructed to steer clear of George Street where the gallows had been erected overnight. On his arrival, Brown entered the building via the back door. In addition to the town's regular officers, 150 special constables had been sworn in for the day, many on a voluntary basis.

As daylight dawned, the weather seemed to accord with the sombre occasion as steady drizzle fell from a leaden sky. Supplied on loan by the city authorities of Aberdeen, the scaffold had been assembled by torchlight in a location specifically chosen to afford the anticipated crowds of spectators a clear and unobstructed view. Throughout most of the forenoon the street remained relatively quiet, the weather perhaps discouraging attendance, and it was observed that far fewer visitors than expected had travelled to Montrose from the outlying areas of Angus and Mearns. As the appointed hour drew closer, however, the crowd swelled to an estimated 3,500 and it did not escape notice that members of the local seagoing community were present in considerable numbers. At the foot of the gallows, a vociferous lay-preacher had to be moved on by officers of the law but he promptly set up his wayside pulpit a short distance away and resumed his high-volume sermonising. Eventually, however, the weather prevailed where the authorities had failed, and the chances are that there were few in the crowd who felt short changed when the soggy evangelist packed up and departed during a particularly heavy shower.

Around half past one the first sign of activity was detected by the crowd when Calcraft appeared on the scaffold where he proceeded to carry out a number of checks and to test his equipment. Clocks were tolling the hour of two when the condemned man himself emerged from the police station, supported by Revs. Stuart and Waterston and flanked by a bevy of policemen, magistrates and other dignitaries. A hush descended on the crowd as they watched the line of men proceed across a wooden gangway, put in place to link the door of the police office with the foot of the gallows, and ascend the flight of twelve stairs that led up to the platform. Those onlookers who were familiar with Brown were shocked by the change in his appearance, and if they thought that he looked thinner, then their supposition was indeed accurate: the reality was that since his court appearance three weeks earlier he had lost an entire stone in weight. Once the group had assembled on top of the scaffold, a prayer was offered up by Rev. Stuart. It looked very much as though the final moment had arrived, but just as the hangman was about to place a white hood over the prisoner's face he spoke out loud and clear. 'Farewell, friends all,' the crowd heard him say. 'The blood of Jesus Christ cleanseth from all sin; the Lord Jesus receive my spirit.'

Shortly after the hood had been placed over Brown's head, there occurred a moment of real horror. Overcome by the occasion, a woman near the front of the crowd emitted a loud, unearthly wail which stretched out over a full minute, a painfully long time in an atmosphere of such tension. Believing that the cry had come from the prisoner himself, there were many in the crowd who felt a shiver run down their spine until, with palpable relief, they realised their mistake. Calcraft appeared unaffected and carried on with his business, adjusting the noose around the neck of the prisoner who meekly complied with the hangman's every instruction.

Once his preparations were complete, the executioner wasted no time in drawing back the bolt and straight away the condemned man plunged an estimated eighteen inches to two feet from the scaffold. Regrettably, death was not instantaneous and, as Brown's body circled slowly at the end of the rope, the crowd was subjected to the morbid spectacle of his agonised facial contortions, clearly visible through the thin cotton of the hood. There were many who averted their gaze. The prisoner hung suspended for three minutes or so until it was apparent that death had finally brought him release. For the best part of the next hour the body was left to hang in the presence of the crowd until Calcraft returned to the scene to cut it down from the gallows. Never a popular figure, the hangman was booed by the crowd and when cries of 'Down wi' him!' began to ring out, a cordon of policeman and special constables was formed to hold the crowd back. In the late afternoon the corpse of Andrew Brown was returned by train to Forfar where it was buried that same night within the precincts of the prison.

Even once the dust had settled, speculation persisted in the Montrose area in relation to the circumstances surrounding John Greig's death. During the court case it was stated more than once that the skipper of the Nymph was a man with whom Brown was on perfectly cordial terms and despite the fact that the law lords, Neaves and Ardmillan, took evidence for a full day, they failed nonetheless to get to grips with the prisoner's thinking or come up with a fully credible motive. In the aftermath of his execution, the story gained traction that Brown's crime had been spurred by his captain's refusal to return to land to enable him to procure alcohol, but, directly contravening his shipmates' evidence, it was not a version of events that stood up to scrutiny. During the course of the trial, various witnesses testified to the negative effect on Brown's personality of the head injuries he had sustained, but at the end of the day their evidence did not carry enough weight to convince the jury that the man in the dock was of unsound mind. Now, a century and a half on, the chances are that we might be more inclined than our forebears were to attribute Brown's actions to the after-effects of brain-damage which in September 1865 sparked an inexplicable moment of madness that he ultimately paid for with his life.

William McDonald : October 1878

In the early afternoon of Thursday 13 June 1878, a young St Andrews fisherman, George McDonald, was working by the seashore when he was alerted to the fact that something had gone badly wrong at his parents' home. Neighbours had heard a series of gunshots coming from inside the attic property, he was told, and one of them had run to fetch him. George hurried home and rushed upstairs as quickly as he could but when he arrived he found the door chained from the inside. He managed, however, to push it open sufficiently to allow him to crane his neck around the corner, and the scene that met his eyes was one that shocked him profoundly.

The history of tension between William McDonald and his wife, Helen, was no secret within the fishing community of St Andrews but it had not always been thus. Born in 1834, McDonald did not have the easiest start in life when his father, a labourer in the town, took his own life after steadily drinking himself into a state of grinding poverty. Probably in reaction to this, his son chose a radically different path, holding office for a time in the St Andrews branch of the Order of Good Templars - an ecumenical brotherhood committed to abstinence from alcohol - and he was known to be a faithful member of the Martyrs' Free Church congregation. Successful as a fisherman, it was clear that he was financially responsible and the chances are that he was viewed as a good catch when in 1858 he tied the knot with Helen Waters, the daughter of one of his associates, and settled down to married life at Shorehead, St Andrews. Initially the partnership appears to have been a happy and prosperous one, and over the next five years McDonald amassed a healthy bank balance as well as becoming the owner of two fishing boats, each worth an estimated £100. Even then, however, black clouds were looming and in the years that followed McDonald's downfall was nothing short of dramatic. His downward slide started when - for whatever reason - his wife, Helen, took to drinking heavily and he was unwise enough to follow her example. Naturally, the couple's savings quickly evaporated and, what was even worse, they piled up debts to the extent that they went in fear of imprisonment. The fact that the oldest of their children chose to leave home as soon as possible to fend for themselves seems likely to have been a reflection of household divisions. Be that as it may, the straw that appears to have finally broken the camel's back was when McDonald found himself unable to pay a fine he had incurred for the seemingly trivial offence of keeping a dog without a licence.

Around one o'clock in the afternoon of Thursday 13 June 1878 the McDonalds' downstairs neighbour, Christina Cross, heard the sound of cries coming from above, followed immediately afterwards by two gunshots. She hurried upstairs and, by peering through the crack between the door and the jamb, she was able to see William McDonald in the act of reloading his gun. Having seen him 'the worse of liquor' earlier that morning, naturally she was worried and cried out, 'Willie, do you know what you are doing?' to which McDonald replied brusquely that, yes, he did. Still anxious, she called out 'Helen!' twice but received no answer on either occasion. She therefore concluded that Helen McDonald must be away from home and that it had been the dog which had been shot, but when McDonald ordered her to leave and threatened to shoot her if she didn't obey, Christina became certain that something even more dreadful was taking place. She continued to watch through the narrow gap beside the door but when she saw McDonald thrusting a ramrod into the barrel of his gun, she made the wise decision to retreat and, as she was hurrying back down the stairs, she heard the sound of a third gunshot. When she gasped out what she had just witnessed another of the neighbours ran to the shore for McDonald's son, George.

The reason why George McDonald had left his parental home in the first place was because his father 'was given to a dram', his mother was fiery and quick-tempered and he knew perfectly well that she routinely drank to excess. She had recently suffered a number of seizures. Despite that, he was totally unprepared for the gruesome spectacle that awaited him behind his parents' door. Pushing it open as far as the chain would permit, what George saw first was his mother lying motionless on the floor with a 'shot bag' and 'powder flask' - items routinely used at the time for loading a gun - on top of a nearby cabinet. She appeared, he thought, to be dead. He placed his shoulder against the door and burst it open, thus opening up the sight of his father lying immobile to his mother's left side with a shotgun partially hidden beneath him. The butt of the firearm rested between his legs while the barrel was pointed directly up towards his head which was cradled in Helen's arms. The fact that he was barefoot attracted no attention, but the significance of this would become clear at a later date. George noticed traces of 'reek', the after-effect of gunfire, rising from the area of his father's chest where his clothing still appeared to be smouldering. By now various neighbours had congregated but George, still reeling from the shock, had no memory of speaking to anyone before he hurried from the scene, though William Cross, Christina's husband, remembered later that he had asked him to run for a doctor, even if it felt a bit like bolting the stable door. If George's memory of events was a little disjointed, then it was entirely forgivable: the depth of his shock and emotional turmoil must have been great. Following his departure, despite initial appearances McDonald showed signs of reviving and William Cross spoke to him, asking, 'In the name of God, what's done here?' According to Cross's recollection, the injured man replied, 'Let her lie, and let me go with her; she bade me do it.' He finished up by adding, 'It should have been done lang syne.'

A few hours earlier the situation was rather different as Helen McDonald was busily engaged in baiting fishing-lines for her husband while he, by contrast, was cosily ensconced not far away in a public-house. When she appeared at the door, asking him to leave, he was unwilling to budge and attempted to persuade her to come in and join him, but she refused and eventually left on her own. If the inn-keeper, Andrew King, was to be believed, there was no suggestion of drunkenness on McDonald's part and during his visit he consumed no more than a single glass of whisky. McDonald's downstairs neighbour, William Cross, had no more inkling of imminent catastrophe than the local publican when both McDonalds, William and Helen, paid him a visit shortly after midday. Cross judged that the couple appeared to be 'on good enough terms', but conceded nonetheless that one or two signs of strain were evident. Helen struck him as entirely sober though he could tell that McDonald had been drinking. When Helen asked her husband to accompany her home he flatly refused and, even though she persisted, he remained unshakeable until she had no option but to leave without him. Not long after this McDonald did get up and follow her upstairs and it was only a few moments later that the sound of gunfire was heard. But if William Cross and Andrew King had singularly failed to anticipate the day's tragic turn of events, one man who was possibly less surprised was Police Inspector William Stuart who over a fifteen-year period had been familiar with the McDonalds' tendency to squabble, often with sufficient ferocity that one would end up reporting the other to the police.

Arriving at the scene, Inspector Stuart's first priority was to take possession of the gun which, with laudable presence of mind, had been removed by William Cross to a place of safety. By the time that Dr Martin entered the house, around half-past one, McDonald had been helped into bed. During the course of his examination, Martin investigated a wound on the left side of the injured man's chest, immediately behind the burns in his clothing. Asked about how he had come by this injury, McDonald stated that he had been shot by his wife, then proceeded to mumble, not entirely coherently, about a pair of scissors and a length of string which she had used to turn the gun upon herself. He went on, however, to offer an alternative version of events, claiming this time that he and his wife had previously made a suicide pact whereby she would take her own life, following which he would immediately follow suit. The wounds he had sustained, he insisted, were the result of two separate unsuccessful attempts to kill himself. But, adding to the confusion, he offered a third explanation, stating that, of the three shots fired, blank cartridges had been responsible for two while his wife had fired the third, simultaneously killing herself and wounding him in the process. Taking a charitable view of matters, it would be understandable in the circumstances if McDonald had been left feeling a little disorientated but, having assessed his speech and manner, Dr Martin for one saw no reason to question his sanity. We may be confident, however, that the glaring inconsistencies in McDonald's various accounts would have been duly noted by Inspector Stuart. It was noticeable that not one of his explanations presented his wife's death as accidental.

If McDonald's recollection of the shooting was - to say the least - muddled, it was hoped that examination of the medical evidence would help to pin down what exactly had happened. As an early priority a post-mortem examination of Helen McDonald's body was conducted by Dr Martin in conjunction with Dr Archibald, also of St Andrews. During their investigation, the two men examined a large, open wound in the dead woman's stomach, one and a half inches long by two inches across, where 'shot' had entered between the ribs, causing damage to the chest area and resulting in a collapsed lung. The wound corresponded with the place where the victim's clothing had been holed, and the doctors concluded that the gun had been fired towards her in an upward direction with the muzzle some two and half to three feet from her left side. Their assessment was that her injuries had been inflicted while she was still alive, that death had been instantaneous, and that suicide could effectively be ruled out. Furthermore, pellets recovered from her body - known as 'duck shot' - were identical to those found in her husband's ammunition bag. In the meantime, McDonald had made his official declaration before Sheriff Beatson Bell but it added little to what was already known. He was 44 years of age, he stated, and had lived with his late wife, Helen McDonald née Waters, at Shorehead, St Andrews for a considerable number of years. When asked directly whether he had shot and killed her, he answered, 'I loaded a gun, but I did not shoot it. There was no murder at all.' Interrogated further as to the cause of his wife's death, his reply was blunt: 'I could answer that question quite well, but as the affair must come to a debate in the court, I prefer to reserve all that I have to say till the end.' To be sure, his decision to remain silent was a puzzling one when presumably he had been advised that he would receive no opportunity during his subsequent trial to speak in his own defence - a legal right that would not be extended to the accused in a Scottish courtroom for some time yet to come.

McDonald's trial took place at Perth Circuit Court over two days in early September. The judge was seventy-year-old Lord Mure. When asked to submit his plea, McDonald stated clearly, 'I am not guilty,' shaking his head as he spoke. The weight of evidence stacked up against him, however, looked formidable and his lawyer, George Omond, chose to focus first on the lack of premeditation or malice aforethought on the part of his client in relation to the death of his wife. He pointed out that the accused had made no effort to flee the scene and raised the possibility that the whole affair might have been based on nothing more than a tragic accident. Alternatively, he argued, the possibility that Helen had taken her own life in accordance with a suicide pact merited serious consideration. By securing the gun against an article of furniture, he suggested, it was possible for her to have used a length of string and a pair of scissors to assist her in pulling the trigger. If the men of the jury thought it all sounded rather desperate, then it probably was - a forlorn attempt at damage limitation which Omond hoped might just be enough to plant a seed of doubt in their minds. Claiming that the circumstances of the case were 'enveloped in doubt', he concluded the defence by suggesting that a verdict of not proven would be the most appropriate outcome. In the aftermath of the trial, however, many commentators believed that McDonald had been ill-served by his counsel on the grounds that some of the strongest arguments that might have been marshalled in his defence had not even been mentioned.

When all was said and done, the jurors were unconvinced by Omond's arguments and, by a majority of thirteen to two, they found McDonald guilty as libelled, though eleven of their number added a recommendation to mercy, alluding to what they described as 'the dissipated habits of Mrs McDonald.' Assuming the black cap, Lord Mure informed McDonald that he would now be removed to prison at Cupar, the county town of Fife, where he would be fed solely on bread and water until Thursday 3 October when, between the hours of eight and ten o'clock in the forenoon, he would be hanged by the neck until dead. In line with customary practice, his body would then be buried within the grounds of the prison, and his property and goods 'escheated' - that is, passed into the possession of the Crown. Throughout his trial, McDonald had appeared stoical, even when the jury delivered its weighty verdict, but during the judge's final address he interrupted proceedings to indicate that he wished to speak to his lawyer. Following a brief conversation, Omond approached Lord Mure and advised him that his client had been unable to hear what had been said. The judge then backtracked, repeating details relating to the jury's recommendation to mercy, and throughout the remainder of his address it was noted that he spoke more loudly. When he finally fell silent, McDonald for the first time showed signs of anxiety, apparently keen to escape the public eye, and he was hurriedly escorted from the dock by two policemen. The court rose at two o'clock, though eleven of the jurors held back to inaugurate a petition, appealing for clemency for the condemned man, which would be forwarded in due course to the Home Secretary, Richard Cross. It was one of several such pleas for mercy.

One of the petitions was accompanied by a letter written by Professor Pettigrew who occupied the chair of Medicine and Anatomy at St Andrews University and who was acting, he said, on behalf of Provost Walter Milton who at the time was 'seriously indisposed'. The petition had been prompted, Pettigrew wrote, by 'a widespread belief that Macdonald [sic] at his trial was virtually undefended' owing to the fact that his defence lawyer, George Omond, had entirely disregarded crucial 'extenuating circumstances'. What the professor indicated that he was referring to were the 'symptoms of insanity in the prisoner and his family' and 'the aggravation he received': the first, an unmistakeable reference to his father's suicide; the latter, to the intemperate habits of his wife. The petition was endorsed with the signatures of many of the great and the good of St Andrews: Provost Milton himself; virtually all of the magistrates and members of the Town Council; several Justices of the Peace; plus many local clergymen, doctors and teachers. It was not, Pettigrew emphasised, 'intended to supersede another and more numerously signed petition', but its signatories were unified by the belief that William McDonald had been given a raw deal.

On the self-same day that Professor Pettigrew signed and dated his letter in St Andrews, a clergyman some fifty-odd miles away at Friarsbrae, Linlithgow, likewise put pen to paper. From the outset, Free Kirk minister, Rev. William Nicolson laid his cards on the table, confidently asserting that the 'so-called murder' at St Andrews was 'nothing of the sort.' He proceeded to lay out his credentials for speaking out. On Thursday 13 June, Nicolson explained, he had happened to be in St Andrews in relation to the half-yearly Fast Day when he was summoned to the scene of an unfolding tragedy. Arriving at Shorehead, he was apprised straight away of the circumstances as they were known and advised that, owing to his injuries, William McDonald was not expected to survive the night. Throughout the rest of the day and on into the hours of darkness the clergyman sat by the injured man's side and, in spite of the precariousness of his situation, McDonald was able during this time to provide him with an account of what had taken place. In his letter, Rev. Nicolson stated candidly that McDonald had 'evidently been drinking hard', but that he had nonetheless been consistently conscious and coherent. The medical consensus was that pellets of shot had penetrated his lungs, therefore McDonald had no reason to doubt that his hours remaining were strictly numbered and, that being the case, Rev. Nicolson concluded that the injured man had nothing to lose by adhering to the truth.

The minister was under no illusions that in some quarters his revelations would be met with scepticism, if not downright incredulity. Published in *The Scotsman*, his letter told of McDonald's 'deathbed' confession in which he described an extraordinary agreement made between himself and his wife to carry out a combined act of suicide. By inserting one of the blades of a pair of scissors through the trigger guard of a loaded rifle and then laying the weapon across the bed with the barrel pointing directly at them, McDonald told Rev. Nicolson that the couple had believed that it would be possible for them to stand side by side in the direct line of fire and, by drawing the barrel towards them, the scissors would become entangled among the blankets, forcing the blades closer and closer together until eventually they applied sufficient pressure to squeeze the trigger. That was the theory at least, but when they attempted to put their plan into practice things didn't work out as anticipated when Helen alone was struck by shot while, standing by her side, McDonald himself was left unscathed. With his wife lying dead at his feet, he tried repeating the process but with no greater success on this second occasion when the pellets bypassed him once again, close enough to shoot the lapels from his coat. For his last desperate attempt, he removed the scissors from the trigger, took off his boots and fired a third and final shot using his toe. This time the lead pellets found their target and McDonald fell wounded to the floor where he was found a short time later by those neighbours who had rushed to the scene. Undoubtedly it was a bizarre tale and, after hearing the details, Rev. Nicolson attempted to verify whether what seemed improbable - some said, impossible - could somehow have been put into effect. Following his investigations, he was satisfied that McDonald had been speaking the truth, and he wrote in his letter to the press, 'I believed his word then, and believe it still.' As to motive, Rev. Nicolson put the whole catastrophe down to 'the act of two persons wearied of a life rendered miserable by the vices of one of them, and latterly of both, seeking relief from an existence which had become intolerable.' He concluded his letter by stating that during the trial he had sent a note of what he called this 'exculpatory evidence' to McDonald's defence counsel but had been disappointed to see that it was never brought to bear. At the end of the day, just how many *Scotsman* readers were convinced by the clergyman's beliefs there is no way of knowing, but what must surely have been beyond doubt was the total sincerity with which he held them.

By the time that Rev. Nicolson's open letter had appeared in print, the original petition in support of McDonald, initiated by the jurors in his case, had attracted a grand total of 1,643 signatures and was duly submitted to the Home Secretary, Richard Cross. Another petition, organised by the Cupar branch of the Society for the Abolition of Capital Punishment, had been endorsed by around 2,000 signatories within the local area. Taken by surprise by such a groundswell of popular feeling, the Home Office instructed police at both St Andrews and Cupar to investigate points raised by the petition regarding the possibility of 'hereditary insanity' and to report back. Completed in the space of a few days, the officers' findings - never made public - changed nothing when word came through in early October that the Home Secretary had ruled out any possibility of a reprieve. From a twenty-first century perspective, we might question, surely, whether the police force was the best qualified agency to pass judgment on the state of a man's mental health. Despite what had come across as 'stolid indifference', McDonald was unable to conceal his anguish when news reached him of the failure of the petitions that had been submitted on his behalf. With the time of his death now settled beyond doubt, he received his last visit in jail from his three daughters and two of his sons, the sole exception being his eldest son, aged about twenty, who was absent on a three-year voyage at sea. It could never have been anything other than a highly distressing occasion for all of those present and McDonald's difficulty in explaining what lay ahead to his youngest child, a wee lass of seven, is scarcely imaginable. In the meantime, the English executioner, William Marwood, had travelled to Cupar and had been engaged since his arrival in superintending the erection of the scaffold, borrowed from Perth for the occasion, in a garden area on the south side of the prison. It would be capable of being seen, it was reckoned, only from the highest of the town's rooftops and from the summits of hills more than a mile away.

The night before his execution, McDonald retired around nine o'clock but for understandable reasons found that he was too restless to sleep. Around midnight the prison governor, Ebenezer Donaldson, entered his cell and exchanged a few words with him, and not long after this McDonald succeeded in getting off to sleep. He did not awake, it is thought, until six o'clock in the morning when he rose, dressed himself and had his final breakfast of tea, bread and butter, and a boiled egg. Shortly afterwards he expressed a desire to smoke and was supplied with a pipe and tobacco which was lit for him by one of the prison warders. Around seven o'clock he was taken to the room of the prison chaplain, Rev. Gibb, who said prayers on his behalf and read aloud a portion of the 5th Hymn - 'The hour of my departure's come'. Hearing the minister's closing line - 'Not in mine innocence I trust' - McDonald commented, 'That's my position - not in mine innocence I trust,' which Rev. Gibb quite reasonably interpreted as an admission of guilt. No doubt McDonald's confession was a bolt from the blue but, given his consistent protestation of innocence and the mental torment he must surely have been experiencing, it seems at least possible that he had simply misunderstood the meaning of the line.

Arriving at the prison shortly before eight o'clock, the Provost, councillors and other officials were shown to a room set aside for pinioning the prisoner who was led in a few moments later. Following the completion of legal formalities, Rev. Gibb read from the scriptures during which McDonald was seen to shed tears but he quickly recovered himself when asked by Provost Milton whether he had any final words that he wished to say. 'I have got nothing to say,' he replied, 'only what I have said already.' He then turned to the prison governor, declaring, 'You have been a good friend to me; mind what I tellt you' - a heartfelt response, it was understood, to an assurance given by Donaldson that he would do his utmost to ensure that McDonald's youngest daughter would be kept secure and well cared for. The hangman, Marwood, began the pinioning process, prompting the prisoner to tell him - 'Don't pinion me so awfully ticht for I have a sore side, and I'll do everything to assist you.' Once the straps had been adjusted and his arms and body were securely bound, McDonald spoke out calmly. 'Now, gentlemen,' he announced, 'although I am thus' - here he indicated his bonds - 'I am quite innocent.' With Provost Milton and Governor Donaldson leading the way, McDonald showed no emotion as he was marched towards the scaffold, flanked by Marwood on one side and a prison warder on the other. He mounted the steps to the platform without hesitation and, despite being pinioned, shook hands there with Bailies Hood and Russell. A mere two minutes later the bolt was drawn, the trapdoor fell and McDonald's time on earth came to an end. Death, it was supposed, came instantaneously. Immediately after the drop a flag above the prison was run up to half-mast and the great town bell pealed out, announcing to all within earshot that the sentence of the law had been carried out. For a decade now executions had been carried out in private, and it was said that, despite the appearance of the flag, there were many in the streets below who were doubtful whether justice had been done.

Jessie King : March 1889

Piecing together the story of Jessie King - or Banks or Macpherson or Stewart, whichever name she chose to go by at any given time - while simultaneously attempting to plug the gaps is no easy undertaking. This was a time when effective contraception was non-existent, abortion illegal and colossal stigma attached to a child born out of wedlock, with the result that an unmarried, working mother had few options open to her other than to hand over her baby to a surrogate parent. In the absence of any properly regulated system of adoption, the resulting gap was filled by unofficial brokers - such as Jessie King - who offered adoption or fostering services whereby they undertook to re-home children, most commonly with childless married couples, in exchange for a given fee. There was, however, a distinctly darker side to the business. With little prospect of being held to account, some of these brokers - known as 'baby-farmers' - resorted to unscrupulous means of disposing of unwanted infants, something that was graphically illustrated in the Stockbridge district of Edinburgh in October 1888.

It all began with a group of lads out looking for amusement when they stumbled across a loosely-tied bundle lying on a patch of waste ground in Cheyne Street. The boys' chance find quickly became a makeshift football which they kicked back and forth in an impromptu match until, tiring of their game, they decided to investigate the contents of the package more closely. When they undid the string and peeled back the oilskin wrappings, they were horrified to find themselves gazing down at the body of an infant, wrapped in sheets of newspaper and severely decomposed. Straight away the boys reported their macabre find to police who promptly visited the scene to remove the child's body to the mortuary and institute an inquiry. On the orders of the procurator fiscal a post-mortem was carried out the following day by the police surgeon, Dr Henry Littlejohn, assisted by his son, Dr Harvey Littlejohn and Dr Joseph Bell (who was, incidentally, credited with being the model for Conan Doyle's fictional detective, Sherlock Holmes). The examination revealed that the body was that of a boy, a year or so old, who weighed little over eleven pounds. A length of cord, possibly apron string, had been wound twice around his neck so tightly as to have become embedded in his skin, leading to the firm conclusion that he had died through deliberate strangulation. The child's appearance gave the impression that a considerable time had elapsed since then.

While this was ongoing, there had been dramatic developments at Cheyne Street. During the course of door-to-door inquiries, Detectives Clark and Simpson had been informed by a local resident, James Banks, that a few months earlier a child he had seen with one of his neighbours appeared to have mysteriously vanished. The neighbour - a Mrs Macpherson - had assured him at the time that the infant in question had been transferred into the care of a suitable adoptive parent and, for a while at least, Banks's suspicions were thus allayed. They were quickly reignited, however, when news spread through the district that a child's body had been found on vacant ground nearby. Based on this information, the two police officers paid a visit to the house occupied by Mr and Mrs Macpherson - the former absent, they were told, at work. When questioned, Mrs Macpherson insisted that the missing child had been adopted by her sister and brother-in-law and was now in their safekeeping. Not yet satisfied, the officers undertook a search of the property during the course of which they came up against a locked closet. Mrs Macpherson stalled for a time before reluctantly handing over the key, but before the detectives had time to unlock the cupboard door she made a dramatic intervention. 'Get a cab!' she cried. 'Take me to the police station. It is there. I did it!' The significance of her words became clear when, lying amongst pots, pans and other household items on the bottom shelf of the cupboard, the detectives found a second corpse, this time of a baby girl, no more than a few weeks old, who had been wrapped up in a canvas sheet. A handkerchief which had been tied around the child's mouth suggested that she had been suffocated. Placed alongside the dead infant was a piece of oilskin, similar to what the dead boy had been wrapped in, as well as a canister containing traces of lime chloride, a substance frequently used at the time to mask disagreeable odours. Straight away the officers placed Mrs Macpherson under arrest and arrangements were made to apprehend her partner at his place of work, Lawson's Nursery, where he was employed as a gardener.

Fairly quickly the unfortunate baby girl's story emerged. Nearly three months earlier, police discovered, she had been born to an unmarried servant girl, Alice Tomlinson, in Edinburgh Maternity Hospital and had been named Violet. Because of her work commitments, Alice had been unable to look after the baby herself, so her mother, Jemima Tomlinson, had placed a notice in a local newspaper on her daughter's behalf in an effort to find an adoptive parent. Among the replies that she received, one stood out from the rest. The respondent was a Mrs Banks (a surname, we might suspect, conveniently borrowed from her neighbour) who stated that her sister wished to adopt a baby girl and, furthermore, that the lady in question's husband held the important post of piper to the Duke of Montrose. Violet, she insisted, would thus be assured of a privileged upbringing in the picturesque surroundings of the Duke's country estate near Loch Lomond. And, if all that wasn't a sufficiently tempting prospect, then the icing on the cake was the fact that the fee demanded by Mrs Banks for her services - a paltry £2 - was the lowest of all that Mrs Tomlinson had been quoted. Negotiations were concluded without hitch and a short time later Mrs Banks arrived to remove Violet from her grandmother's home and convey her - allegedly - to Loch Lomondside to embark on her idyllic new life. Perhaps it all sounded a little too good to be true and certainly in the weeks that followed Mrs Tomlinson began - too late, alas! - to smell a rat when, no matter how often she visited Cheyne Street to inquire after her granddaughter's welfare, she found that she was unable to elicit any information whatsoever. She would later discover that the woman she knew as Mrs Banks was neither who nor what she claimed to be.

It didn't take long, however, before police were able to root out the fact that the woman's surname was neither Banks nor indeed Macpherson, and that Violet Tomlinson was not the first unwanted child she had been paid to take care of. Hailing originally from Anderston, Glasgow, 27-year-old Jessie King had moved east to Edinburgh where she found employment as a washerwoman at Craigmillar Laundry. Things, however, did not go entirely smoothly and by early 1887 she found herself pregnant and homeless in what to her was a strange city. This was the point where William Thomas Pearson stepped in. Whether or not the 59-year-old gardener was the father of Jessie's child is uncertain but, becoming aware of her plight, he offered her a roof over her head in exchange for domestic duties, almost certainly with sexual favours thrown in. Such, we might imagine, was Jessie's vulnerability at this stage that she was prepared to accept his terms. After the birth of her child Pearson and she remained together as a couple, moving regularly from address to address throughout the city. By the autumn of 1887 they were installed in lodgings at 24 Dalkeith Road where, for public consumption, Pearson chose to portray himself either as Jessie's father or alternatively her uncle, whichever happened to take his fancy on any particular occasion. The partnership was not, however, consistently cordial and neighbours on Dalkeith Road overheard quarrelling from time to time as well as boisterous drinking sessions.

Acting under the surname of Stewart, Jessie replied during the autumn of 1887 to a notice seeking adoptive parents for a five-month-old boy whose background story was all too common. An unmarried young woman called Elizabeth Campbell had fallen pregnant and until her child was born had moved in with her sister, Janet, and brother-in-law, John Anderson, at Prestonpans, east of Edinburgh. Tragically, Elizabeth died a week after giving birth to her son, Walter, but the Andersons indicated a willingness to adopt the boy, provided that his father, David Finlay, a postman in Leith, undertook to contribute to his upbringing. Unwilling to do so, Finlay opted instead to advertise for adoptive parents and, on receiving Mrs Stewart's expression of interest, he turned up at Dalkeith Road, gave her lodgings a cursory once-over, handed over £5 for his child's maintenance and departed without further ado. His final act was to pen a brief note to Janet Anderson, informing her rather coldly that 'a party [would] call for the child tomorrow forenoon', and, with that, he bowed out, having - in his own eyes, at least - met his paternal responsibilities in full. By the time of their visit to Prestonpans, Jessie and Pearson had their lines well-rehearsed: Jessie was a widow, so the story went, whose own young son, of a similar age to Walter, had passed away, and ever since that unhappy event she had been unable to shake off an intense depression. The 'Stewarts' handed Janet Anderson a letter of authorisation written by the child's father, David Finlay. During the course of their dealings, Janet was surprised that the couple were unwilling to give her a note of their address but she had no authority to do anything other than comply with Finlay's instruction, so tiny Walter Campbell was duly passed into the Stewarts' care and removed to Dalkeith Road. As it turned out, his stay there would be a fairly short one and when he disappeared a few months later - in April or May 1888 - Jessie's explanation to her neighbours was that he had gone to live with an aunt. It was, of course, precisely the same story that she would use later in relation to Violet Tomlinson but, as far as baby Walter was concerned, his small body was never traced or accounted for. Sadly, his fate is all too easy to imagine.

There was more to come. In late May 1887 an unmarried domestic servant, Catherine Gunn, was delivered of twin boys whom she named Robert and Alexander. The children's father, whoever he might have been, appears to have shown a clean pair of heels at the first opportunity but for a time Catherine managed to glean enough from her own wages to pay for childcare during her working hours. Money was scarce, however, and after a year she found that she had no option other than to seek a more permanent solution. In response to an advertisement in the press, she received a total of 29 replies from potential adoptive parents, many of them making high-flown claims regarding the rosy future that her children might expect. Perhaps it was Jessie's modest fee - £3 - that influenced her in making the decision that, when the twins went to separate homes in early April 1888, Alexander would pass into her care. Back at Dalkeith Road, Jessie paid a few coppers to a local thirteen-year-old, Janet Burnie, to take charge of the toddler during daytime, but when he vanished a few weeks later she had a ready explanation at her fingertips. His mother had died in the Royal Infirmary, she claimed, and the boy had now gone to a permanent home. His father had come during the night, she said, and had taken him away. Pearson's version of events, by contrast, was that Alexander had been taken 'across the water' to Canada for the good of his health. Of course, neither of these stories had the tiniest grain of truth in them, and when Pearson and Jessie flitted from Dalkeith Road to Cheyne Street Alexander's tiny corpse formed part of their luggage. It was his decomposed body that turned up abandoned on a vacant plot a stone's throw from their accommodation and, as we already know, it didn't take long for the police to come chapping at their door.

Questioned at the time of her arrest, Jessie admitted to the Sheriff that she had been responsible for the deaths of two children - Alexander Gunn and Violet Tomlinson - but she remained silent concerning Walter Campbell. In the case of Alexander, she claimed to have had no means of supporting him and had strangled him while under the influence of alcohol. Whether out of love, loyalty or - somewhat unlikely - as a simple matter of fact, she went out of her way to exonerate Pearson of any involvement in the murders. Never at any stage, she declared, had he even been aware of Violet Tomlinson's presence in the house. The very afternoon she had taken possession of her, the baby girl had died, so she said, after choking on a small quantity of medicinal whisky and, for fear that Pearson might hear the infant's gasps, Jessie had placed a hand over her mouth and had thus stopped her from breathing. Secreting the child in a closet, she had stuffed a cloth into her mouth in case by some remote chance she had revived. It was a rum tale, no doubt, but, credible or otherwise, the effect of Jessie's declaration was that all charges against Pearson were dropped, leaving him free to testify in court without fear of conviction. Regarding baby Walter Campbell, Jessie was prepared to reveal nothing and, despite a thoroughgoing search of her lodgings at Cheyne Road during which the very floorboards were taken up and the coal cellars searched, police were unsuccessful in finding any trace of the boy. Owing to the difficulty of securing a conviction without a body, charges relating to Walter Campbell were subsequently dropped.

Flying in the face of her earlier statement, Jessie opted to plead not guilty when her case came to court on 18 February 1889. Her neighbour, Joseph Banks, testified that she had brought a baby home to Cheyne Street which she claimed to have been paid £25 to adopt - and which, in retrospect, must have been Violet Tomlinson. When the infant was never seen again, she explained to Banks that, for a payment of £18, she had arranged for 'another party to take it off her hands', thus netting for herself a tidy profit of £7. A credible story, maybe, but it was, of course, entirely fictitious and at that very moment tiny Violet was lying dead a few yards away. When Pearson's turn came to take the stand, he directed all of his efforts towards keeping himself in the clear, in spite of his guarantee of immunity from prosecution, and he flatly denied any knowledge of the killings. He claimed to have known nothing of the presence in his home of the baby girl, Violet Tomlinson, but when it came to the case of Walter Campbell it was less easy for him to wriggle out completely since he had accompanied Jessie (in the guise of her 'father') to Prestonpans to take possession of the child. In relation to Walter's disappearance, Pearson testified that Jessie had assured him that she had placed the boy in Miss Stirling's Home, a local establishment for the care of unwanted children. She had used the same story in relation to Alexander Gunn and when he had asked to visit the boy there she had put him off, telling him that male visitors were permitted only at certain times and he had accepted this without question. Predictably, Pearson denied any knowledge whatsoever of the contents of the closet and stated that he had no idea as to whether or not it was normally kept locked. Questioned about his oilskin coat, he stated that he had been irritated when Jessie told him that she had thrown it out. Regarding the tricky question of aliases, Pearson claimed to have no recollection of ever using the surname *Stewart* - despite his being shown a document which he had signed with precisely that name - and *Macpherson*, he explained, had stood him in good stead in former years when taking part in Highland games. Speaking on Jessie's behalf, her lawyer, Fitzroy Bell, did his best to argue the case that, despite Pearson's rather lame protestations of innocence, Jessie had been acting under his pernicious influence and that the charge against her should more rightly be culpable homicide rather than murder. Bell had, however, an uphill struggle on his hands, given that the version of events he was peddling ran directly counter to the official statement given by Jessie immediately after her arrest. At the end of the day, when both Crown and defence arguments had been aired, the fifteen men of the jury retired to consider their verdict at three o'clock in the afternoon.

It was a short process. They returned within minutes - three to be precise - to report that they had reached a unanimous verdict of 'guilty as libelled' on both charges. Jessie listened in silence throughout, though a nervous twitching of her mouth betrayed her inner anxiety. In his summing up, the judge, Lord Kingsburgh, started out by stating that the prisoner's formal declaration of guilt plus the weight of evidence against her had made a guilty verdict well-nigh inevitable. Jessie stood up in the dock as he turned to address her directly, reminding her that her days were now numbered and urging her to devote what time she had left to preparation for the afterlife where, if genuinely repentant, she could be confident of divine forgiveness. As proceedings wound to a close, he donned the customary black cap and announced to her that she would be returned to the Calton Jail and there, between eight and ten o'clock in the forenoon of Monday 11 March, she would be hanged by the neck until dead. Her remains, he continued, would be buried within the precincts of the prison, and 'this I pronounce for doom, and may the Lord have mercy upon your soul.' Of all those present, Jessie, it seemed, was the only one to whom his words appeared to come as a shock and her groans of distress were clearly audible as, dismissed from the dock, she had to be carried downstairs to the cells.

Shortly after Jessie's conviction a letter appeared in the press under the address 'Buchanan Castle' and dated Monday 25 February 1889. Its author was one John McDonald, 'Piper to His Grace the Duke of Montrose', and the gentleman in question wished to let it be known that Jessie King was 'entirely unknown' to him and, as to his being married to her sister, the blunt fact was that he was a bachelor. The letter drew to a close by reinforcing the fact that Jessie's assertions about a fictitious sister and brother-in-law were thus shown to be 'entirely erroneous'. Assuredly McDonald's claims would have been difficult to counter, and how Jessie dreamed up a connection with Douglas Beresford Malise Ronald Graham, 5th Duke of Montrose, is anybody's guess.

During the three-week gap between her trial and the date set for her execution Jessie's spiritual welfare was catered for by Canon James Donlevy of St Mary's Cathedral, Edinburgh, who reported that she showed signs of deep remorse for the crimes she had committed. Rumours circulated at this time to the effect that on more than one occasion she had attempted to strangle herself in her cell, using strips of material torn from her skirt, but this would later be denied by Canon Donlevy. Arguing the case that Jessie was of very low intelligence and that she had been put up to her actions by one or more others, a petition to secure a reprieve from execution managed to attract more than 1,800 signatures but, following consideration by the Secretary of State for Scotland, Lord Lothian, ultimately it proved unsuccessful. The truth was that Jessie had little sympathy among the population at large, and one Edinburgh woman went so far as to say that she 'would rather pull the rope [herself]' than hear that the sentence had been commuted. On Saturday 9 March - two days before her execution - Jessie received a visit in jail from two ladies, formerly her employers, who later reported her words that she was 'quite ready to meet her God.' In the meantime, the hangman, James Berry, had arrived in Edinburgh in anticipation of his duties and was currently being accommodated within Calton Jail. It was thanks to Berry's influence that it was now regarded as more humane to provide the prisoner with a longer rope than in former times in order to ensure the likelihood of an instant death.

On the eve of her execution Jessie was understandably emotional when nursing her son, Thomas, still only six months old, for the last time. Comforted by Canon Donlevy, she retired to bed at ten o'clock and slept soundly, it was said, until half past five in the morning when she awoke and made her way to the prison chapel. There, in the company of two Franciscan nuns, she celebrated mass and received her last communion before returning to her cell where she ate a light breakfast. To the prison doctor's offer of assistance - some form of sedative perhaps - she gave a dignified response: 'I have nothing with which to thank you for your great kindness to me,' she told him. 'All I can say is may God bless you for all you have done for me.' She proceeded calmly to say goodbye to all of the officials who had attended her during her time in jail, and shortly before eight o'clock James Berry arrived to set about the business of pinioning her arms. Canon Donlevy handed a crucifix to Jessie which she clutched tightly though her wrists were bound while the white hood was placed over her head and face. Flanked on one side by the prison chaplain and on the other by the matron, she was led to the scaffold, replying all the while to the litany recited by Canon Donlevy, robed in white and purple. Jessie's final words were spoken from the platform: 'Into thy hands, O Lord, I commit my spirit. Lord Jesus, receive my soul. Jesus, son of David, have mercy on me.' At that, the drop fell and, mercifully, she died instantaneously and with no sign of struggle. 'She has never moved since the drop,' was Berry's comment. The black flag was raised to intimate to the crowd waiting outside that the execution had been carried out, and in the early afternoon Jessie's body was laid to rest within the prison grounds in a short ceremony conducted in accordance with the rites of the Roman Catholic church. Interviewed later, James Berry described Jessie as the most courageous woman he had ever encountered: 'Such bravery I never in my life witnessed before. I am very, very sorry for her; but, of course, it had to be done.' For a hardened executioner, the hanging appeared to have affected him deeply. In relation to executing women generally, he said, 'It always made me shiver like a leaf.'

After Jessie's death it came to be known that, in the weeks prior to her execution, she had devoted time to jotting down on a slate an account of her background, early years and subsequent life which she had then dictated for transcription by Canon Donlevy. The content of this document was not made public but, even so, there was no let-up in interest in Jessie and the details of her life among the public at large. It was reported that she had been born in March 1861, the daughter of a Glasgow weaver. She had two brothers named Peter and John. Sadly, her mother passed away when she was only eighteen months old and her father died while she was still in her teens. Perhaps these painful losses were what led to an unsettled, seemingly aimless, existence in the years that followed. She left Glasgow and moved to the Vale of Leven where she worked for a time in the mills at Bonhill. For whatever tragic reason, the next we hear of Jessie is as an inmate of the Magdalene Asylum in Edinburgh, an institution for 'fallen women', where she remained for an eighteen-month period during which she was instructed in the rudiments of laundry work. Discharged from the asylum, she returned to Glasgow where it has been suggested that she served a short prison sentence for 'concealment of pregnancy', viewed as a serious offence at the time when doing away with an unwanted new-born baby was not uncommon. From Glasgow she moved farther west to Gourock, working as a laundress there for approximately one year, before she drifted back east and found employment in Edinburgh as an 'ironer' in a laundry business until, pregnant and near destitute, she was - as we know - taken in by Thomas Pearson: a fateful encounter if ever there was one. In Edinburgh Maternity Hospital in late spring 1887 she was delivered of a baby girl, Grace, whose birth was registered according to form and who was duly vaccinated four months later. Thereafter - nothing. What became of baby

Grace is unknown. A year and a half later Jessie returned to the Maternity Hospital where her son, Thomas, was born. As things turned out, she had less than six months left to devote to her baby boy.

Several weeks after the execution Canon Donlevy revealed that the evening prior to Jessie's death she had in his presence made a full and frank confession which he had written down at her bidding and which she had subsequently checked and approved. The confession starts out by stating that Jessie 'wishes it to be made public that she acknowledges the justice of her sentence', but it quickly moves on to more controversial territory. She 'accepts with a humble and contrite heart the punishment of death *for her share in these crimes.*' She was not guilty, she continues, of all that she had confessed to in her official declaration - lending credence to the view that she was badly advised to admit everything she was accused of in order to be given a more lenient sentence. Jessie's confession finishes off by stating that she 'freely forgives the companion who participated in these crimes, and prays for his conversion.' Whom she carried the can for she does not specify but his identity is not hard to guess. Given that revelation, it should come as no surprise that in her last will and testament Jessie chooses not to place the future of her young son in Thomas Pearson's hands. Her will is headed 'HM Prison, Edinburgh, 8th March 1889' and reads thus: 'I, Jessie Kean [*sic*] at present in the above prison, hereby appoint as the guardian of my child, Thomas Kean, the Very Reverend James, Canon Donlevy, priest in charge of the Roman Catholic Cathedral, Broughton Street, Edinburgh, and ... may he be brought up faithfully in the faith of the Roman Catholic Church.' Jessie had previously told Canon Donlevy that providing for her baby son's future was 'the work which, after her salvation, she [had] most at heart.'

Inevitably, suspicion was rife throughout Edinburgh that Jessie had been responsible for the disappearance of more than three children, including perhaps the infant whose body had turned up recently among left luggage at the North British Railway Station or another found abandoned under the seat of a railway carriage in the Abbeyhill district of the city. However, had she but known it, Jessie's name was not universally reviled and comparisons with Florence Maybrick, much in the news at the time, brought her a considerable degree of sympathy in spite of the fact that the two women's crimes were markedly different. The daughter of an American banker, Florence was convicted in April

1889 of murdering her husband, James Maybrick, a wealthy Liverpool merchant, but - unlike Jessie - she was successful in gaining a reprieve. The gulf in social status - and, of course, disparity in financial clout - between the two women was glaringly obvious and led, some contended, to their contrasting fates. It was, of course, too late for Jessie but if her sad fate led to any positive consequences it was perhaps the spotlight it shone on the urgent need for child protection, much neglected until then, and the influence it had in opening up debate regarding the morality of capital punishment, an issue which had been simmering under the surface for some time but which would not be finally settled for another seventy-odd years.

From a historical standpoint, whether Jessie deserves to be viewed more as victim than villain is possibly a moot point, and disentangling the two would undoubtedly be a tricky proposition. The role played by her partner, Thomas Pearson, remains unclear and the extent of his involvement in the whole sorry affair still stands as an irksome loose end to the story. In the aftermath of Jessie's execution, it has been suggested that Pearson retreated to his native Glasgow, most likely to escape his notoriety in the capital, where he lapsed into a life of dissolution and alcoholism. When his lifeless body turned up some time later with his skull caved in, it may, of course, have been no more than the outcome of a drunken misadventure, but there is always a temptation to suspect that his shady past had perhaps caught up with him in the end.

William Bury : April 1889

In the century and more that has passed since the murderer known as
Jack the Ripper perpetrated his gruesome atrocities in the Whitechapel
district of London, a broad array of suspects have come under the
spotlight, some more plausible than others and ranging from petty East
End villains on the one hand to an unhinged grandson of Queen Victoria
on the other. More surprising than that, however, is the fact that, in the
aftermath of the Ripper's brutal killings, there was no shortage of
individuals who came forward to admit responsibility for his crimes.
Sentenced to death for multiple murders, Dr Thomas Neill Cream's
alleged parting claim - 'I am Jack the...' - was stifled when the noose
tightened around his neck and choked off his final words for ever.
Hanged in London in 1892, the Glasgow-born poisoner was by no means
the only suspect with a Scottish connection to come under scrutiny.

By the time of his arrival north of the border, William Henry Bury had
already had an undeniably chequered existence. Varying accounts have
been given of his early years but one thing which features consistently is
their tragic nature. Born in the English Midlands in 1859, he was still
only a baby when his father, Henry, fell beneath the wheels of a fish-cart
he was in charge of and was fatally crushed when the horse took fright
and bolted. A few weeks later, Bury's mother, Mary Jane, was diagnosed
as suffering from 'melancholia' and duly committed to Worcester Lunatic
Asylum where she remained until her death, aged 33, in 1864. During the
course of an epileptic seizure, his eldest sister, Elizabeth Ann, died at the

tender age of seven, and neither of his two remaining siblings, Joseph or Mary, lived much beyond thirty. It has been suggested that Bury himself was brought up by a maternal uncle, Edward Henley (though this is disputed) who enrolled him as a pupil at Blue Coat School in Stourbridge, a charitable institution which educated children from impoverished backgrounds. Thrown early on his own resources, after leaving school he was employed for a time as a warehouse clerk but was obliged to move on after defaulting on a loan. He found work with a locksmith in Wolverhampton but once again things went awry when he was dismissed by his employer when caught stealing. Details of his next few years are fairly sketchy but it has been suggested that he led a peripatetic life during this time, moving from job to job throughout the Midlands and Yorkshire. In the 1881 census his surname is listed under the spelling *Berry* - a name that ironically would later prove highly significant - and by 1887, it seems, he was settled in the city of Birmingham where he gleaned a living on the streets by selling small items from a pack.

Before the year was out, however, he had relocated once again, this time south to London where in the East End district of Bow he found employment with James Martin, a dealer in sand and sawdust, commodities in demand at the time for spreading on the floors of shops, business premises and public houses. Initially accommodated in his employer's stable, Bury eventually worked his way up and indoors where he met his future wife, Ellen Elliott, a domestic servant who was three or four years his senior. As a lucrative side-line, James Martin was known to have an interest in an East End brothel where it is rumoured that Ellen did a spot of moonlighting, not by any means unusual for an attractive working-class girl struggling to make her way in Victorian London. Her financial situation eased, however, when she fell heir to a substantial holding of stocks and shares, left to her in the will of an unmarried aunt, and Bury, no doubt, was fully aware of her fortunate windfall when they were married in Bromley Parish Church on Easter Monday of the following year, 1888. It didn't take his new bride long to rue the day, however, when within a week of the couple's wedding their landlady, Elizabeth Haynes, was disturbed by sounds of a violent commotion emanating from their room and, on rushing in to investigate, was confronted with the sight of Bury kneeling over his wife and brandishing a knife with which he was threatening to kill her. The threat of police involvement restored calm, for the time being at least, but Ellen took the precaution thereafter of asking Mrs Haynes to keep a room key close at hand in case her husband might lock the door in future before repeating his outrages. Her kindly landlady assured her that if she heard her cry out she would certainly rush to her aid. By this stage it was clear that alcohol had secured Bury in its grip and the motive for his assault, of course, was to gain control of Ellen's money. Before long he found himself out of work once again, this time for failing to hand over his takings to his employer, and only after Ellen had cashed in a number of her shares and repaid her husband's debts was he reinstated in his job.

If Bury was grateful for his wife's intervention, he showed little sign of it. In an attempt to extort yet more of her money, he continued to abuse her both in public and behind closed doors with the result that their landlady, Mrs Haynes, insisted that they vacate their room and find new accommodation elsewhere. By the end of 1888 he was forced to sell his pony and cart - purchased some time earlier using Ellen's money - in order to continue to fund his debauched lifestyle, yet strangely he appears to have been blind to the fact that by now the greater part of his wife's inheritance by far had already been squandered. More than once he stole her purse from her pocket and, for fear that he might pawn her jewellery, she was obliged to hand it over for safekeeping to her older sister, Margaret Corney, who advised her that in order to be rid of her abusive husband she should seek the advice of a magistrate. Ellen agreed to do so but, in the event, it never happened. In the new year of 1889 Bury put it about that his wife and he were contemplating emigrating to Adelaide in Australia - details were vague but he went so far as to commission two large, wooden trunks for their proposed journey. The reality of Bury's plan, however, was a good deal less ambitious. When she learned that his intention was to relocate to the Scottish city of Dundee, Ellen was less than enthusiastic and her sister, Margaret - fearful of her brother-in-law's frequent violent rages - did her best to dissuade her from accompanying him. As a means of countering his sister-in-law's influence, Bury produced correspondence which he claimed to have received from Dundee jute manufacturers, Malcolm, Ogilvie & Co., Limited, offering a seven-year contract of employment both to himself and his wife at wages of £2 and £1 per week respectively. Of course, it later transpired that the document had been forged - most likely by Bury himself - but Ellen, barely literate, could hardly have been expected to notice its amateurishness or detect his slip-ups in spelling.

Why, of all places, Dundee? On the face of it, there would seem to be no obvious reason for his choice when neither he nor his wife had any previous connection with the city, but perhaps the most likely possibility is that he had learned of its connection with the jute business from workers employed at Ritchie's Jute Mill in Whitechapel or the Wallace Works, a London factory which had recently been taken over by Malcolm, Ogilvie & Co. Whatever his thinking, he went ahead and bought two second-class tickets aboard the steamer, *Cambria*, departing from Dundee Wharf, London, in the forenoon of Saturday 19 January. Having tried one last time to persuade her sister not to accompany Bury, Margaret Corney would later recall her deep sense of foreboding as she watched the vessel depart, convinced that she would never see her sister again. (Her premonition was justified, as it turned out, and the last she would ever hear from Ellen would be a brief note, posted two days later from Dundee.) Heading out into the open sea, the *Cambria* tracked north, berthing at her destination the following evening - Sunday 20 January - but Bury and his wife opted to remain aboard until morning before disembarking to tramp the city streets in search of accommodation. Late in the afternoon they were successful in finding a vacant room in Union Street, located - all too conveniently, perhaps - immediately above a public house, but Bury insisted on moving out a mere eight days later, deeming the rent of eight shillings per week too expensive, which came as a surprise to the landlady who had noticed Ellen's fine jewellery. To secure replacement lodgings, Bury posed as a prospective tenant and obtained a key to view a rather squalid unfurnished basement flat in Princes Street where he and Ellen promptly set up home, ignoring repeated requests for the return of the key. At a local market Bury purchased an iron bedstead, bedclothes and other household items which he had delivered to his new address and he paid two men to uplift those goods that he had left in his previous lodgings. Struggling to manhandle a heavy wooden crate, one of the men was heard to mutter, 'It's like as if there was a dead man in it.'

Many of his Dundonian neighbours and new acquaintances appear to have found Bury's English accent well-nigh impenetrable, and he seems to have created rather a mixed impression. It did not escape their notice that he appeared to make very little effort to find work, applying himself instead to the task of becoming acquainted with the public houses of his adopted city, in particular the Prince Regent Bar where he was in the habit of portraying himself as a well-to-do man of means. When questioned on one occasion about what he did for a living, he replied breezily, 'Oh, nothing,' and casually referred to a local Episcopalian clergyman of his acquaintance, Rev. Edward Gough, who, he said, 'will find something for me to do.' Strangely enough, he never appeared short of money and the fine clothing and gaudy rings that he wore attracted a degree of admiration. At times he let it be known that he had come to Dundee for business reasons and intended to remain in the city until late summer, but on other occasions he indicated that his move north had been to benefit his wife's health, and he went on to express relief at the mildness of the weather, having been told in London to expect a great deal of snow in Scotland. Yet, for all his apparent casualness, when shopping locally for everyday items he soon established himself as an inveterate haggler whose habit it was to make unfavourable comparisons with London prices, and who angled, persistently if unsuccessfully, for 'tick'. A good deal more industrious than her husband, Ellen managed to find employment as a cleaner in Baxter's jute mill but, for whatever reason, she gave the job up after a single day. 'She don't like that kind of work,' Bury explained to a neighbour. In response to a mischievous suggestion that he might be on the lookout for 'some bonnie Scotch girl', Bury gestured toward his wife, saying, 'This is my girl; she's plenty for me.'

Often by closing time he was visibly the worse for drink and his treatment of his wife was a good deal less affectionate in private. Although he had assaulted Ellen consistently throughout their time together, Bury's level of violence escalated steadily after his arrival in Dundee until matters finally came to a head some three weeks later. Around seven o'clock in the evening of Sunday 10 February the officer on duty at Dundee's Central Police Station, Lieutenant Parr, watched an unfamiliar man - slightly stooped, sparsely bewhiskered and little more than five feet in height - who entered the building in a state of some excitement and proceeded to introduce himself as William Henry Bury, a dealer in sawdust. In an unmistakeably English accent, the visitor asked to speak in private and, when taken aside, he confessed with high drama to being fearful that he would be arrested as Jack the Ripper. He then went on to recount to the listening policeman a bizarre series of events.

Throughout the previous Monday, he stated, he and his wife had engaged in a prolonged drinking session until, thoroughly inebriated, they had retired to bed, at what time exactly he was uncertain. Surfacing the following morning, he was surprised to discover that his wife was no longer beside him in bed and when he called out to her there was no reply. Puzzled, he set about searching the apartment and was shocked at what he discovered. His wife, he related, was lying on the floor in a state of insensibility with a length of cord twisted firmly around her neck. In desperation he tried speaking to her but obtained no response. This was the point where Bury's story grew even more outlandish. After gazing down at his wife for some time, he claimed that, for reasons which he could not explain, he was seized by 'a mad impulse' that impelled him to take up a knife - apparently conveniently to hand - which he proceeded to plunge repeatedly into her lower body. Immediately afterwards, when the enormity of his actions struck him, he had taken fright and, in fear of being suspected of murder, he had crammed the body into one of his wooden crates where it had remained until now. His shocking tale at an end, Bury surrendered his house key to a speechless Lieutenant Parr.

Two police officers, Lieutenant Lamb and Detective Campbell, set out immediately to investigate Bury's claims and, searching his flat by candlelight, they found - just as he had indicated - a large wooden box at the rear of the property. When they prised the boards apart, a crack appeared sufficient for them to see the foot and leg of a woman, twisted at what appeared to be an unnatural angle. On a windowsill nearby was a knife which still had flesh, blood and hair adhering, and in the grate the policemen detected signs that an attempt had recently been made to burn articles of clothing. A length of rope lay discarded on the floor. Straight away they sent word of their gruesome discovery back to their headquarters with the result that a police surgeon, Charles Templeman, was dispatched to Bury's flat. He wasted no time in arranging for the corpse to be transferred to the city mortuary where, assisted by a local doctor, Alexander Stalker, he embarked upon a post-mortem examination. The men found that, in order to be made to fit into the box, the woman's body had been crushed and compressed, and her right leg had been broken at the calf and then doubled over. She was virtually naked and, among a number of other cuts and bruises, the marks of a rope were clearly visible around her neck. In spite of close to a dozen horrifying incisions on the lower part of her body - one sufficiently deep as to permit her intestines to protrude - it was the doctors' opinion that death had occurred through strangulation and that the woman's body had been mutilated with a knife immediately afterwards. That said, they conceded that it was by no means impossible that the wounds had been inflicted while the victim was unconscious but still breathing. Any suggestion of suicide, they believed, could be dismissed.

The evidence, of course, was more than enough to justify Bury's being placed behind bars. When he was searched, officers found in his possession twelve or thirteen shillings in cash, a bank book showing a modest credit balance and a quantity of jewellery - a watch, a necklace, various brooches and earrings - which he stated were the property of his late wife. Police conjectured that the most obvious motive for the killing was to facilitate Bury's inheritance of what money Ellen still retained in her name. Appearing at the Police Court the following forenoon, he seemed agitated as the charge of murder was read out but, interrogated later by Sheriff Campbell Smith, he remained unshakeable in his conviction that his wife's death was the result of suicide. When questioned as to why he had mutilated her body and concealed it inside a box, he remained resolutely silent. Hoping to shed light on Bury's past, Chief Constable Dewar made contact with the London police by telegram and received a reply in due course which informed him that the dead woman had been known as a quiet, unassuming soul who more than once had had to be rescued from her husband's barbaric cruelty. Shockingly, the reply from London added that the walls of a room which the couple had occupied in the East End were still discoloured by her bloodstains. Why, we might wonder, did Bury choose to present himself on Sunday evening, 10 February, at Dundee's Central Police Station, rather than simply sit tight? The assumption must surely be that, unable to devise a plan to dispose of his wife's body, the pressure simply became too great until he finally panicked.

Though the authorities did their best to keep a lid on Bury's shocking revelations, almost inevitably word leaked out within a matter of hours and spread rapidly through the city, fuelling rumours that Jack the Ripper had been apprehended in Dundee and was now confined behind bars. On Monday 11 February groups of sightseers congregated in Princes Street to gaze down through the railings at the basement flat where the tragedy had occurred, and, during meal breaks at the jute mills, eager crowds flocked to newsagents' premises, impatient for what the latest edition of the newspapers might reveal. 'Ay, it's true,' new arrivals were assured. 'He's gi'en himsel' up - he's a Londoner too!' Prowling youths were thought responsible for chalked graffiti that appeared at Bury's lodgings, indicating that 'Jack the Ripper is at the back of this door' and 'Jack the Ripper is in this sellar [sic].' Only once the factories and mills had closed down for the night and heavy snow began to fall - as though in confirmation of Bury's anxious forebodings - did people finally disperse to their homes.

Perhaps surprisingly the police case against Bury did not go entirely to plan and received an unexpected setback when a second post-mortem examination, carried out by local doctors, David Lennox - a veteran of the Sudanese war - and William Kinnear concluded that 'the strangulation was suicidal.' Their findings, however, were put in the shade when new information surfaced which cast yet more doubt on Bury's version of events. It went badly for him when a close neighbour in Princes Street recollected that in the early hours of Tuesday 5 February he had been disturbed by three loud screams, ringing out one after another in rapid succession. David Duncan stated that he had listened intently for the next half-hour or so but with nothing more to be heard he had simply dismissed the matter from his mind. On top of that, a final three-hour post-mortem examination, carried out by one of Scotland's most eminent surgeons, Dr Henry Littlejohn of Edinburgh, categorically ruled out suicide as the cause of death and concluded that Ellen had been strangled from behind. In addition to abdominal knife wounds, other marks were visible on her body that strongly suggested that she had put up a struggle before being overpowered. And if all that wasn't damning enough, it soon emerged that Bury's statement to Lieutenant Parr had contained at least one major omission. What he had conveniently neglected to mention was the fact that on Monday 4 February he had entered a shop on Princes Street and explained that he was looking for a length of cord. When just such an item was produced by the shopkeeper, Janet Martin, he examined it and remarked, 'That will do nicely.' She had no reason to suspect that he was anything other than sober.

The public gallery was full to bursting on the morning of Bury's trial, Thursday 28 March. Tidily groomed and dressed in a dark suit, he entered the dock at around ten o'clock. Leading for the prosecution was the Advocate-Depute, Dugald McKechnie, while Bury's defence was to be conducted by two lawyers, David Tweedie and William Hay. Presiding on the bench was Lord Young. 'The charge against you,' Lord Young told him, 'is that on 5 February 1889 ... you did strike, stab and strangle Ellen Bury, your wife, and did murder her.' Invited by the judge to respond, Bury replied with a firm, 'Not guilty.' As proceedings got underway, a number of witnesses were called who had travelled all the way from London: Margaret Corney, who had recently faced the harrowing task of identifying her late sister's body and who was in a position to give a vivid account of her brother-in-law's cruelty and habitual drunkenness; James Martin, who testified to having witnessed his employee's violent temperament on more than one occasion; East End landlady, Elizabeth Haynes, in whom Ellen had confided her fears for her safety. Other witnesses lived closer at hand: David Malcolm of jute manufacturers, Malcolm, Ogilvie & Co., who recognised instantly that Bury's supposed job offer was a fake; Janet Martin, the Dundee shopkeeper who had inadvertently supplied Bury with what became in his hands an instrument of death; David Duncan, whose night had been disturbed by Ellen's chilling screams, ringing out through the darkness. Representing the police service, Lieutenant Parr described the agitated man who entered Bell Street Police Station on Sunday 10 February, fearful of being apprehended as Jack the Ripper; while Parr's colleague, Lieutenant Lamb, recalled his gruesome findings as he searched Bury's flat. Drs. Templeman, Stalker and Littlejohn explained for the court the conclusions they had drawn from the post-mortem examinations they had carried out.

When the turn of the defence came round, Rev. Gough of St Paul's Episcopal Church was called and indicated that, since Bury's arrival in Dundee, he had approached the clergyman twice to seek his assistance in finding a job. Following on, Drs. Kinnear and Lennox explained why their reasons for concluding that Ellen had died by suicide. In an attempt to counteract the testimony of David Duncan, another of Bury's close neighbours, Jane Duffy, was called upon to tell the court about her watchdog and how its sleep had been unbroken on the night of the alleged murder. Duffy's evidence, however, was undermined somewhat when she confessed that the creature in question had also slept soundly through the commotion caused by the discovery of Ellen's body and its removal to the mortuary - an admission that provoked a degree of hilarity in the public gallery. Summing up for the prosecution, the Advocate-Depute spoke briefly, suggesting that Bury 'had been of the opinion that Scotland was hardly a civilised country' where, hopeful of evading the law, he had brought his wife with the sole intention of doing away with her and inheriting what was left of her fortune. For the defence, William Hay argued in turn that strangulation by suicide and by homicide were virtually indistinguishable and, if the jury entertained the least doubt about the guilt of the accused, then they would be justified in returning a verdict of not proven. In his own summing up, Lord Young spoke for more than an hour concerning the circumstances of the case but he emphasised that the jurymen's verdict would have to be based entirely on their own judgment. A few minutes after ten o'clock he dismissed them to consider what they had heard.

It took the thirteen men of the jury fewer than thirty minutes to reach a verdict, but it turned out to be one which generated a degree of consternation. It fell to their spokesman, John Ramsay, to deliver the outcome of their deliberations. 'The jury have considered the evidence brought before them,' he announced, 'and they unanimously find the prisoner guilty of the charge brought against him but strongly recommend him to mercy.' Unable to conceal his surprise, Lord Young sought clarification. 'May I ask,' he inquired, 'the grounds of the strong recommendation for mercy?' A second juryman, Alexander McPherson, stepped in to explain that their equivocal verdict reflected the conflicting medical evidence that had been presented. McPherson's response, however, did not satisfy Lord Young who intimated that if the jurymen had any doubt concerning the reliability of evidence, then the right thing would be to reconsider their decision. There were, he stated categorically, no grounds for a recommendation for mercy. Perhaps a little chastened, the jury retired once again and took little more than five minutes to return with a verdict of guilty, plain and simple. Their job now completed to his lordship's satisfaction, the judge thanked them for their day's work - thirteen continuous hours - then turned his attention to the man in the dock.

An expectant hush descended on the courtroom as Lord Young prepared to address Bury. He opened his remarks by pointing out that the matter had effectively been removed from his hands by the guilty verdict that the jury had reached, and the sentence which he was required by law to impose was now set in stone. Nothing he could say at this stage, he continued, would be likely to benefit the prisoner or anyone else present, and for that reason he was reluctant to prolong 'this painful scene ... with unprofitable and idle remarks.' Listening intently, Bury remained impassive throughout, even when Lord Young assumed the black cap before pronouncing his fate: ' I do therefore in the language and in the form prescribed to me by law and custom, order and adjudge that you be carried from the bar to the prison of Dundee, and therein be detained until the 24th day of April next, and upon that day, between the hours of eight and ten o'clock forenoon, within the walls of the City Prison of Dundee, by the hands of the common executioner, be hanged by the neck from a gibbet until you be dead, and that your body be thereafter buried within the walls of the prison. And I ordain your whole moveable goods and gear to be escheat and indraught [i.e. confiscated by the state] to Her Majesty's use, which is pronounced for doom. And may God have mercy on your soul!' On hearing these grim words, Bury betrayed no emotion but, as he was led from the dock, he clearly signalled his gratitude to his legal representatives, Tweedie and Hay, for their efforts, albeit unsuccessful, on his behalf. When the court finally rose an hour before midnight an estimated 5,000 people were waiting outside in the dark, keen for news of the verdict. A number of editions of the local newspaper, the *Dundee Courier*, had been published with regular updates throughout the day, and the final issue, on the streets within minutes of the court's rising, was said to have sold several thousand copies within half an hour.

Held in solitary confinement and kept under constant suicide watch, Bury was ministered to daily by Rev. Gough but outside the walls of the prison there were other moves afoot. A petition on the condemned man's behalf was sent by David Tweedie to Henry Matthews, the Home Secretary in London, appealing for clemency. Since no new facts had emerged to be considered immediately prior to the jury's second recess, argued Tweedie, and given their earlier qualms about conflicting medical evidence, a 'not proven' verdict would surely have been a more fitting and just outcome. He made a point of highlighting the fact that little more than five minutes was all the time they took to revise their original decision. Not only that, he also pointed out that no account had been taken during the trial of a possible family disposition towards mental disorder and, in the wording of his petition, the solicitor referred to the sad fate of Bury's mother, raising the possibility that, at the time of Ellen's death, his client might well have been 'labouring under extreme mental excitement' - a fairly obvious code for insanity, temporary or otherwise. The absence of signatures on the petition Tweedie explained away by pointing out that Bury was an unknown newcomer to Dundee and could hardly be expected to generate much local sympathy, on top of which the shortage of time he had remaining meant that any delay could prove critical.

Meanwhile the city authorities were equally active, anticipating Dundee's first hanging in forty years. On Saturday 30 March the death warrant, duly signed by Lord Young, was received by the Town Clerk, William Hay (the father, as it happened, of Bury's counsel in court), and the recently-elected Bailie Stephenson deputed to take charge of logistical arrangements relating to the execution. It was noted with wry amusement that, when elected to office several months earlier, he had referred jokingly to his responsibilities as junior magistrate 'to act as hangman.' Unseen since 1872 - when the murderer, Thomas Scobbie, had been granted a last-minute reprieve - Dundee's municipal scaffold had been stored in sections in a dusty vault beneath the sheriff court and required now to be reassembled and checked over. In early April the services of the hangman, James Berry, were secured for Dundee's execution to come. During this time the condemned man, it is said, remained calm for the most part, was given a say in what he ate and slept soundly at night. In the days prior to his trial he had produced a 44-page written memoir of his background and early years, and he had now apparently undertaken the task of completing the process by recording the events of his adult life. He also spent time reading the Bible and other religious works.

When Lord Provost Hunter of Dundee received a black-bordered envelope in the post on Tuesday 23 April, its contents can hardly have come as a shock. 'With reference to the case of William Henry Bury,' wrote the Secretary of State for Scotland, the Marquis of Lothian, 'I have to acquaint you that, after careful consideration, I am unable to discover any sufficient grounds to justify me in recommending Her Majesty [Queen Victoria] to interfere in this case.' At that, the message concluded decisively in stating that 'The law will therefore take its course.' As prayers were offered up in Episcopal churches throughout the city, it was left to David Tweedie and Rev. Gough to break the news to the condemned man, but Bury, it was said, retained his composure and looked to his impending fate with a degree of fatalism. In the evening of Monday 22 April James Berry and his assistant, Scott, arrived in Dundee by rail. Unrecognised by the populace at large, the executioner was said to have informed his startled cab driver that his reason for visiting Scotland was for the purpose of dispatching William Bury. On the day immediately prior to the execution the final preparations took place as the scaffold was assembled and tested in the presence of magistrates and accordingly deemed satisfactory. For understandable reasons, Bury's composure cracked somewhat during his final afternoon and his last night's sleep was said to have been fitful, in anticipation, we might assume, of his forthcoming appointment with fate.

He rose shortly after five o'clock, dressed himself in the same suit of clothes in which he had appeared at his trial and ate a light breakfast of tea, bread and butter and poached eggs. Lighting up a cigarette, he spent some time reading the Bible and, in conversation with one of his warders, was heard to remark, 'This is my last morning on earth. I freely forgive all who gave false evidence against me.' The identities of who these might be were not made explicit but, resentful or not, Bury gave the impression of being calm and resigned to what lay ahead. Around half past six the ringing of a bell heralded the arrival of Rev. Gough, and the clergyman was followed by a steady stream of magistrates and other officials who were required by statute to be present. Bringing up the rear came representatives of the press who were also to be permitted to attend. Whilst the final bureaucratic preliminaries were being dealt with, Berry and Scott attended to more practical matters, trying out the rope and giving the scaffold a final once-over on the spot where it had been erected within the prison grounds. A bantam cock of a man, William Bury stood at just five feet three inches tall and weighed less than ten stones, and it was estimated that a drop of just over six feet would be required in order to ensure instant death. Berry's meticulousness with regard to calculations and arrangements was well known: 'I tests my ropes before I uses them,' he was quoted as saying. A few minutes before eight o'clock the condemned man met his executioner who pinioned his arms and wrists to his body while, standing alongside, Rev. Gough recited aloud the Episcopal service for the dying. Once the pinioning process was complete, the condemned man indicated that he wished to say a few words to express his gratitude for the treatment he had received since entering prison, and to bid his warders a final farewell. As he was escorted from his cell, he was preceded by Rev. Gough, attired in white clerical vestments and bearing a prayer book in his hands, and it was observed by those in attendance that the prisoner appeared to be in better physical shape than some weeks earlier when he was first locked up - the result, almost certainly, of enforced abstinence from alcohol and a regular wholesome diet. When given the opportunity to speak, Bury declined, opting instead to remain silent.

The march to the scaffold was led by two warders, with the condemned man following on behind, accompanied by Revs. Gough and Robertson, this latter the prison chaplain. Next in line came the executioner, various magistrates and officials and, at the back of the queue, a group of journalists. As the procession passed between the condemned cell and the scaffold, Rev. Gough intoned once again the prayer for the dead and the firm voice of the prisoner was clearly heard in response. Before reaching the scaffold, his collar and tie were removed and a rope put in their place; the customary white hood was drawn down over his features; and he was guided, blindfold, to the foot of the scaffold. He climbed the stairs without hesitation and, arriving on the platform, was positioned directly below the beam. While Berry's assistant, Scott, strapped his legs together, the hangman himself concentrated on making a few last-minute adjustments to the noose. Despite his face being covered, it was possible to see that Bury continued to mouth his responses to Rev. Gough's prayer for the dead until the very end when, just as the clergyman fell silent, the executioner stepped forward and drew the lever, thus releasing the trapdoor. As the prisoner dropped from sight all that was visible was a sudden jerk when the rope reached its fullest extent. A dull thud was heard simultaneously. The rope, it was noted, never gave a quiver which pointed to the fact that death had come mercifully swiftly. With no time wasted, the black flag was hoisted over the prison gate as a signal to the waiting crowd - reportedly amounting to several thousand, many of them female - that the murderer, William Bury, had departed to meet his maker. After being left to hang for an hour or so, at around nine o'clock the body was raised to the platform once again where an examination was carried out by the prison surgeon, Dr James Miller, which confirmed that the spinal cord had been snapped cleanly, resulting in a painless and instantaneous death. The corpse was then placed in a plain wooden coffin for interment that evening within the prison grounds. Adjacent to the graves of his fellow-murderers, the spot where Bury was laid to rest was subsequently marked by a stone engraved - *W.H.B. 24/4/1889.*

Not long after the execution Rev. Gough revealed that, two days prior to Bury's death, he had made a 'full and frank confession' of his guilt and, at the clergyman's behest, had agreed to put his words in writing. 'I admit that it was by my own hands that my wife Ellen Bury met with her death,' he wrote, adding enigmatically that he was not prepared to divulge his motive since it 'concerns so closely the character of my wife.' The letter closed with a request for 'the Pardon of Almighty God.' It was forwarded by Gough to the Secretary of State for Scotland but never subsequently appeared in print. Around this same time a strange little anecdote circulated throughout Dundee involving a young woman who had formed part of the crowd awaiting news outside the prison on the morning of Wednesday 24 April. Visibly upset at the sight of the black flag being raised, she had apparently broken down while uttering the words, 'Oh, Harry! I did not think it would come to this.' Questioned by those around her, she had confessed that she and Bury had been married nine years earlier, thus accounting for her present distress. Accompanying her was a small child of some eight or nine years who was, the woman claimed, the daughter of the newly hanged man. She had remained silent up till now, she went on, in order to spare her child the ignominy of having had a convicted murderer for her father. Reportedly resident in Dundee for several years, the unnamed young woman supported herself and her daughter from the wages she earned at a local factory. That the story sounds dubious is hard to deny but, that said, it does raise the intriguing possibility - however remote - that the crime of bigamy could be added to Bury's catalogue of vice. And, if true, it might go some way to explaining why, after leaving London, Dundee had been his destination of choice.

A mere three days after Bury's conviction, a crime was committed in the city which many considered a copycat action. On Saturday 30 March Bridget Redmond was serving a customer in the small grocery store in St

Mary Street, Dundee, which was run by her husband and herself when, completely without warning, he approached her from behind and plunged a knife into her back. Joseph Redmond was bravely disarmed by Charles Anderson, a bread delivery man, while Bridget staggered to the door, crying, 'Oh! I am stabbed! Take hold of me!' Out on the street she fell to the ground where she was comforted by neighbours who placed a pillow under her head and moistened her lips with brandy, but to no avail. Before a doctor could be summoned Bridget Redmond passed away approximately half an hour after her husband's murderous assault. Redmond, it turned out, was an army veteran who had seen service in India where he had been severely afflicted with sunstroke and this, it was believed, had had a negative long-term impact on his mental health. The previous day he had read in the newspaper details of William Bury's trial and this, it was surmised, had been the instrument by which he became unhinged. Declared insane, he was duly committed to Perth Prison during Her Majesty's pleasure where he died of natural causes three years later, still in his early fifties.

Within a matter of weeks there was a curious sequel to Joseph Redmond's case when his brother, James, was arrested in Edinburgh when found drunk and incapable. Detained by police, he attempted unsuccessfully to commit suicide in his cell by strangling himself with his handkerchief. Following examination by doctors, he was pronounced sane and defended himself in court by claiming that he had been mentally destabilised by news of his brother's committal to jail. A veil was quickly drawn over the matter when he was admonished by the presiding magistrate and dismissed.

As for William Bury, at the end of the day we might imagine that his trial, execution and belated confession would have effectively put a lid on matters but, no, the rumour mill continued to grind. The nub of the matter was the question of whether William Bury and Jack the Ripper were, in point of fact, one and the same person. Certainly the *modus operandi* of the two killers might lead to such a conclusion and what was inescapable was the fact that the Whitechapel atrocities had ceased around the same time that Bury moved north. On the far side of the Atlantic, the American press ran with the story, reporting that 'Bury has confessed to all the Whitechapel murders', while, nearer home, a Scottish newspaper confidently asserted three years later that 'the Dundee authorities are still of the opinion that the William Henry Bury who died in Dundee at the hands of the common hangman was no other than the much spoken of Jack the Ripper.' In 1895 that same hangman returned to Dundee where over several nights he lectured to packed-out audiences in the People's Palace. It was rumoured that Berry let slip that, back in 1889, London detectives had told him that 'We are quite satisfied that you have hanged Jack the Ripper. There will be no more Whitechapel crimes.' And, as it turned out, there weren't. If, however, the story had any truth in it, what is puzzling to say the least is why in his 1892 autobiography, *My Experiences as an Executioner*, Berry failed even to mention Jack the Ripper or, for that matter, the Dundee murderer, William Henry Bury.

William McKeown : January 1893

West Lodge was an extremely desirable property situated in the up-market Glasgow suburb of Pollokshields. One of the largest villas in a district that abounded in large villas, it stood in Maxwell Drive amid two acres of its own grounds, overlooking the recently-completed courts of Pollokshields Tennis Club. The owner of West Lodge was the widow of the late Bailie Wilson who, finding the house too large for her needs, took the decision to decamp to her country house at Prestwick, leaving the Pollokshields property in the hands of a firm of estate agents. For obvious reasons a substantial sandstone villa lying empty in one of Glasgow's best addresses would be vulnerable to break-in, so the agents took the precaution of putting a watchman in place who was accommodated in a ground floor kitchen-cum-bedroom, accessed via its own external door. The caretaker appointed was a 31-year-old jobbing gardener by the name of William McKeown.

During his time at Maxwell Drive, McKeown (or McEwen) was on cordial terms with Alexander McDougall, the gardener from two doors down at Mount Blow Villa, who formed the habit of knocking on his friend's window each morning to waken him, after which the two men would often have breakfast together. When McDougall arrived at West Lodge shortly before 6 a. m. on Tuesday 11 October 1892 he was surprised to find that there was no light in his friend's window. He gave it a tap and heard McKeown's voice crying in response, 'Is that you, Sandy?' McKeown went on to explain that he was still half-asleep and in his shirt-tails, and that therefore he would not be out till after breakfast. Suspecting nothing amiss, McDougall replied that he would return at nine o'clock, then turned around and headed back to Mount Blow where he spent the next three hours working in the garden. A curious little incident occurred just as he returned to West Lodge at nine o'clock. Finding a bird caught up in a bush, he took some time to disentangle the small creature which he then carried into one of the outhouses in the hope of finding a cage. Unsuccessful in his search, he stepped back outside and walked towards McKeown's door which he found, to his surprise, was wide open though there was no sign of the caretaker himself. He called out more than once but received no answer, so he entered the narrow passageway that gave access to the bedroom itself. Glancing down as he did so, he was puzzled to see what looked like smears of blood on the floor but it was only when he stepped into the bedroom itself that he came face to face with a sight that stopped him in his tracks. The room, he found, was in a state of total disarray, both of its beds unmade and various items of women's clothing strewn over the furniture. Worst of all by far, on the floor between the two beds he saw a large puddle of what appeared to be blood. At this, McDougall had seen enough and turned on his heel and left West Lodge with the intention of alerting the police. The small bird in his hands, we may assume, was probably granted its freedom.

Meeting another local gardener, McDougall inquired whether he had seen McKeown but the answer was no. When McDougall revealed to him what he had recently found, the two men went inside and examined McKeown's room, taking care not to touch anything or disturb the contents in any way. When McDougall stepped out on to the street again a few minutes later, he was fortunate to encounter two local policemen, Constables Sampson and Sim, who, hearing his tale, returned with him to West Lodge. After they had investigated McKeown's room, the officers noticed traces of blood on the gravel of the driveway which led them towards a water trough where they found a spade, a hamper and a wooden box, all of them stained with blood. By now it looked very much as though they had a serious case on their hands and therefore they alerted their senior officers, Chief-Constable John Boyd and

Superintendent Thomas Muir, who descended on West Lodge shortly after midday. Where an area of cultivated ground showed signs that the soil had recently been disturbed, these officers authorised Alexander McDougall to start digging and within moments a series of grisly finds began to emerge. Twelve inches or so below the surface McDougall uncovered two severed human legs, while loosely buried in a second hole a short distance away he unearthed a bundle of intestines and internal organs with the sole exception of one kidney. A third hole was found to contain one arm and the trunk (with the left kidney remaining in place), and buried in the fourth and final hole were the victim's head and remaining arm. Looking for the weapon, or weapons, involved in the crime, officers discovered an axe stained with blood in the coal-cellar and, concealed among sticks in an outdoor tool house, they found a broken hand-saw with ragged strips of flesh still attached to its teeth. This, they surmised, had been used in dismembering the body. On top of that, they came across a joiner's hammer, hidden below McKeown's bed, and recovered a razor from an ash-pile in the garden.

Following these gruesome discoveries, the Glasgow police force swung quickly into action. In an effort to prevent the suspect, William McKeown, from fleeing the city, officers were directed to monitor all travellers preparing to leave by rail, while others were posted at the Greenock ferry terminals in an effort to thwart his chances of escaping by sea. It was believed that McKeown had very little money in his possession, and for that reason police were confident that he would be unable to travel far from the city without being detected. As a precaution, however, neighbouring forces were alerted by telephone - advanced technology at the time - and messages sent by telegraph to more distant locations. Meanwhile, descriptions of the suspected murderer were copied and distributed in large numbers: 'William McEwan [sic], jobbing gardener; from 30 to 35 years of age; 5 feet 8 inches in height; ruddy complexion, prominent nose, heavy eyebrows, sandy-coloured hair, reddish whiskers and moustache, shaved on chin. Dressed in dark serge or corded shooting coat, single-breasted vest of dark tweed, dark tweed trousers, with greenish stripe, and double-peaked tweed cap; has a shambling gait, and throws his feet well out when walking; has a rather dissipated appearance, and is a native of County Down and speaks with a strong Irish accent.' Although McKeown had been doing odd jobs in the Pollokshields area for some two to three years and had been employed at West Lodge since the early part of 1892, little appeared to be known of his personal history. Based on his colouring and complexion he was known to his associates by the nickname of 'Red Wull', and when questioned by police they described him as 'a nice, quiet fellow' who was - as far as they knew - 'of a very cheery disposition'.

Gathered together in a basket, the body parts found at West Lodge were forwarded to the Southern Police Office mortuary where a post-mortem examination was carried out by two eminent medical men, Professor Dunlop and Dr Moore, the latter the medical legal examiner for Glasgow. As they pieced together the various parts of the corpse on their table, the doctors noted that all of the cuts through the flesh had been made roughly, as though in great haste. What they saw led them to conclude that the woman's head and limbs had been detached from her body after her death using a saw. From the entire body's bloodless condition, they deduced that her carotid artery had been severed while she was still alive which would have resulted in a loss of blood from the brain so sudden and so great as to cause the heart to cease functioning immediately. Gashes on the woman's cheeks and forehead gave the impression that a struggle had taken place during the attempt to cut her throat, and the angle of the cuts suggested that her head had been pulled well back at the time. The doctors found no evidence that the woman had been stunned prior to her death, and the uniform nature of the cuts suggested that they were likely to be the work of a single individual. Initially the body was identified as that of Mary McCallum, a dark-haired woman in her mid-thirties, but a correction had to be made after the corpse was recognised in the mortuary by Alexander McIntyre of Byres Road who recognised a mark on the woman's lower lip which identified her conclusively as Eliza Connor (or O'Connor), a 25 or 26-year-old Irishwoman with whom he had been cohabiting now for several months. McIntyre was able to fill in a few details relating to her background. Eliza had formerly been employed as a domestic servant, he said, but her life had spiralled out of control through misuse of alcohol. Obstreperous when drinking, she had been evicted from her home at least once and locked up by police on several occasions, most recently when arrested for fighting. The last time McIntyre had seen her alive was when the two had parted company at the corner of North Street at around nine o'clock in the evening of Monday 10 October. As far as he knew, McKeown was a stranger to her.

During the course of the day various stories began to circulate concerning Eliza's death. It was rumoured that McKeown and she had been seen entering a cab the night before in the company of a third man, this latter believed to have been arrested and to have provided police with valuable information. For the time being, however, officers remained tight-lipped as they worked hard behind the scenes to establish McKeown's movements during the previous evening and the early hours of the morning. It emerged that around 7.30 p.m. he had paid a visit to his fellow countryman, a sailor named Thomas McNeilly - the rumoured third man - who lived with his wife and four children in Finnieston Street, just north of the River Clyde. Another two of McNeilly's associates - his brother, John, and his friend, John McMullan - were also present. After downing a substantial quantity of whisky and beer, the men left Finnieston Street at around half past ten and walked to a public house known as McIntyre's where they continued drinking. When the landlord refused to serve them any further on the grounds that they had already drunk enough, the four men moved to a second public house at Queen's Dock and here they separated into two groups. McKeown and McNeilly left to have supper in a cheap late-night restaurant before wandering the city streets for more than an hour. They ended up in George Square where they fell into conversation with a young woman unfamiliar to either of them - Eliza Connor, as it turned out - who was out walking the streets. Presumably suspecting her of prostitution, a policeman shone a light in Eliza's face but, for whatever reason, he decided to take no action and moved away. At this point McNeilly was ready to walk home, but McKeown gave him a shake, saying, 'Come on!', and persuaded him to share a cab with Eliza and himself. Following negotiations over the fare, the three piled inside and were driven the short distance south over the River Clyde and on to Pollokshields where they asked to be dropped off at the corner of St Andrew's Road and Maxwell Road, a few minutes' walk from West Lodge. Obviously in high spirits, McKeown took it upon himself to foot the cabman's bill of two shillings as well as tipping him an extra threepence on top. The two men and their female companion then walked the short distance to West Lodge where McKeown lit a fire in his room and all three settled down to drink whisky. At around half past two or three o'clock McKeown offered to make tea, but McNeilly declined. Most conveniently, the room contained two beds and, removing his jacket and boots, McNeilly fell into the one nearer the window, while McKeown and Eliza made themselves comfortable directly opposite.

Almost certainly alcohol contributed to the fact that all three dropped off pretty quickly and apparently slept soundly until six o'clock when, as we already know, the gardener from Mount Blow tapped on the window. Awakened by the sound of McKeown's voice, McNeilly glanced at the clock and realised with a jolt that he would be late for his work as a lamp-trimmer aboard the *Furnessia*, an Anchor Line steamer due to depart for America in two days' time. McKeown set about brewing a pot of tea, but McNeilly had no time to wait and he left West Lodge at around a quarter past six while Eliza was still in bed. Police would later conclude from studying the teacups that McKeown and she had taken tea together before the murder took place. What happened after McNeilly's departure was witnessed by no-one, but shortly before eight o'clock McKeown was seen leaving West Lodge by milkmen who had just arrived in Maxwell Drive to carry out their deliveries. One of the men, Joseph Beattie, knew him by sight and asked whether he had any grass for sale to be used as fodder for his horse. In reply McKeown shook his head and muttered unintelligibly, something that Beattie thought was out of character since previously the two men had often enjoyed a joke together. The last that Beattie saw of McKeown was as he strode off quickly in the direction of Bellahouston.

McKeown, of course, was not the only suspect in relation to the case, and Detective Inspector Carmichael called at Thomas McNeilly's home that afternoon to be told by his wife that he was still at work and not expected back until early evening. The policeman informed her that a murder had been committed and questioned her about William McKeown who she confirmed was a regular visitor to her home. Carmichael returned at around seven o'clock to find McNeilly lying on top of his bed, awaiting his arrival. After confirming his identity, McNeilly provided him with a full account of his movements during the previous evening and overnight. When charged with Eliza Connor's murder, he was vehement in protesting his innocence but was inevitably arrested nonetheless and taken into custody. According to standard procedure, at the police station he was required to strip to allow his clothing to be examined for traces of blood but, in the event, none were found. Sometime later Inspector Carmichael returned to McNeilly's house where he found more articles of his clothing, washed and hung out to dry, but like the garments previously examined none of these showed any sign of blood. Based on the openness of his manner and the fact that he had raised no objection to his possessions (including a pocket-knife) being examined, Carmichael's instinct was that McNeilly had given a truthful account of his involvement. At the end of the day, however, it would take more than a detective's hunch to clear his name in court.

The following morning - Wednesday 12 October - McKeown remained at large, though no shortage of sightings had been reported, often in different locations at precisely the same time. At the end of the day, however, it turned out that he was apprehended little more than a mile from Maxwell Drive when three gamekeepers on the Pollok Estate were patrolling fields on East Henderston farm, a short distance south of the main Paisley road. One of the men, Samuel Wright, spotted a stranger acting suspiciously and immediately the gamekeeper's thoughts turned to the recent murder. He approached the man - none other than McKeown - who immediately made off at a run, then, as the keeper looked on in horror, drew a knife from his pocket and, holding his chin with his left hand, attempted to cut his own throat. Wright called upon him to stop but McKeown paid no heed and by the time that the gamekeeper drew level with him, he had dropped to his knees - pale, bleeding and trembling, but still alive. As Wright wrested the knife away from him, McKeown grasped his collar and tie with a surprisingly strong grip but the keeper managed nonetheless to roll him on to his back and keep him secured there until his colleagues caught up with the action. Taking charge of the situation, the head gamekeeper sent Wright and his colleague to the Half-Way House, a few hundred yards to the north, where Sub-Inspector Cowie had been stationed in expectation of possible sightings. Cowie accompanied the two keepers back to the spot in the fields where the injured man lay, and they were joined there soon after by Constable Mellon of the Queen's Park division who had spent the morning scouring the area by bicycle and who was familiar with McKeown by sight. Word was sent to Dr Hunter of Paisley Road who arrived promptly on the scene and, after examining the injured man, ordered that he be removed to hospital without delay. Throughout this time McKeown remained conscious but did not say a word.

Constable Mellon set off on his bicycle to make arrangements for an ambulance wagon to be despatched from Govan and, when it arrived at the Half-Way House, the wounded man was carefully lifted aboard and escorted by Inspector Murray and Constable Mellon to the Royal Infirmary. News of McKeown's arrest had spread through the city with astonishing rapidity and by the time that the ambulance reached the Royal Infirmary a large crowd, consisting mainly of young people and women, had gathered at the hospital entrance in eager anticipation of his arrival, but if they were hoping for a glimpse of the suspected murderer then they were to be disappointed. The ambulance wagon passed quickly through the external gateway whose doors immediately closed behind it, and only when it was behind the perimeter wall was the curtain drawn back to reveal the pallid, drawn and haggard form of McKeown inside. He was lifted from the ambulance by hospital attendants, assisted by a burly policeman, who carried him into the hospital building where he was placed in a ward and examined by Dr Henderson, with a group of nurses and medical students looking on. McKeown's self-inflicted wound, it transpired, extended diagonally from his left ear to the middle of his throat and measured three inches in length by one inch deep. Blood had clotted around the ragged edges of the laceration and it was feared that administering any treatment might lead to an artery giving way. Some hours later, however, the cut was able to be washed and dressed and McKeown's condition improved steadily as the day went on.

When Detective Inspector Carmichael learned of the arrest he made his way immediately to the Royal Infirmary where doctors assured him that McKeown's condition had now stabilised, and that charging him with murder would be unlikely to put his health at risk. Coming face to face with his suspect, Carmichael verified his name and address before reading out to him the charge of murder. McKeown showed no reaction and stayed silent throughout. As his clothing was being removed for examination, the contents of an inside coat pocket struck Inspector Carmichael as potentially significant. From a used envelope addressed to 'Wm. McKeown, caretaker, West Lodge', the detective withdrew a piece of paper on which the following words had been written in pencil - 'I am put to do this; may the Lord have mercy on my soul'. The short message ended with the suspect's signature - 'W. McKeown'. On the outside of the envelope the words 'I am pressed' appeared to have been scrawled in haste, plus a number of other marks which were impossible to decipher. Brief and nebulous though they may be, it is hard to avoid interpreting these inscrutable, pencilled messages as some kind of a confession.

Once fit to be discharged from hospital, McKeown was accommodated pending trial in Duke Street Prison, notorious for its harsh conditions. Though by no means fully recovered, he was sufficiently well by Saturday 17 December to stand at the bar alongside his friend, Thomas McNeilly, to be charged by Sheriff Birnie that 'on 11th October 1892, in an apartment of the house called West Lodge, Maxwell Drive, Pollokshields, Glasgow, you did assault Elizabeth Connor or O'Connor, sometime residing in Stockwell Street, Glasgow, now deceased, and did beat and stab or cut her, and did murder her'. The two men's trial came to court in Glasgow a fortnight later and was held over two days during the last week of December. In an attempt at plea bargaining, McKeown's lawyer indicated his client's willingness to admit to culpable homicide if the murder charge against him were to be dropped, but the offer was rejected out of hand by the Advocate-Depute, acting for the prosecution. McNeilly, for his part, tendered a plea of not guilty, and his lawyer intimated a special defence of *alibi* on the grounds that he was not present when the murder was committed at West Lodge, but was either aboard or on his way to the vessel *Furnessia*. As the case proceeded, it became clear that a crucial plank of the defence's case was its attempt to refute the findings of the two surgeons who had carried out Eliza Connor's post-mortem examination by demonstrating that there was a considerable body of medical opinion who opposed their belief that it was possible to be certain as to whether wounds had been inflicted before or immediately after death. This was a very important point in the case since if it could be established that Connor's wounds might theoretically have been inflicted after her death, then it stood to reason that it would not be safe to convict McKeown of murder. Various medical men were brought in as witnesses. Dr Love, who had been present at West Lodge, suggested that wounds inflicted within two minutes of a person's death would be indistinguishable from those inflicted immediately beforehand. Invited to give his opinion, an experienced police surgeon, Dr Johnston, agreed that 'it was a matter of doubt', and Dr A. M. Moffatt, who had visited McKeown in jail on several occasions, was equally dubious. As well as attempting to cast doubt on the validity of the post-mortem examination, the defence also raised the question of McKeown's mental state. When called to the stand, Dr J. F. Sutherland of Duke Street Prison recounted how McKeown had attempted to kill himself in jail more than once and had therefore been placed on constant suicide watch. Questioned regarding his mental health, Sutherland replied that '[McKeown's] mind is to a considerable extent deranged' and 'he does not seem to realise the gravity of his position' - a little odd in the light of his repeated suicide attempts. Dr Moffatt testified in turn that McKeown 'exhibited mental peculiarities which one would not expect to find in a person of good health'. By merging these twin lines of argument, the defence mooted the possibility that McKeown might have mutilated Connor's body shortly after her death while 'in a state of frenzy' caused by some or other mental abnormality. The point, of course, was that, if he had been acting with diminished responsibility, then it would be unjust to convict him of murder.

There was, of course, more than one man in the dock, though the case of Thomas McNeilly had been relegated to something of a sideshow throughout much of the trial. During the course of the second day the judge, Lord Adam, addressed the members of the jury, pointing out to them that no evidence had been brought to bear against McNeilly and that a number of factors pointed in his favour. By his own account, he had left West Lodge shortly after 6 a.m. and had arrived aboard the *Furnessia* around one hour later without a speck of blood about his person. Furthermore, after being told by his wife that he was wanted for questioning for murder, he had made no attempt to abscond but remained calmly at home, awaiting Detective Inspector Carmichael's arrival. According to medical experts, the dismemberment of Eliza Connor's body could have been accomplished by a single person within roughly the space of an hour, and they had deduced from the manner in which she had been wounded that it was likely to have been the work of one man. For all these reasons, the judge stated that he was certain that there was no case against McNeilly and, if the jury agreed, then he would no longer require to be detained. After deliberation, the jury's spokesman agreed with Lord Adam and a formal verdict of not guilty was then delivered. At that, McNeilly was released from the dock, and it was noted that, when he glanced briefly across at his former companion, the look on McNeilly's face was unreadable.

Summing up for the prosecution, the Advocate-Depute suggested that by tendering a plea of culpable homicide at the start of the trial, McKeown's counsel had effectively accepted his responsibility for Eliza Connor's death, and all that remained to be decided now was whether she had died accidentally or murder had been committed. He contended that a quarrel had flared up between the two and a struggle had ensued in McKeown's bed during the course of which he had pulled back Connor's head and slit her throat. Faced with the problem of disposing of her body, he knew full well that any attempt to remove it from West Lodge could not fail to be noticed by neighbours, so he plumped for the only other option - dismemberment and burial. This, the Advocate-Depute concluded, could be viewed as nothing other than an act of murder, and accordingly he requested that the jury return a guilty verdict. When it came the turn of the defence, McKeown's lawyer countered by highlighting the absence of either premeditation or motive on his client's part, arguing that it had not been established beyond doubt that Connor's injuries had been inflicted while she was still alive and, indeed, the fact that bloodstains on her clothing did not correspond with the wounds on her body indicated rather the opposite. He postulated a scenario where, during the course of an altercation, McKeown had accidentally killed Connor by a single blow to the head, panicked and attempted to conceal her body in the garden. Hinting at his client's inherent decency, he pointed out that from the outset McKeown had absolved his friend, McNeilly, of any involvement in the death of Eliza Connor. For these reasons, he concluded that a verdict of culpable homicide would be appropriate and just.

Following Lord Adam's summing up from the bench, the jury retired to consider their decision but returned to court within the space of half an hour. Asked for their verdict, the foreman announced that the members of the jury found the prisoner guilty as charged. McKeown, it seemed, had not heard and leaned over to consult one of the police officers beside him in the dock. On learning his fate, he remained quite impassive, his face devoid of expression, and he quickly resumed his former casual attitude, leaning his left elbow on the front bar of the dock with his head resting on his hand. Called upon to stand for sentencing, he appeared dazed and detached from his surroundings. Lord Adam told McKeown that, as 'the mouthpiece of the law', he had no option other than to sentence him to death, announcing that he would be hanged within Duke Street Prison on Wednesday 18 January 1893 between the hours of eight and ten o'clock in the forenoon. Then, assuming the black cap, the judge concluded with the words, 'And this I pronounce for doom'. At this, McKeown was led from the dock and escorted to the cell where he would spend his final three weeks.

For Thomas McNeilly, of course, the outcome was a good deal more cheerful. Looking remarkably composed after leaving the dock, he was greeted by his wife, sister and brother in an emotional reunion, but as the four attempted to leave the court building by the front door they were engulfed by crowds of well-wishers who cheered heartily and insisted one after another on shaking McNeilly by the hand. Unable to escape, the McNeillys retreated into the courthouse with the exception of his brother, John, who slipped out in search of a cab. Owing to the striking similarity he bore to Thomas, John McNeilly found himself mobbed yet again and only with the greatest of difficulty did he persuade the crowds that he was not their man. Eventually all four McNeillys managed to slip unnoticed out of the back door and, as he left, the acquitted man was reported as saying, 'I'll never lift liquor to my mouth again.' Whether he kept his word is unknown.

In spite of the bloodthirstiness of his crime, a petition appealing for clemency was submitted on McKeown's behalf to the Secretary of State for Scotland, Sir George Trevelyan. While awaiting its outcome, he was said to have been receptive to the ministrations of Father Polycarp Clifford, who attended him in prison and advised him on spiritual matters. The wound on his throat continued to heal satisfactorily and he was able to eat wholesome meals. But if it had not done so already, the reality of his situation had definitely sunk in and his only hopes now were pinned on a successful outcome for the petition. On Monday 16 January - two days before the day set for McKeown's execution - the hangman, James Billington, arrived from England on the first of three professional visits he made to Scotland during the course of his career. A former Sunday school teacher, Billington's lifelong fascination with hanging was rumoured to have led him as a boy to experiment with stray dogs and cats in his parents' garden. Arrangements had been made to accommodate him in one of the gatehouses to Duke Street Prison, and it was noted that he had brought with him his own rope from Holloway

Prison, London, and the various other items in connection with his trade. Meanwhile inside the prison McKeown waited on tenterhooks for the Scottish Secretary's reply, but not until the day immediately prior to his execution were copies of a letter from Sir George Trevelyan received respectively by Lord Provost Bell of Glasgow, Governor Alston of Duke Street Prison and McKeown's legal counsel. The letters contained no good news, stating that 'after careful consideration, [Trevelyan] regrets that he is unable to discover sufficient grounds to justify him in recommending any interference with the course of the law.' The unenviable task of conveying the bad news to McKeown fell to the Town Clerk, Sir James Marwick, who, seeing the devastating effect it had on him, beat a rapid retreat and left Father Clifford to play the part of comforter as McKeown lay on top of his bed, sobbing bitterly. What sympathy is due to a man who acted so brutally, we might ask, even under the influence of alcohol? It is hard to know what to make of William McKeown. Inevitably comparisons were made with the recent Whitechapel atrocities of Jack the Ripper, both in terms of Eliza Connor's place in society and also the murderer's methods. Worthy of any sympathy or not - and opinions are likely to vary - what was now beyond doubt was that McKeown's fate was well and truly sealed.

Understandably, his final night in Duke Street Prison was an unsettled one. Around one o'clock he suffered a panic attack and had to be calmed down by warders to whom he confessed his fears of breaking down during his ordeal ahead. He lay down again, but rose every so often to pray at a small altar that had been placed in his room the previous day. He gave up trying to sleep at four o'clock and got up, washed and dressed himself in the same clothes that he had worn for his trial. An hour or so later Governor Alston visited his cell but, lying on top of the bed, he kept his eyes closed and refused to speak. He was more responsive when Father Clifford arrived at six o'clock in the company of a second priest, Father Cornelius McGrath, and a third man, McGrath's assistant. The clergymen celebrated Mass in the condemned cell where McKeown's final Holy Communion appeared to provide him with at least some degree of comfort. Unsurprisingly, he showed no appetite for food and refused breakfast when it was offered but he did manage to drink a small quantity of tea. By the time that the prison bell started tolling shortly before eight o'clock a body of twenty policeman were already in position whose job it was to maintain good order and ensure that proceedings went without hitch. Also present were two Glasgow magistrates, Bailies Alexander and Parnie, the prison chaplain, the prison surgeon plus a number of other officials. The joiner whose job it had been to erect the scaffold had been permitted to wait in order to see his handiwork put to the test.

A few minutes after eight o'clock the prison governor and the executioner, Billington, entered the condemned cell. McKeown made no effort to resist as his arms were securely pinioned to his sides, but tears flowed down his cheeks as the bandages were removed from his self-inflicted neck wound. Preceded by Father McGrath's acolyte holding a lighted candle, he was accompanied to the scaffold by the hangman, Governor Alston, Fathers Clifford and McGrath and a number of prison warders. Other than the low tones of the priests, reciting the prayers for the dying, and McKeown's subdued responses, the solemn group proceeded in silence. Meanwhile, a second procession of magistrates and the Chief Constable of Police, escorted by city officers bearing halberds, was making its way to the scene of the execution. It was a well-established procedure, set by historical precedent, though we may assume that the man at the centre of it all would have remained unimpressed by the ceremonial. From the foot of the scaffold he was obliged to climb a sloping gangway, draped with black cloth, that led on to the platform where he stood motionless to have his legs bound tightly together with a leather strap. At his side, Father McGrath held up a crucifix which he leaned forward to kiss while uttering his last ever words - 'Jesus, have mercy on me.' At that, the white hood was drawn down over his face, the noose given a final adjustment, and at nine minutes past eight o'clock precisely, Billington drew back the bolt, the trapdoor fell and William McKeown plunged downwards from the platform. Mercifully, death appeared instantaneous and, as his body dangled at the end of the rope, no sign of movement could be detected. It was left to hang there for an hour before being cut down and examined by doctors who observed that, such had been the strain on his neck, that McKeown's wound had reopened and that his larynx had been torn right through. There was, however, no sign of bleeding.

Throughout the city and beyond, McKeown's case had generated enormous public interest and, despite the fact that it was a gloomy, wet, winter morning, an enormous crowd of men and women had gathered outside Duke Street Prison whose gaze without exception was directed up towards the roof where the notorious black flag would soon be raised. Variously estimated at somewhere between 12,000 and 20,000 individuals, the spectators filled the entire west side of Cathedral Square, the east end of Rottenrow, plus an area of vacant ground adjacent to the High Street. Weaving to and fro in their midst, the chanting and hymn-singing of evangelical preachers went largely unregarded. When there was a slight delay in hoisting the flag, a rumour ran through the crowd to the effect that something untoward had taken place and, when it did finally make its appearance, it failed to open out immediately and a few seconds passed before it was definitively identified as the signal of death. Knowing that justice had been served, the crowd's reaction was curiously muted and within a few moments the spectators, for the most part, simply melted away. Meanwhile, inside Duke Street Prison the last part of the process to be carried out was the identification of McKeown's corpse by the various officials and other individuals involved - including his former friend, the gardener of Mount Blow Villa, Alexander McDougall. For his part, the hangman, Billington, wasted no time in leaving Glasgow and, his task now efficiently carried out, he caught the mail train south shortly before midday.

As it turned out, McKeown's night-time fears of breaking down when standing on the brink of eternity had proved unfounded, and in fact he went to his death with firmness, perhaps even a degree of dignity. What is odd is the fact that at no stage, either before or after his conviction, was he prepared to make a full and frank confession and, while it seems fair to assume that no-one at the time entertained any serious doubts as to his guilt, what exactly it was that lit the touch-paper at West Lodge and prompted McKeown to commit his horrific crime is something that must remain for ever a mystery.

John Herdman : March 1898

It all started out innocently enough. An attractive girl in her late teens, naturally Jennie Soutar had no shortage of admirers, the foremost of whom was a 22-year-old trade apprentice, John Herdman, whose fine singing voice had earned him a degree of acclaim in the Edinburgh area. Despite his musical talents, however, there was a distinctly darker side to Herdman's personality. Quick-tempered and inclined to jealousy, he quarrelled with a rival over the pretty laundress's affections and when he chanced one afternoon to meet the two of them strolling in the Meadows an initial exchange of insults soon developed into fisticuffs and Herdman, as it turned out, came off second best - no great surprise, perhaps, for a bantam cock of a man weighing less than ten stones. Later, when chaffed over the incident by his rival's brother, he grew inflamed to the extent that he launched a knife in his direction, injuring the man's back and earning himself a criminal record in the process.

Turn the clock forward three decades or so and - whatever might have taken place during the intervening years - Jessie Soutar and John Herdman had now been keeping company for some two to three years. In her late forties, Jessie was still working in a local laundry and, though native to Edinburgh, she apparently had no living relatives in the city while Herdman, for his part, was a 52-year-old widower with a grown-up family who earned his living as a printer's machineman. By the end of

1897 the couple had been cohabiting for several months in a sixth-floor garret at 7 Milne Square, just off the High Street, though their relationship was a consistently stormy one and on more than one occasion they had parted in acrimonious circumstances. The tenement building they occupied was fairly dilapidated and their single room was divided from its immediate neighbours by nothing more substantial than a flimsy wooden partition, meaning that James and Ann O'Connor and their children, living a few steps away on the other side of the divide, were all too familiar with the noisy squabbling that inevitably followed in the wake of the couple's heavy drinking. Even worse, sounds of violence were a common occurrence. On Hogmanay of 1897, following an absence of several weeks, Jessie returned to Milne Square at around four o'clock in the afternoon, apparently quite sober. When Herdman arrived home a little later the couple took to drinking and, shortly after the New Year bells rang out, raised voices and abusive language were to be heard coming from their flat. The quarrel continued well into the night, dying down occasionally before flaring up again.

Living in such close proximity, none of the residents of the four sixth-floor flats at Milne Square was oblivious to what was going on that Hogmanay. During the early hours of New Year's morning one of James and Ann O'Connor's daughters was awakened by the sound of a woman's voice crying out 'Murder!' while another neighbour, a widow named Catherine Budge, had her sleep similarly disturbed by screams coming from across the landing. Around this time Jessie, her face bloodied and beaten, knocked at the door of Ann Kidd, also a widow living alone, and blurted out: 'He has been abusing me all night.' Ann Kidd advised her rather tersely to seek police protection and promptly closed the door. Four hours later Jessie had grown increasingly desperate and turned up this time on Ann O'Connor's doorstep, begging for admittance, but Ann refused her, wary perhaps of becoming embroiled in someone else's domestic dispute. A brief lull during the forenoon offered hopes of a reconciliation but - no - before long hostilities resumed with renewed vigour. Shortly before midday Catherine Budge was working at the communal *jaw-box* - or sink - on the sixth-floor landing when Jessie's door burst open as she fled from her flat with Herdman in near pursuit, cursing violently. Taking pity on her neighbour, Catherine gave Jessie refuge but she could not fail to notice that her mouth was badly swollen, her face cut and bruised and her clothing heavily bloodstained. She offered to report matters to the police but Jessie apparently talked her out it - understandably afraid of what the consequences for her might be. Sometime later the two women heard Herdman's door banging as he left the flat and went downstairs, giving Jessie the courage to emerge from Catherine's room and return to her own home. He returned, however, more quickly than expected. When an eleven-year-old girl, Johan Sorlie, climbed the stairs in the early afternoon with a message for Catherine Budge she was shocked at the sight of Jessie lying supine on the landing while Herdman grabbed her by the hair and repeatedly dashed her head to the floor, bawling, 'This is another time you have not got my supper ready!' Had the situation not been so deathly serious the grim banality of his words would surely have been darkly comic. Five or six times Johan saw Herdman kick Jessie on the head and each time heard her cry out in response, 'Oh, my poor mother!' Shocked and horrified, the child ran downstairs where she told her friends, ten-year-old Mary and nine-year-old Christina, what she had just witnessed. 'Oh, come on upstairs,' she urged them. 'There's a woman lying on the passage, and you can hardly see her hands or face for blood.' The three girls stole quietly to the head of the stairs and watched in horror as Herdman savagely stamped on Jessie's head with the heel of his boot. It was more than the children could stomach and, terrified, they fled back downstairs. At this same time Catherine Budge heard screaming on the landing, followed by a loud thud, just such a sound as a body might make when thrown to the floor, before all went silent. A few hours later Margaret O'Connor, James and Ann's daughter, overheard Herdman calling, 'Come awa' in, Jessie,' but heard no voice in reply. Margaret and her father carried a light out on to the landing where they found Herdman kneeling alongside Jessie who appeared to be unconscious. Herdman raised her by the armpits and, assisted by James O'Connor, trailed her into his flat. At first O'Connor thought that Jessie had merely fainted but when she failed to revive within a reasonable time he told Herdman, 'I doubt she's dead.' At this Herdman cried out, 'Oh, no, Jessie!', and O'Connor left the building to contact the police.

When Constable Robert Combe arrived at Milne Square and entered Herdman's flat he found Jessie's body lying in a pool of blood but there was no sign of her partner. Hurrying back to the Central Police Office, he reported details of what he had seen and straight away returned to the crime scene, accompanied by a second officer, Detective Frew. As they entered the building, the policemen saw a man in front of them on the stairs and, despite never having seen John Herdman previously, Frew had a hunch that the man ahead might possibly be the suspect they were looking for. Just on the off-chance he called out - 'Herdman!' - and when the man turned immediately in response to his name the officers placed him under arrest. Proceeding to the top floor, they passed through the cramped and gloomy passageway that gave access to Herdman's flat. Lighted only by a small skylight window, the room was minimally furnished and little more than ten feet square. Not yet cold, Jessie's body lay sprawled on top of blankets and her head and face had been bludgeoned almost beyond recognition. Her hair was thickly clotted with blood and what appeared to be a stab wound had penetrated the area close to her left breast. All around the room blood-smeared fragments of a broken chair lay strewn, and the floor and walls were likewise grotesquely splattered with blood. From his observations, Detective Frew surmised - not entirely accurately - that Jessie had been assaulted on the landing, perhaps while attempting to make an escape, and had been dragged back inside the room where she had been beaten to death by a leg, or legs, of the broken chair. While it was at least possible that her breast wound had been inflicted by a fragment of shattered wood, it seemed more likely that a sharp instrument such as a blade had been responsible. As things stood, it looked bad for Herdman whose hands and clothes were stained with blood and when he was searched back at the police station a knife was found in his possession. And if he harboured any hopes that further inquiries might provide him with grounds for optimism, then he was to be sadly disappointed. According to the findings of the two eminent surgeons who carried out the post-mortem examination of Jessie Soutar's body, Professor Sir Henry Littlejohn and Dr Joseph Bell, there was no doubt that her wounds had been 'inflicted by wilful violence.' The injuries they listed formed a catalogue of horror: body bruised all over with a number of severe wounds on the head; bones of the nose fractured and driven inwards by a violent impact; several broken ribs and a stab-wound on the chest that, at three quarters of an inch deep, was sufficient to have punctured the lung. Professor Littlejohn stated later that, in all his fifty years of medical practice, this was one of the very worst cases that he had ever been involved in.

Dressed in a dark suit, John Herdman appeared in the Edinburgh Police Court on Monday 3 January before Bailie Kinloch Anderson where he was charged with having attacked and murdered Jessie Soutar on Friday 31 December 1897 or Saturday 1 January 1898, and his case was sufficiently serious to be referred automatically to the High Court. Bailie Anderson could not help noting that the prisoner never raised his eyes from the ground. Given the weight of evidence stacked up against him, Herdman's decision to plead not guilty to the charge of murder was always likely to be a long shot - but, then again, in the circumstances he had little to lose. At the High Court of Justiciary on Monday 21 February the Solicitor-General, acting for the Crown, insisted that there was no question that Jessie Soutar's death had been caused by anything other than 'a case of deliberate, brutal and wilful murder.' When the turn of the defence came round, the best that it could offer in reply was to quote Hugh Hamilton, Herdman's boss at the printworks, who described his employee as 'a quiet and inoffensive man' (presumably when sober) but 'inclined to be soft' - a not so veiled reference to the prisoner's low intelligence. The defence went on to highlight the fact that Herdman was a chronic alcoholic and suggested that, since much of the evidence marshalled against him had been provided by young children, 'the safe path for the jury' was to dismiss the murder charge and to deliver a verdict of not proven. In the judge, Lord Young's, summing up he reminded the jury that, as medical evidence had demonstrated the impossibility that Jessie Soutar's injuries had been self-inflicted, the only point they need address was the question of who had been responsible for inflicting these injuries: namely, either the accused or alternatively some other person, hitherto unidentified and unnamed. He went on to clarify that the fact of a person's being under the influence of alcohol at the time of committing a crime was viewed under Scots law as no excuse for his actions, on the grounds that drunkenness was a self-induced condition. In addition, he added, the public at large was entitled to expect protection from persons drunk as well as sober. If, he concluded, the jury was satisfied that the accused had perpetrated Jessie Soutar's fatal injuries, then the law would have no hesitation in characterising his actions as murder. Shortly after four o'clock Lord Young dismissed the jury to deliberate, reminding its members that their verdict must be based on the evidence in its entirety.

By a margin of two to one, the fifteen men of the jury took little more than half an hour to find Herdman guilty of murder. In addressing the prisoner, Lord Young made it clear that, with the verdict of the jury now settled, he himself at this stage in the proceedings was merely following the requirements of the law. 'The law itself prescribes to me the sentence that must follow the verdict which the jury have just returned,' he told Herdman, 'indeed [it] presents the very words in which I shall pronounce it.' At that he donned the black cap and sentenced the prisoner to be returned to the Calton Jail where on Monday 14 March - three weeks hence - he would be hanged until dead. On hearing Herdman's fate thus spelled out, a young woman in the public gallery, believed to be one of his daughters, broke down and wept while he was removed to the cells in a similar state of distress. By a curious quirk of timing, the day when he was sentenced happened to be the third anniversary of the death of his wife.

If it was surprising in the circumstances that as many as one third of the jury - a total of five men - remained unconvinced of the prisoner's guilt, possibly even more unexpected was the establishment of a petition, circulated in the days after his trial, which sought to bring about a commutation of the death sentence. Among a number of highly questionable points it raised was a reference to Herdman's previously 'irreproachable character' (which, of course, conveniently ignored the knife-throwing incident, albeit many years earlier, as well as his more recent persistent drunkenness and tendency to domestic violence) before going on to highlight the (irrelevant) fact that both Herdman and Jessie Soutar had been inebriated in the hours leading up to her death - 'as persons of their rank in life,' it sniffily suggested, 'often are on Hogmanay Night and New Year's Day.' Milne Square was an area where many 'low people' were to be found, the petition continued - any one of whom might possibly have been responsible for Jessie Soutar's gruesome death. Far-fetched though its claims might sound, the petition attracted more than 11,000 signatures from Edinburgh and beyond, though it was widely accepted that few of those signing had acted out of genuine sympathy for the condemned man but were simply taking advantage of an opportunity to voice their opposition to capital punishment in general. One such signatory was John Morley, Liberal Member of Parliament for Newcastle-upon-Tyne, and for similar reasons Herdman's case attracted a degree of sympathy among some sections of the Scottish press. Others endorsed the petition, it was suggested, out of a misguided, if understandable, sympathy for Herdsman's three daughters, all of whom were married and living in Edinburgh. In the event, 'after full consideration' the petition's demands were rejected by the Secretary of State for Scotland, Lord Balfour of Burleigh, who indicated that he saw no justification for preventing the law from taking its course. News of its failure was transmitted to the condemned man on Friday 11 March.

During his time in the Calton Jail, Herdman was found to be a quiet and biddable inmate, dividing his attention more or less equally between attending to the spiritual ministrations of the prison chaplain, Rev. Hugh Mackenzie Campbell, and focusing his attention on the more pressing matter of what his next meal might consist of. Regarding the crime of which he had been convicted, he claimed no memory of it whatsoever: 'I must have done it,' he was quoted as saying, 'there was no other body to do it; but, before God, I don't recollect anything about it.' Regarding his own bleak prospects, he commented - with some degree of restraint - that it looked like a 'bad job'. Not sufficiently literate himself, he sought the assistance of Rev. Campbell in penning on his behalf a number of farewell letters as well as taking charge of a few trifling possessions which he wished to be distributed among friends and family members. On Sunday 13 March, the day immediately prior to his execution, he took his final leave of those who were closest to him and retired to bed at around eleven o'clock. But even if Herdman was calm and resigned to his fate, elsewhere in the jail there was another prisoner who was a good deal less so. Convicted in the High Court several months earlier - on Monday 25 October 1897 - of something in the order of forty cases of fire-raising in Aberdeen, a sixteen-year-old labourer, John Thomson, had contrived to commit suicide in his cell. Apparently during his trial much play had been made of Thomson's low intellect, a trait he was alleged to have shared in common with the rest of his family, but he was savvy enough for all that to have misappropriated a length of cord while engaged in mat-making, and this he had used to hang himself. It was widely believed at the time of his arrest that what had spurred the impressionable teenager to step aside from the straight and narrow was his addiction to 'penny dreadful' magazines - tawdry, sensational storybooks that were highly popular throughout much of the nineteenth century.

But if Herdman got wind of his fellow inmate's suicide, it appears to have done nothing to prevent him from sleeping. He awoke at five o'clock the following morning and a short time later Rev. Campbell arrived in his cell to guide him in prayer. For the first time since his arrival in prison, Herdman displayed a poor appetite for breakfast but, despite this apparent show of nerves, he was successful in maintaining his composure while communicating a number of private messages to the chaplain which he wished to be conveyed to members of his family. Dressed in a brown tweed suit, he was then escorted from his top-floor cell to a room on the ground floor which was located immediately above an underground chamber, used as a punishment cell and accessed via a narrow descending staircase. The scaffold had been suspended over the stairwell so as to allow a drop of six feet and five inches, reckoned to be sufficient to dispatch a man of Herdman's smallish build and stature. When he reached this spot, he turned to shake hands with those prison warders with whom he had become acquainted during his three weeks in the Calton.

Meanwhile a group of officials and other dignitaries had gathered in the room of the governor, Captain Christie, including city magistrates and heads of various municipal departments, accompanied by two ceremonial halberd bearers; Dr Henry Littlejohn, surgeon, and his son, Dr Harvey Littlejohn, following in his father's distinguished footsteps; and some half a dozen or so representatives of the Scottish press. At around a quarter to eight the assembled group left the governor's office and made their way to where Herdman was currently being held. Once the necessary formalities had been attended to, a profound hush descended as, on the prisoner's behalf, Rev. Campbell read out the following statement: *I, John Herdman, about to pass into the presence of my God, say farewell to all my friends outside. I offer my most sincere thanks to those who interested themselves in my reprieve. With God I have made my peace, and relying on His mercy, I go forward to meet Him. God bless my children.* When he finished reading, Rev. Campbell turned to the prisoner and asked if this was his final message to the world, to which Herdman replied simply, 'Yes.' A short religious service then followed, during which the chaplain invited those in attendance to join with him in singing the Scots hymn, 'The hour of my departure's come'. This, he indicated, had been a favourite of the condemned man's since childhood. For a time Herdman participated in the singing but he eventually broke down, unable to continue, and covered his eyes with his hand. Standing alongside, Rev. Campbell rested a supportive hand upon his shoulder and before the hymn had ended the condemned man succeeded in recovering himself. After various readings from the scriptures, the chaplain brought proceedings to a close with a final prayer in which he invited God to 'Look in pity on the temptations of [Herdman's] life, on the companionship and surroundings which encircled him [and] on the physical weakness of his brain' - this last an unmistakeable reference to Herdman's low intelligence that had previously surfaced during his trial. The pernicious effect of alcohol, the negative influence of bad company and the squalid social conditions of the poor had all conspired, the minister seemed to suggest, to combine with Herdman's weak intellect and lead him with a tragic inevitability to this place at the foot of the gallows. His victim was not forgotten: 'He goes before Thee,' Rev. Campbell stated, 'sorrowing for the life of her who in his great sin he sent into Thy presence,' and finally he ended by beseeching the Almighty to 'Pity his sorrow ... and lend an ear unto his prayer.' Just how many of his listeners were convinced by the clergyman's social theorising and came around to his depiction of Herdman as victim as well as villain it is impossible to know. The point Rev. Campbell made remains a contentious issue to this day.

Within the confined space of the narrow stairwell many of the officials and dignitaries found themselves uncomfortably close to where the drop would fall. Brought from England for the occasion, the executioner was James Billington, whose mastery of his craft no-one could have doubted. As the prison bell tolled sonorously in the background, he deftly pinioned Herdman's arms and positioned him on the appropriate spot over the trapdoor, then - virtually unseen by any of the onlookers - he slipped behind the prisoner and strapped his legs firmly together. Next, he produced a long white hood from his pocket which he drew down over the condemned man's face before finally fitting the noose around his neck. Throughout this time Herdman's only visible movement was a slight shake of the head as he felt the rope tighten, and then, just as the clock struck eight and the chaplain concluded the words of the benediction - 'Lord Jesus, receive this man's soul' - Billington drew back the bolt. There was an almighty crash as the trapdoor opened and Herdman plunged downwards, followed a split second later by a sickening thud as the weight of his body tightened the rope to its fullest extent. The work of the executioner was efficiently done since death appeared to be instantaneous.

For more than an hour before the execution people had been assembling in groups at various locations throughout the city. Outside the prison; on the North and Waverley Bridges; on the heights of the Calton Hill - anywhere, in fact, that would offer a suitable vantage point - an estimated 500 men and women stood in silence, overseen by a large body of policemen. When the prison bell rang out at a quarter to eight a ripple of anticipation ran through the crowd, and fifteen minutes later the black flag was hoisted over the prison, confirming to those waiting that the dictate of the law had been followed to the letter. As they began to disperse to their homes and jobs throughout the city, the townsfolk of Edinburgh were not to know that John Herdman would be the last man - or woman - to face the death penalty in nineteenth-century Scotland, or for that matter that he would achieve the parallel distinction - if such it might be termed - of being the last to be hanged north of the border under Queen Victoria's reign.

Afterword

During the course of writing this book I was repeatedly struck by the truth of the old adage that there are few blacks and whites in this world, only a broad spectrum of shades of grey. Against a backcloth of poverty and hardship in the nineteenth century, in a society that offered few if any prospects for ordinary folk and where the rich exploited the poor as a matter of course, we shouldn't really be surprised that from time to time the lives of those occupying the lower rungs of the social ladder went badly awry. That, of course, isn't the whole story. Then as now, alongside good there was straightforward evil, and as I compiled these accounts of past lives this was something that refused to be ignored. Not everyone in these pages was utterly impoverished - take, for instance, the notorious Dr Pritchard - and some of the crimes committed were, regardless of circumstances, well-nigh unforgivable.

This, of course, isn't necessarily a justification for the death penalty. Throughout the course of the nineteenth century an undercurrent of public opinion gained steadily in momentum which was opposed to capital punishment in principle. In particular, the notion that watching men and women in their death throes could be classed as a form of entertainment became increasingly abhorrent, though it was not until 1868 that the Capital Punishment Amendment Act finally did away with the unwholesome spectacle of public executions.

During the twentieth century, the death penalty was used less and less often in Scotland, but nonetheless more than thirty hangings were carried out before capital punishment was effectively removed from the statute book in 1965. The last execution took place in Aberdeen on 15 August 1963 when Henry John Burnett was hanged for murder. Since that day more than half a century ago the words 'judicial hanging' have never appeared on any death certificate issued in Scotland and, despite ongoing debate, the likelihood of that changing seems decidedly slim.

Index